CHANGE UP

CHANGE UP

AN ORAL HISTORY
of 8 KEY EVENTS *that*
SHAPED MODERN BASEBALL

LARRY BURKE
and
PETER THOMAS FORNATALE

with Jim Baker

RODALE

Rodale books may be purchased for business or promotional use or for special sales. For information, please write to:

Special Markets Department, Rodale, Inc., 733 Third Avenue, New York, NY 10017

Printed in the United States of America

Rodale Inc. makes every effort to use acid-free ⊗, recycled paper ♻.

Book design by Christopher Rhoads

Library of Congress Cataloging-in-Publication Data

Burke, Larry.
    Change up : an oral history of 8 key events that shaped modern baseball / Larry Burke and Peter Thomas Fornatale with Jim Baker.
        p.   cm.
    ISBN-13 978–1–59486–189–5 hardcover
    ISBN-10 1–59486–189–7 hardcover
    1. Baseball—United States—History.   2. Baseball players—United States—Interviews.   I. Fornatale, Peter.   II. Baker, Jim.   III. Title.
GV867.B87   2008
796.357'640973—dc22   2007044923

Distributed to the trade by Macmillan

2   4   6   8   10   9   7   5   3   1 hardcover

RODALE
LIVE YOUR WHOLE LIFE™

We inspire and enable people to improve their lives and the world around them
For more of our products visit rodalestore.com or call 800-848-4735

DEDICATION

To the memory of the man responsible
for the biggest change of all,
Jackie Robinson

CONTENTS

ACKNOWLEDGMENTS

The writing of this book was a true team effort. We were very fortunate to be able to rely on many writers and researchers who are accomplished in their own right. At the top of the list is Richard Lally. He is a consummate professional who helped with many of the interviews and provided invaluable editorial insight as well.

Bernie Corbett's help was also indispensable. When it came to tracking down the toughest-to-find players and ex-managers, he was truly the man.

Chris Wertz also went above and beyond the call of duty in the interviews he did for us.

Many thanks also to Pete Abraham, Albert Chen, Richard Deitsch, John Hickey, Jon Malki, Tim McDonough, Jim Salisbury, Melissa Segura, and Jeff Zrebiec for their talent, effort, and diligence.

This book wouldn't have happened without Scott Waxman and Zach Schisgal. Kevin Smith, who joined the process later on, has also been very generous with his time and ideas.

The Burke family—Beth, Casey, Maddie, Charlie, Teddy, Mom, and Dad—deserves a huge thank-you for its unwavering patience and support.

Susan Van Metre also gets major kudos for putting up with her husband during the writing of this book.

INTRODUCTION

A host of books have been written with the thesis that baseball reached its zenith in New York in the 1950s. It is sometimes said that Golden Ages exist in the memory of the teller, but, if nothing else, 1950s New York baseball is certainly the game's most celebrated historical era. Ironically, as wonderful as it was supposed to be, it ended when two-thirds of its participants abandoned the city. This abandonment of New York was the second major change to come baseball's way in the postwar era. The first was the breaking of the color line by the Brooklyn Dodgers—an event that adds some genuine heft to the Golden Age argument. Those two bookends, coming a decade apart, were the first steps in a long line of changes that have shaped the game as we see it today.

When this project began, all we knew was that we wanted to tell the story of baseball over the past half century in the words of the people who were there: the players, the managers, the coaches, and the members of the media covering the games. As we began our interviews with a couple of topics in mind, certain themes began to develop. As much as anything else, it became apparent that baseball has matured in the last 50 years in ways that it did not in the previous 50.

Consider this: From the beginning of the 20th century through the end of World War II, baseball on the field went through various eras: Deadball, Liveball, and wartime deprivations, but the game itself and the way it was conducted off the field stayed largely, if not entirely, the same. Eight teams made up of white men in two leagues and 10 cities played 154 games each year, the winners in each league meeting in the World Series.

After the war, this regimentation slowly began to unravel. The profound impact of integrating the big leagues has been written about eloquently and often, to the point where no reasonable baseball fan can argue that there was ever any "golden age" of the game that didn't include players of color. As far as we're concerned, the first step toward the creation of Major League Baseball as we know it started when Jackie Robinson walked on the field.

It's safe to say that the national expansion of the game really began with the westward moves of the Dodgers and Giants. No more major-league teams were added until 1961, but in '58, for the first time, there was baseball from coast to coast, instead of just baseball as far west as Kansas City. (It can be argued that expansion comes in two forms: the expansion of movement and the expansion of numbers. Baseball finally began to experience the first in 1953, when the Boston Braves relocated to Milwaukee, the first of three such moves that saw a two-team city lose one of its clubs [within two years the St. Louis Browns would move to Baltimore and the Philadelphia Athletics would jump to Kansas]. The relocation of the Dodgers and Giants, however, truly broadened the game's reach in a way that moving to places like Milwaukee, Baltimore, and Kansas City could not.)

From 1958 through 2008, the changes have come for baseball in many different forms. Some have come swiftly and some gradually, some by fiat, some by reaching a tipping point, some because they were forced by prevailing cultural norms, and some because it was time for the game to catch up with the rest of society. If we wrote about everything that has happened in that time frame, you'd be looking at a three- or four-volume set, a baseball answer to Donald Kagan's *History of the Peloponnesian War*. We therefore decided to limit our topics in a couple of different ways. For one, we decided to leave out detailed discussions of the topics mentioned in the previous paragraphs, figuring that they've been covered extensively elsewhere and predate our time line. Second, we set aside, at least for now, the discussion of the game on the field. This book will not cover topics such as why pitchers don't throw nine innings anymore, or the change in the way relievers are used, or improvements in equipment, or the various things that players may be doing to themselves in order to improve their performance on the field.

Instead we wanted to focus on the external changes that have shaped the game we know and love. Some of the chapters are very direct discussions of the changes themselves; others use a key event as a lens with which to view change.

- We look at the physical expansion of the number of teams by discussing the 1962 Mets, the most famous last-place team of all time.

- Our chapter on the Latino players coming into baseball in the 1950s tells a story of great perseverance that has taken the game to new heights.

- The way baseball is covered by the media and how the population at large perceives modern athletes represents another major difference in the game today. We examine that through a look at Jim Bouton's classic 1970 book, *Ball Four*.

• Our history of the players' union puts the reader right in the thick of what it was like to be a professional trying to make a living as a baseball player in the 1960s and traces the arc of change right up through the present day.

• The designated hitter is perhaps baseball's most controversial change, either loved or loathed by players and fans, depending on whom you talk to. We present both sides of the debate in our chapter on this most famous/infamous of all rule changes.

• Frank Robinson broke the color line for managers when he took the helm for the Cleveland Indians in 1975. It was a significant moment in the game's history, and one that hasn't gotten the attention it deserves in baseball literature. Our goal was to put the reader in the dugout alongside Robinson.

• Cal Ripken Jr. changed baseball people's preconceptions of what a shortstop is supposed to be, as much as any player has ever done at his position. We look at Ripken, the Streak, and what he meant to the game in a time of great need.

• The second major wave of internationalization in baseball started in the 1990s and is still going strong: the Asian players coming into the game. We examine the origins of this wave and also cover the emergence of Hideo Nomo and Ichiro Suzuki and what their success has meant to baseball fans around the world.

Our idea was to present each chapter as if it were a discussion around the dinner table between old friends, each with his own perspective and insights. Their words, woven together, tell each story in new and interesting ways. We believe that what emerges is more than just a book about change, but one about why everyone we spoke with, from Dave Anderson to Earl Weaver, Frank Robinson to Alex Rodriguez, loves baseball the way we do. Certainly not all our interviewees would agree with this next statement, but we believe that on balance, the changes that have come into baseball over the years are a good thing, and that there has never been a better time to be a fan. Sure, there are still problems as there always have been, but in many ways, thanks to some of the men in this book, the Golden Age of Baseball is now.

THE 1962 METS

Featuring

ROGER CRAIG: Veteran starting pitcher who had spent a dozen years with the Dodgers organization.

JIM HICKMAN: Rookie center fielder from the Cardinals organization.

JAY HOOK: Starting pitcher from the Reds organization who got the victory in the Mets' first win ever.

ED KRANEPOOL: Local high school phenom signed by the Mets and brought to the majors at the end of the season at the age of 17.

ROBERT LIPSYTE: A young writer who did feature stories on the team for the *New York Times*.

KEN MacKENZIE: Reliever acquired in a trade with the Braves.

FRANK THOMAS: Veteran slugger obtained in a trade with the Braves but most often identified with the Pirates.

WHEN THE AMERICAN LEAGUE doubled the number of big-league clubs to 16 at the turn of the 20th century, the U.S. population was about 77 million. Within 50 years that number had in turn doubled to 155 million and had grown an additional 25 million by 1960. In spite of those massive gains in potential ticket buyers, baseball remained as it was, a 16-team operation at the big-league level. And the recently transplanted Los Angeles Dodgers and San Francisco Giants were the only major-league teams west of Missouri.

That number seemed almost sacrosanct and, as has so often been the case in baseball's attitude toward change, it was going to take external pressure for it to move forward. Because so much of the population was not being serviced by major-league baseball other than via television, the door was open to fill that need. The pressure on major-league baseball came in two forms. First, the Pacific Coast League made some noise about becoming a third major league, going so far as to change from a lettered classification to an open one in 1952, but a general decline in minor-league attendance and the westward franchise shifts of the Giants and Dodgers put an end to that talk. Secondly, the void created in New York by the Giants' and Dodgers' moves could not possibly go unfilled. It inspired William Shea, a New York attorney, to first make overtures about moving existing teams such as the Pirates and Reds to the city and then to create the Continental League, a third major league cut from whole cloth.

Whatever Shea's intentions—and some have suggested that the whole enterprise was a leverage move to get the National League back into New York after his attempts to land an existing team had failed—the Continental League did exist on paper for a full year. From July 1959 to August 1960, ownership groups were in place for seven cities. (All, save for one—Buffalo—would eventually get major-league franchises, some sooner rather than later.) This presence was enough for the major-league owners to finally increase their franchise number to better reflect the market realities around them. The Washington Senators would move to Minneapolis-St. Paul—a Continental League city—and be replaced by a new Senators franchise. The Minnesota Twins would be joined in the American League by a second Los Angeles franchise; both of those teams began play in 1961. (The Continental League had some prescient choices among its locales, but it did not extend itself to the West Coast.) The following year the National League would move into the Sun Belt by awarding a franchise in another CL city, Houston. The second National League expansion team would go to New York.

And therein begins this tale. While the other three new clubs managed to create rosters that would win at least 60 games in their first year of existence (the Angels were especially successful, getting outscored by only 40 runs in 1961 and finishing in third place in '62), the architects of the Mets managed to create a perfect storm of a ball club, one that lost a record 120 games. Although their counterparts did a much better job of hitting the ground running, it was those Mets, under their colorful manager Casey Stengel, who became legendary.

GETTING STARTED

The new teams' rosters were stocked by an expansion draft, the players for which were provided from the major- and minor-league rosters of the existing eight teams. In the first phase of the draft the Mets and Colt .45s would select from lists of 15 players submitted by each of the eight established NL teams. Eight of the 15 players had to have been on the 25-man major-league roster as of August 31, 1961, while another seven could come from elsewhere in the organization. The Mets and Houston Colt .45s were required to take two men from each team at a cost of $75,000 each. It was from this phase that the Mets landed their first player, catcher Hobie Landrith. (Baseball's most recent expansion teams, which joined the majors in 1998, began operating minor-league teams in the seasons leading up to their debut. Houston and New York had no such luxury.)

The second phase of the draft was dubbed the "premium" phase. Each team designated two more players from its major-league roster, and the Mets and Colt .45s could select no more than one from each club at $125,000 each. The first player the Mets got in this round was Cardinals pitcher Bob Miller. In all, the Mets spent $1.8 million on expansion draft day, a fairly sizable amount of money given the level of talent made available and the fact that this money wasn't included in the franchise fee. The Mets' premium picks were Miller, Reds pitcher Jay Hook, Cubs infielder Don Zimmer and Phillies corner infielder/outfielder Lee Walls. Two months after the draft New York shipped Walls to Los Angeles for Charlie Neal and a player to be named later, who turned out to be pitcher Willard Hunter.

Of the four premium choices, only Zimmer could have been considered a regular in 1961. Two of the players the Mets took in the initial draft were deemed expendable by their respective teams after they had been struck by routine maladies the year before. Cardinals catcher Chris Cannizzaro had lost playing time to appendicitis in 1961. Jay Hook had been hit by the mumps. Ironically, it was during a turn as a baseball goodwill ambassador that he caught the disease.

JAY HOOK: When [the Reds] wanted somebody to speak at schools or something where they didn't pay anybody to do it, they thought of me. So we were out in California and I had gone out to speak at the school—actually the guy had been the principal at the grade school I went to in Illinois but had moved to California. I must have contracted [the mumps] there but they really knocked me out for that 1961 season, which was a shame, because I ended up with mono; at the end of the season they insisted I go get a physical and my blood count was still high. So anyway, I had a terrible year in 1961 [1–3, 7.76 ERA in 62⅔ innings] when we won the pennant. I really didn't get to pitch very much after I got sick. But I think they put me in the draft—they put me as one of the premium draft choices— because they probably didn't think anybody would pick me. My wife Joanne and I were driving home from the World Series in our little Austin-Healey—the kids had gone home early— and we heard over the radio that we'd been sold to the Mets.

ROGER CRAIG: [The move to the Mets] had some possibilities because in 1960 I had had a collision with Vada Pinson and broken my clavicle and I came back and pitched after a doctor said I'd never pitch again. I came back eight weeks later and nearly had a complete-game victory against the Cardinals. I didn't really feel that bad because baseball is a business and sometimes you just have to move on.

JIM HICKMAN: Like anybody, I was glad to go to the big leagues; I was glad to get there.

ROGER CRAIG: I saw it as a chance to get a new start and pitch every fourth day. I was looking forward to playing for Casey Stengel—which, as it turned out, I really enjoyed for those two years. I knew we were going to lose a lot of ball games because we had a lot of guys—including me—that were near the end of their careers. I learned a lot that really helped me when I became a pitching coach and a manager later on.

Some were disappointed that they weren't taken in the draft, like Braves pitcher Ken MacKenzie, who turned out to be the only '62 Met who fashioned a winning record (5–4).

KEN MacKENZIE: I'm actually part of Mets history as the first non-draftee to join the team, although that requires a bit of explaining. The expansion draft occurred while I was playing in Puerto Rico and I remember being really depressed when neither the Colt .45s nor the Mets chose me. To put it more accurately, I wanted to get away from the Braves. I was stuck in a logjam in Milwaukee: the pitching staff had Warren Spahn, Lew Burdette, Bob Buhl, Carl Willey, Don Nottebart, Bob Hendley, and Don McMahon. Moe Drabowsky was also on that team. There was no place for me and I knew it. I hadn't pitched much for the Braves in '60 or '61 (15⅓ innings total), and I was going to be 28 in '62. In '61 (Milwaukee manager) Chuck Dressen sent me down to make room for this young catcher named Joe Torre. I told Braves general manager John McHale that I was going to quit. Now back then someone like me was worth money to the club—about $25,000 would be the going rate. I was sold a couple of times for that amount. Players were being moved all over the place for numbers like that; it was the bottom price. So McHale said, "No, you go to Louisville and have a good season and I'll do something with you at the end of the season if you don't figure in our plans." That sounded good to me.

I did pitch well in Louisville and the Braves put me in the expansion draft. I was ready to quit when I didn't get picked. But, a few weeks later, while we were still in Puerto Rico, I got a letter from New York. The letter informed me that I had been purchased from the Braves by the New York Metropolitans Baseball Club. They had bought me from Milwaukee along with Johnny Antonelli, another lefty. The letter was on *Continental League* stationery—they were recycling the stationery. I didn't think to save it . . .

Slugger Frank Thomas came to the Mets via a trade with the Braves on November 28, 1961. The deal angered him, but not because it was to an expansion team.

FRANK THOMAS: I was kind of disappointed because, number one, I was promised that wouldn't happen. When I went in to talk contract with John McHale, I said to him: "If you have the intention of trading me, please, don't let me sign. Let me dicker with the club I'm going to go to." Then I asked him, "What are your intentions for me come 1962?" And he said, "Well, you're going to be our left fielder." I said, "If that's the case, then you bring out whatever contract you want me to sign and I'm doing it, because you're giving me the chance to play regularly again." That was in September. In November I was up hunting with my friends when my wife called and said, "You just got sold to the Mets." He lied to me.

Ed Kranepool came to the team later, signed for a nice bonus at mid-season right out of high school in the Bronx, and was brought up through three levels of the minor leagues, and finally to the big club, in the course of one summer.

ED KRANEPOOL: When I reached the majors the final bonus was over $100,000—a lot of money back then. We didn't have a draft back in '62; you could sign with whomever you wanted to and you negotiated your own deal. The talks went very quickly. Bubber Jonnard [the Mets' chief scout] wanted me and he made no secret of it. I did give [White Sox scout] Steve Ray the last option. I told them what the Mets had offered so Hank Greenberg [a part-owner] and the White Sox could match it, but they didn't. That was fine with me. I wanted to stay in New York and the Yankees hadn't really pursued me. They knew the Mets were at every game and it was a foregone conclusion that they would go at me hard.

SPRING TRAINING AND A ROUGH START

It is not generally remembered that the '62 Mets played fairly well in spring training, further proof that anyone who puts stock in spring games is missing the point of the exercise. New York finished exhibition play with a .500 record. While no one thought they would contend, few saw what atrocities were in store for the team.

ROGER CRAIG: There were a bunch of really good ball-players there: Gil Hodges, Frank Thomas, Richie Ashburn, Gus Bell, Felix Mantilla. We felt that even though we all came from different places we might be able to blend together and do something. It was a fun feeling. Casey Stengel brightened up the clubhouse even during the season when we were really losing. He would make you feel like today's another day and we have a chance to win. In spring training it was a lot of fun. It was a novelty.

JAY HOOK: It was a pretty optimistic feeling, because we had a number of guys who had had wonderful careers already. We had a manager who had won a number of pennants with the Yankees; Casey had a great relationship with all the writers; so, you know, as Mets we probably got as much publicity, if not more publicity, than the Yankees did.

ROBERT LIPSYTE: I went down there assuming that they were going to be terrible. What did I know? I was not a baseball writer. I was not particularly a sports fan. I had not followed this stuff closely.

The general feeling at the *Times* was that this team was going to be so bad that it would be a feature writer's delight. It was not going to be a good assignment for sports guys who had been hunkering in the corner since 1957 when the Dodgers and Giants left town. It was seen as a feature writer's story rather than a real baseball writer's story, which is why they sent me.

KEN MacKENZIE: None of us suspected what would happen with the Mets that first year. We had some names on that club, you know. Charlie Neal, Don Zimmer, Frank Thomas, Felix Mantilla—whom I knew could hit from when he was with the Braves—Richie Ashburn, Gil Hodges, Gene Woodling, Gus Bell, Roger Craig. We also had guys like Elio Chacon, but he was really a fringe player. We thought we had a baseball team.

ROBERT LIPSYTE: To my shame, along with my little portable Olivetti typewriter, I brought along my glove. What kind of insanity was that? Joyce Carol Oates once said that the comparison between the fighter in the ring and the ringside reporter was maybe as great as the difference between men and women. Professional athletes are like another species. I remember the first time I went to bat during spring training. This was batting practice thrown by Cookie Lavagetto, one of the Mets coaches; kind of soft, little tosses but they were the fastest thing I had ever seen. Later I went onto the field with the glove I had brought and kind of gathered in a soft fly which felt like a bullet in my hand. As mediocre or bad or as second-rate as this expansion team might have been, you can't forget that these were professional athletes. They had been stars since they were 12 years old and they took an enormous amount of pride in themselves. At that level, particularly then, before there was such an explosion of talent, the difference between a guy who was on the world championship team and the cellar team really wasn't all that great. They were all wonderful, superb talents.

ROGER CRAIG: On paper, with all those names, we looked halfway decent. Then the games started. We lost nine in a row to start, then we won one, then lost a bunch more. We were a bad defensive ball club and the pitching was so-so at best. We found out pretty soon that it was going to be a long season.

CASEY

Never an entity to pass up a chance to trade on a local favorite, the Mets tabbed for their very first manager Casey Stengel, a man whose New York baseball roots went back to his playing days with the Brooklyn Dodgers beginning in 1912. He had also played with the Giants in the '20s and had managed the Dodgers to no good end a decade later. Most famous and recent, though, was his incredible run at the helm of the Yankees. Beginning in 1949 and ending with Stengel's unceremonious dumping at the end of the 1960 World Series, when he was 70 years old, his Yankee teams had won 10 pennants and had gone on to grab the world championship seven times. In a more litigious era Casey would have been able to make a strong case against his former Yankees employers for age discrimination. As it was, he departed with dignity and the Yankees kept on winning. His affiliation with the new Mets franchise made him one of the few people who could say that he'd been an employee of all four New York ball clubs.

Actually it was Stengel's old boss, George Weiss—himself a victim of Yankee ageism—who in his new role as Mets team president hired him to pilot the expansion club. Stengel had turned down the Tigers' opening and seemed ready for retirement when Weiss convinced him to return to the National League. (It's interesting to note that had Stengel taken the Tigers' job prior to the 1961 season and kept it through July 24, 1965, the day he broke his hip and retired for good, his career winning percentage as a manager would have been some 35 or 40 points higher.)

There is a tendency to think of Stengel's tenures with the Yankees and Mets as being polar opposites in terms of seriousness. After all, it was said that rooting for the Stengel-era Yankees was like rooting for U.S. Steel. Certainly there was no greater contrast for such a team than the happy-go-lucky expansion Mets. Really though, how completely serious could any team be with a character like Stengel running the show? This was, after all, the man who over the years had fired off such wry pearls of wisdom as, "The secret of successful managing is to keep the five guys who hate you away from the five guys who haven't made up their minds." In his biography of Stengel, Robert Creamer tells of the time in 1960 that the Yankees took part in a staged group satire. He writes, "In Chicago one night, Stengel and his players mocked [Bill] Veeck's famous exploding scoreboard (the first to put on an extravagant display when a home-team player hit a home run) by lighting sparklers after a Yankee hit one over the fence and parading around in front of the dugout waving them at the crowd." That certainly sounds like a '62 Mets anecdote—except for its obvious American League pedigree, of course.

FRANK THOMAS: I enjoyed playing for Casey. You know, you hear a lot of stories about Casey and everything like that, but I was in the field most of the time and didn't know some of the things he pulled on the bench. Casey was the type of manager that if he wanted to light a fire underneath a ball-player he would make sure that in the clubhouse with the writers around him he would be close enough to that particular ballplayer to make sure that the ballplayer heard what he had to say. This is something that he did with Jim Hickman. I kind of told Jim that he was trying to light a fire under you and that you were a better ballplayer than what you were showing. And Casey thought that by doing this Jim would say, "I'll prove to that old son of a gun that I am a better ballplayer." But Jim went the other way. Casey used reverse psychology with him and it didn't work. After he left the Mets, Jim had a great year with Chicago. Hit a lot of home runs [32 in 1970, with 115 RBIs].

JIM HICKMAN: Playing for Casey was great. Everybody doesn't get that opportunity and I didn't realize what a great opportunity it was until after it was over. I had a hard time understanding him. He'd give us some of those little talks in spring training that year and I just wondered what he said when he finished. You know, maybe in a couple of days it would kind of come to me. Sometimes it would take a day or two for it to hit you.

KEN MacKENZIE: We were coming back from the airport on the bus one night. Casey and I were probably the only two Mets who lived in Manhattan. So there were probably only two or three writers on the bus with Casey and me. Casey was getting off at the Essex House up on 59th and I was going to take the bus down to Grand Central, the last stop, and from there go on to the Village where my wife and I were living.

Casey is a row in front of me and he starts talking about this pitcher he's got and how he had thought he might fire him, but then he talked to a guy from Vanderbilt and he decided to give this player another chance and now he's pitching pretty good so he's going to keep him.

This went on for 15 or 20 minutes until I finally realized he was talking about me! The guy from Vanderbilt had been

Ben Garrity, my former manager at Louisville. I knew I had
been on the hook, but I never knew until then just how close I
had come to getting sent out. Obviously I had a game or two
in the interim that had changed his mind. I guess, in a way, he
was sending me a message.

ROGER CRAIG: Casey was a heavy drinker and he'd be
out drinking a lot at night and we'd be playing these hot day
games in spring training and he'd fall asleep on the bench
all the time. The crack of the bat would wake him up and
he would jump. One time he jumped out of a nap and said,
"Get me Blanchard down in the bull pen." Of course, Johnny
Blanchard had been his catcher with the Yankees.

Whenever we flew, our trainer Gus Mauch carried a small
suitcase and Casey would hide different kinds of liquor in there.
One time I went to the back of the plane to use the lavatory
and Casey said, "Mr. Craig, I'd like to talk to you. What would
you like to drink?" And he opened up his suitcase and there
was all this whiskey and stuff in there.

ROBERT LIPSYTE: I loved covering Casey. I think
he's one of the great misunderstood guys in all of sports.
He was extremely smart and very aware of what was going
on. I liked him enormously. If you spent a whole day—or a
whole night as was often the case since he would close the bar
every night—listening to him very carefully and would catch
who he was talking about at the beginning of the monologue
and kind of follow it through the twists and the turns and
the riffs and the diversions, he would tell a wonderful story
with a lot of wisdom and a lot of great baseball history. There
was this tendency, particularly on the part of columnists who
would kind of breeze in and out and didn't have a lot of time,
to listen to him for just an hour and scribble down what he
was saying about ". . . this guy . . . that guy . . . this feller . . ."
and call it "Stengelese" and make him "the old Professor,"
this kind of nutty old guy. This was fine with Stengel because
I think he saw his function at that point was to divert the press

from just how bad the team was while still keeping the Mets in the news.

ED KRANEPOOL: He was a consummate PR man for the Mets 24 hours a day. They needed that. The great thing about Casey was that he took the press off the players, away from how badly the team was doing. So the reporters wrote about the losing—they had to—but it wasn't really negative.

ROGER CRAIG: Casey was a media delight. He could entertain! Everybody talks about Stengelese, but I have to say, he was very intelligent and very sharp. He was in his 70s then and he could carry on 10 different conversations with 10 different sportswriters at one time and that confused some people, but he knew exactly what he was saying. He'd be talking to one guy, remember what someone else had asked him, and go back to that on the fly.

JAY HOOK: He was a legend and he loved the game. I analyzed Stengelese and came to realize that he'd be talking about one subject and thinking about the next subject he was going to talk about and he'd jump to that subject, but he hadn't finished the first one so he'd go back to it. So he'd have two or three lines of discussion going on at the same time.

ED KRANEPOOL: That act he put on in front of the cameras before the game was just that. All show business. The red light went on and you might as well walk away from him because he was going into that double-talk, rambling about stuff that happened 50 years before for the reporters. But when he talked to you one-on-one or in the clubhouse, you knew exactly what he was saying. He was not only clear but articulate. I hope I'm as sharp as he was at 75.

KEN MacKENZIE: One day Roger was on the mound and Casey took him out after Roger got into some trouble and brought in Galen Cisco. On the way back to the dugout, Roger said to Casey, "So you're going to blow this one too, you old goat." He and Casey sat next to each other in the dugout and Casey put his hand on Roger's knee and said, "You know, you've lost a few yourself."

After the game Roger—his locker was next to mine—said, "You know I really feel like shit, what I said to the old man. What should I do?"

I said, "I think you should apologize." He goes into Casey's office for a few minutes and when he came back I asked him what had happened.

Casey had told him, "Forget it, Roger. I know you want to win and so do I."

ROBERT LIPSYTE: He could be very sarcastic and nasty. We had taken over this big, old formerly posh hotel in St. Petersburg. The team was staying there and they had some black players. There were some complaints from some of the old-line guests about black players in the pool. So Casey ruled the pool off-limits for all players. So I asked him about that story and he said, "That's right, and I also said they can't screw the whole season. Now you put that in your *New York Times*." More pointedly he was likely to introduce a couple of second rate rookies to the press as "the future of the Mets! I want you guys to look at these guys carefully and interview them because on their shoulders is the future of this team." So everybody would spend time with them and, of course, they'd be cut or sent back to the minors the next week.

KEN MacKENZIE: Casey was guilty of using pitchers who had a hot hand too often. He'd keep running you in there until you got your brains beat out and then you sat for nine days or two weeks. He would overwork you, then underuse you, and you can't establish a pitching rhythm that way. That's an advantage relievers have today. It's all scripted. They pretty much know in advance who will pitch the fifth, the sixth, and so on unless someone gets their ears pinned back early. To my mind,

Casey was a seat-of-the-pants manager, at least with us. There didn't seem to be any great plan from one game to the next. He just made it up as he went along. He managed the way he talked.

ED KRANEPOOL: I loved playing for him. Casey was a gentleman who spent a lot of time with the young players, passing on all the information he had. He kind of took me under his wing. He didn't want to expose me too quickly.

JAY HOOK: He was probably the most quick-witted person I have met. He was *so* quick-witted.

ROGER CRAIG: A lot of managers can't handle a great ball club like Casey did with the Yankees. He was so witty, so funny, and so sharp that he kept us very loose and I'm sure he did that with the Yankees, too.

ED KRANEPOOL: He spent a lot of time with the younger players like me and Larry Bearnarth, taking us around the bases and making us sit next to him in the dugout to learn the game. He wasn't going to teach anything to Frank Thomas or Richie Ashburn. They already knew.

KEN MacKENZIE: In one of the last games of the season, Casey put Jim Hickman in center field and Richie Ashburn at second base. Richie had been in the major leagues for over 14 years and he had never played anywhere but center field before. I'm not sure but I think someone might have been hurt. But to tell you the truth, it didn't matter. On that club, Ashburn was as good a second baseman as anyone else they could have put out there. Really, I didn't notice any difference.

JAY HOOK: My wife and I had two kids at the time and they looked at Casey and his wife Edna as a third set of grandparents. They never had any children. She was a silent-movie star and they lived out in Glendale, California. When we'd go to a press luncheon or something, he'd come and get our two kids and take them and they'd sit with Casey and Edna. When I got traded to Milwaukee, his first comment was, "Well, Edna's going to be upset with me."

ROBERT LIPSYTE: The most telling moment with Stengel came one day before a spring training game. We were just standing there talking when an old man came down to the railing dragging a surly teenager. He reaches out and touches Stengel. He said, "Excuse me, Casey, do you remember me? I played against you in Kankakee." [As a player, Stengel had spent a season there in 1910, 52 years before.] Stengel looks at me and kind of rolls his eyes. Then he turns and he looks up at the guy and he immediately sees the situation with the surly teenager and he says, "Yeah, it's you! The old fireballer! I was glad when you left the league, you gave me such a hard time!" He grabbed the guy's arm and he talked for a while about the old days and the minor leagues and then he says, "Whoops, I gotta go now. I've got this really bad team I have to manage. So listen, if you decide to make a comeback I could use you, and if that kid of yours is half as good as you are, send him around. I'll give him a bonus."

I watched him walk away and the dynamic between the kid and the old man had changed. So I said to Casey, "Do you really remember that guy?" And he just shrugged his shoulders. Here's the kicker: Later on I told this story to one of the other reporters, an older guy who was one of the men responsible for creating the Old Professor/"crazy old Casey" stories. He said that he does that sort of stuff when you're around because he sees you as this young, liberal guy. "You also might notice that when you're around and he sees people that are quadriplegics or blind people, he'll go talk to them."

And I said, "Okay. If you agree that he's this manipulative genius, then why do you keep writing this crap about him?"

"My editor and the fans really like this nutty Old Professor stuff," he said. That was kind of a journalistic revelation for me. I was still a kid. I said to myself, "So this is how we do this stuff?"

KEN MacKENZIE: The reporters knew how to play off Casey and it was great fun. One night in Milwaukee I threw a pitch to Del Crandall, the weakest hitter in the Braves lineup, and he hit a shot that Frank Thomas just caught at the left field fence. Casey told the reporters afterward, "If you're going to throw high, you've got to have lightning." And one of the reporters said, "No, Casey. He's been hit by everything *but* that."

ROGER CRAIG: The main thing I learned from Casey was that you have to keep a good clubhouse atmosphere. In his own way he was strict. I think that for most successful managers it all starts in the clubhouse. You've got to let them know you're the boss and don't let things get out of hand. If you see a problem you've got to nip it in the bud. There will be certain players that are not going to like you and they will try to get you fired. One time I asked my coach with the Giants, Norm Sherry, if my players liked me. He said, "They're afraid of you but they respect you." And that's how I wanted it. Casey was different. Unlike him, I would show my frustration at times. Not during a game. I would never show a player up. After the game or maybe before the next game I might have a meeting to discuss it. Casey, though—maybe because he was older—I never saw him mad.

FINALLY, A WIN

The Houston Colt .45s won their first game 11–3 and the two after that by shutout. The year before, the brand-new Los Angeles Angels also won their first game, while the new version of the Washington Senators got their first win in the second game of the '61 season. This sort of good fortune did not grace the Mets. They lost on Opening Day in St. Louis and kept right on losing for the better part of the next two weeks. Symptomatic of this nine-

game opening drought was starting third baseman and former Dodger Don Zimmer. He started all the games, often at the top of the order, and managed three singles and two walks in 37 plate appearances. He scored one run and had no runs batted in.

The Mets finally got their first win in Pittsburgh when Zimmer sat down and Jay Hook tossed a five-hitter at a Pirates lineup that differed little from the one that had clinched the world championship in Casey Stengel's Yankee swan song just 18 months before. Hook also had a two-run single in the game. His other legacy from that season was the revelation that he, practically alone among all the men who have ever thrown one, could actually explain why a curveball curves.

JAY HOOK: When I was going to grad school at Northwestern University the Russians were launching the Sputnik satellite. Sputnik was a spheroid and we got to talking about the dynamics of a spheroid coming back into the atmosphere. It's the same dynamics that govern a baseball curving and it's the same dynamics that govern an airplane's wings. Basically wing theory. So over coffee some of the grad students and I worked up the dynamics of a curveball. Bob Lipsyte came up to me one day and said, "I've got 13 inches of column space in the *New York Times* to fill. Explain to me why a curveball curves." So I drew a ball with a boundary layer buildup and the force vectors and all this and I wrote out Bernoulli's Law.

ROBERT LIPSYTE: Jay Hook was very smart and he drew me diagrams about the gas dynamics law for an article I did for the *Times*.

JAY HOOK: Of course, who's going to believe a ballplayer on something like that? So he goes over to Columbia University and gets the head of the physics department and gets him to look at my stuff and the guy said, "Yeah, that's Bernoulli's Law of Basic Wing Theory. He got it right." Later on, a company called Sarcoscope probably saw Lipsyte's article and contacted me and had me expand on it. They used Bernoulli's Law in the manufacturing of their steam traps. They paid me a little money to write a thing that they put in this little publication that they sent out to their distributors. It was called *The Dynamics of the Curveball.*

I think the Bureau of Standards did some calculations one time and discovered that a ball could curve 16½ inches or something like that within the 60 feet, 6 inches—and that was the maximum amount it could curve. You look at the things that affect it: the density of the air, the amount of moisture in the air, how fast you throw it, how much spin you've got on the ball—there's a bunch of optimums that have to come together to get the maximum break on a curveball.

So Lipsyte won $100 for the best article of the month in the *New York Times* and about a week later I'm pitching in the Polo Grounds and get knocked out in the fourth or fifth inning. After the game Lipsyte came into the locker room to talk to me, and Casey Stengel came by, and he looked at me and he looked at Lipsyte, then he looked back at me and said to Lipsyte, "You know, if Hook could only do what he knows." I've used that line in business and I used it when I taught at Northwestern. I've used it in church talks.

ROBERT LIPSYTE: Casey saw the curveball piece and said, "It's wonderful that he knows how a curveball works. Now if he could only throw one."

THE LOSSES PILE UP

The high-water mark of the Mets' season came at the conclusion of an impressive 9–3 run that lasted from May 6 to May 20. New York began play in that fortnight at 3–16 and finished it 12–19. All nine victories required the Mets to come from behind, which might seem to be a testament to their fortitude but is probably more an indicator of how close to failure they were even when things were seemingly going well. The run proved to be nothing more than a prelude to disaster, however, as the comebacks stopped coming and the team promptly lost its next 17 games to fall to the prescient winning percentage of .250. A 13-game losing streak came later in the season as well as two seven-game skids. Individual achievements were easily superseded by such group futility. For instance, Frank Thomas, who hit 34 home runs for the season, had three consecutive two-homer games in August—and the Mets lost all three.

FRANK THOMAS: As a ballplayer, every day is another day. You have so much pride in yourself and that's what makes the game of baseball so great. In other words, if you're playing football and lose on Sunday, you have all week to brood about it, whereas if you're playing baseball, you can get beat 15–0 and start fresh the next day. It's altogether different.

JIM HICKMAN: Nobody likes to lose. You know, even though we knew we didn't have a real good ball club, nobody likes to lose, and we didn't enjoy going to the park and losing every day. At that time there wasn't too much we could do about it.

ROGER CRAIG: A lot of guys would give anything to be in the major leagues, so I don't think there were too many people on the team that weren't happy to be there. I do think, though, that as the season went on and it got tiring to lose all the time, that there were a lot of guys who were thinking, "Well, maybe I'll get picked up by some contending ball club and get out of here." There was some of that going around. There were some decent players that could have played a different role with a better club and helped them.

FRANK THOMAS: If you look at my career—I played 18½ years, and 12 of those were spent in last place. Through the minors I was with the Pirates organization and they were almost always last. It doesn't get old if you love the game of baseball. A ballplayer has so much pride in himself, he'll just go out and give 100 percent and let the chips fall where they may.

JAY HOOK: I never felt that we were down. I guess the neat thing about baseball is that there's a new game every day. And I always felt that people were fairly optimistic, that we thought we could compete, and, you know, you hate to be honest but while you're going through it you've still got a game tomorrow.

ROBERT LIPSYTE: These guys were not happy being on a terrible team, especially the older players like Thomas, Gil Hodges, and Ashburn. These were guys who had a taste of what it meant to be a real ballplayer on a real team and they did not like to be made fun of. On the other hand players like Rod Kanehl and Choo Choo Coleman were just happy to be there.

ED KRANEPOOL: We were bad in the sense that we had a lot of name players past their primes and it was tough to compete in the National League, particularly with an older club. We were an expansion team but we weren't young. Remember, in 1962, you got to be 32, 33, they thought you were ancient. Not like today.

ROGER CRAIG: It became more of a job than it was a fun thing. I knew when I walked out there that I wasn't going to get many runs and that I had a good chance of losing. That didn't affect my positive thinking as far as trying to win, but it became more of a job as it went along.

THE DODGERS-GIANTS CONNECTION

It is sometimes said that while expansion teams like the Angels and Colt .45s tried to put together the best team possible, the Mets seemed a little too concerned with reliving New York's baseball past, and it cost them on the field. Their very colors were a combination taken from the uniforms of the departed teams. There is no denying, however, that the specter of the Dodgers and Giants loomed large over the Mets, and nowhere did that manifest itself more than at the turnstiles. The average attendance for the Mets' games against San Francisco and Los Angeles was 31,538. Against the other seven visiting clubs it was a budget-busting 9,432. The former New York teams went a combined 15–3 at the Polo Grounds in 1962, a year that found them tied for first when the regular season ended. These were teams loaded with stars worth paying to see, regardless of who they were playing: Sandy Koufax, Don Drysdale, Tommy Davis, Maury Wills, Willie Mays, Willie McCovey, Juan Marichal, and Orlando Cepeda.

There was a strong desire to stock the Mets roster with as many former Dodgers and Giants as possible. Don Zimmer, Charlie Neal, Gil Hodges, Roger Craig, and Johnny Antonelli were of this stripe. In the case of Antonelli, a 31-year-old left-hander who had won 19 games for the Giants in '59, it didn't work out.

KEN MacKENZIE: Antonelli almost immediately decided to retire. He was in the tire business or something up in Syracuse and he decided to pursue that. So that left me as the only non-draftee on the Mets. If Antonelli had showed up, I probably wouldn't have made it to Opening Day. They really wanted him. He had been a big winner with the New York Giants, and the Mets were naturally attracted to players who had starred with the Giants or Dodgers. They were good for box office.

ED KRANEPOOL: My teammates were pretty much all helpful. Frank Thomas was my first roommate and my closest friend on the club. We still talk. I'm fresh out of high school and now I have to dress like an adult; I've never stayed in a hotel or been exposed to much travel. Never set foot on a plane until we went to California. Frank helped with that. Gil Hodges worked with me on defense at first base. I was a raw kid who had played first base with a limited knowledge of everything the position demanded. And I played it well, but Gil taught me the fundamentals and secrets. He was always stressing positioning, where to throw the ball. How to block and scoop the ball. Things you don't learn in high school. Gil polished me into a good first baseman. I already had good hands. Gil could see that. But there are ways of stretching out and giving with the ball so that it drops into your glove rather than throwing your glove forward and pounding it away from you. If your hands are loose when the ball hits your glove and you're extended—as opposed to jabbing at it—then you draw your glove back toward your body and the ball hits the pocket and stays there. My footwork was fair but there are positions that you're supposed to take on and around the base to have an advantage; Gil worked on all that stuff. When the throw was coming from third, I could position myself in one area, from second or short, I'd set up somewhere else. He taught me not to stretch too soon, not to anticipate. If you stretch out and the ball is offline, you'll never be able to recover.

JIM HICKMAN: Every time the Dodgers and Giants came to town the place was full, and it was a different atmosphere as far as the game itself. It was sort of a play-off atmosphere to us, and everybody talked about the two teams that left town. They were tough games. Both the Dodgers and Giants had real good ball clubs. We knew we were in for it when they came to town.

JAY HOOK: One of the advantages I think we had versus, say, Houston, was that the Dodgers and Giants had been there and they had their own cadre of fans, and they moved out to California and there was a four-year hiatus there where there wasn't National League baseball. I think when the Mets came they were kind of adopted by a lot of Giants fans and Dodger fans. And sure, they could be brutal at times, but most of the time they were really cheering for the Mets.

FRANK THOMAS: We always wanted to play the spoiler.

ROGER CRAIG: Maury Wills was going to run, and you just had to figure out when. He was on his own most of the time, so he would go when he thought he had the jump. By throwing to first base a lot it made him more cautious and it helped my catcher when he did run. He had the knack of knowing when I was going to throw over there. He and Joe Morgan were the best I ever saw at that. Maury and Joe were often able to steal signs to know when you were going to throw over. One thing about Maury was that when he was going to go, his lead wasn't quite so big. When he was going to go, he'd back off a couple of steps and knowing that helped me hold him there.

JAY HOOK: I remember facing Sandy Koufax. I batted left-handed—and I didn't strike out very much. He threw me a four-seam fastball that kind of rode up that I fouled off. The next pitch he threw me a two-seam fastball that sunk, which was a strike, and the next pitch he threw me was a curveball and I knew it was a curveball and it started out like it was going up behind my head. I knew it could get over the plate, but I didn't think it could get down into the strike zone. But it did. It *really* broke. He had a great curveball.

KEN MacKENZIE: Koufax didn't have one of his greater years that season because he faced us only twice. Struck out 18 the first time and pitched a no-hitter the second time. I've always said he was unfair. I don't know how many people are aware of this, but Sandy has these enormous hands. From the butt of his palm to the tips of his fingers, his hand was at least an inch and a half longer than mine. So when his wrist comes forward, think of where that baseball goes when compared to my stubby hands. I'm back in the arc. Koufax's fastball was a couple of feet faster than mine and it was all there in those longer hands. Which is why his ball would land in the catcher's mitt while mine was still out there getting whacked. He threw a four-seam fastball, straight backspin. His curveball had straight forward spin, so you really had difficulty differentiating the spin between the two pitches. They looked the same coming in because there was no seam showing, whereas with most curveballs there's usually a dot you can pick up. You hear about 12-to-6 curves that break straight down but the true 12-to-6 is very, very rare. Most of them go 1-to-7. Sandy had that 12-to-6, straight over the top. Maybe Ernie Broglio had one, Clem Labine, and that fellow who pitched for the Washington Senators, Camilo Pascual—great curve. When it has that tight spin, you can hear the ball go *sizzzzzzz*. Koufax's curve would start high, say, around your shoulders and would be down around your knees when it finished up. A real curve. But none of those curveballers could match Koufax's velocity. He would throw a fastball up in the letters and it would look good, but no one could hit it. No one. The key was he not only threw the ball hard—I'm sure he could reach 100—but it had great movement. His fastball wasn't straight and it would hop.

ED KRANEPOOL: With Koufax we knew what was coming. I could read his pitches. For years he gave away his pitches with this little thing he did in the stretch. But it didn't matter when you're that overpowering with a dominating curveball. Right-handers took a lot of those curves for strikes because the pitch started high and broke so late. But when a left-hander sees something high in his eyes, he's going to swing and you can put it in play. I think lefties had better luck against Koufax because they didn't take as many curves. The curveball was his strike-out pitch.

THE MARV MYSTIQUE
AND THE "NEW BREED" OF FAN

To say that the '62 Mets were a "cult team" is only a bit of an exaggeration. They were popular beyond their level of achievement, but not as popular as they would become two years later when Shea Stadium opened and the turnstiles really began to whir. The '62 team's attendance of 922,530 is the second-lowest in club history (not counting the strike year of 1981), besting only the New Dark Ages team of 1979. As noted, when the Dodgers and Giants weren't visiting, the '62 Mets drew as poorly as any team in baseball except perhaps the Chicago Cubs and Kansas City Athletics. In the midst of this, though, a change was occurring, a division between old and new that was epitomized in the difference between attending a Yankees and Mets game. There was an almost romantic cynicism about the proceedings, perhaps best exemplified in the development of the Marv Throneberry mystique.

Marv Throneberry, who died in 1994 and is known for his appearance in Miller Lite commercials, was perhaps most famous for a play that smacks of urban legend. It really did happen, though, on June 17 in the first game of a doubleheader against Chicago. After botching a rundown—a Throneberry specialty—in the top of the first that was instrumental in giving the Cubs four runs, he came to bat with men on first and second and one out in the bottom of the inning and creamed one.

FRANK THOMAS: He hit a triple and got called out for missing first base, and Casey came out to argue and the umpire, Dusty Boggess, said, "Don't bother, Casey. He missed second, too." The next man up hit a home run and we ended up losing by a run.

KEN MacKENZIE: Marv thought he was Mickey Mantle. Really. When he jogged, he kept his elbows up behind him like Mickey. At the time some of the guys got their shirts tailor-made. Mickey always wore a wide-collared white shirt. So did Marv. He wore his helmet the way Mickey did. And every once in a while Marv would hit a ball like Mickey—a long way. But not nearly as often. In the field, zany things just seemed to happen around him. He wouldn't get his foot on first base, he wouldn't catch balls hit right to him. I also remember him lunging for bad throws and looking awkward when it really wasn't his fault. Our infielders weren't known for their consistent accuracy. A lot of those throws put him on the spot.

ROGER CRAIG: I had a good pickoff move, and that year I had a lot of targets for it over there at first base. Now, when Marv Throneberry was playing first, a lot of the time my pickoff throws would hit him in the chest. Finally, he came over to me one day and said, "Don't throw to first base because I can't see the ball coming at me because of the white shirts in the background." So, I looked behind me and all I could see was empty seats on the third-base side and I said, "There's nobody over there!" He was touted as being the next Mickey Mantle. He kind of copied Mantle the way he swung. He was a nice guy, but he didn't like me to throw the ball over there.

ROBERT LIPSYTE: Throneberry was interesting. The writer Stan Isaacs did a lot to help create the Throneberry legend. Throneberry was never going to be a superstar, but he was brought up by the Yankees and was in the outfield with Mickey Mantle. He was one of those guys who had given up a college football scholarship to become a baseball player. He was a very proud baseball player who years and years later told me that he had not enjoyed that time when he was being mocked and he had really always thought of himself as a former Yankee rather than a former Met. Within the dynamic of the team the guys got it and ran with it, especially Richie Ashburn. By then Ashburn had had a successful career with the Phillies. He was the one who really talked to Throneberry about relaxing into this role as the kind of goat/spokesman for this goat team. I remember one time Frank Thomas made a couple of errors at third base and, at Ashburn's instigation, Throneberry said so that the press could hear, "What's Frank trying to do, steal all my fans?"

KEN MacKENZIE: He wasn't very receptive to the Marvelous Marv thing at first. He didn't want any part of it. It was Ashburn who instantly recognized what was going on with Marv. He took Throneberry aside and said, "No, Marv, this is good, just go along with it." It was really Ashburn who encouraged Throneberry to play back with the writers and tell them what he thought about things.

ROBERT LIPSYTE: In many ways what was really colorful was not the team but the response to the team. Had it been happening in Milwaukee or Cleveland or somewhere, it would have just been lost in the fog of sports. But here you had a very hungry and very clever press contingent led by Dick Young of the *Daily News* and his sidekick Jack Lang from the Long Island paper. So they kind of built this into a totem or mythical worst team of all time and they created a whole body of negative statistics. They called them "neggies" in the press box—stuff the Mets were obviously not going to give us. [The '62 Mets] also created "the new breed" of sports fan and in many ways the things that we saw then, the banners that appeared in the stands, the fans marching around . . . This was the beginning of the rock-and-roll era and somehow there was this kind of melding of this starchy, traditional old ballpark. People in those days went to ball games as if it were church. They behaved. Meanwhile, you had this other thing that was happening, this participatory audience at rock concerts. I think that's what happened: the idea of the celebration of the Mets as the people's team; the celebration of the Mets as part of a new era with their fans, a new breed that had a right to participate. Not to make too much of it, but I'm not so sure that a lot of the bad fan behavior or the madness of fans that we see now in every sport did not begin there.

AS BAD AS ALL THAT?

The Mets scored 617 runs and allowed 948 in 1962, a gap that would anticipate about 50 wins instead of 40. For whatever reason the team was especially bad in the second games of doubleheaders that year. While they went 11–19 in openers, their record dropped to 4–26 in nightcaps, as if to point out a lack of depth in the pitching staff. Only once in 19 tries did they lose the opening game of a doubleheader and manage to come back to win the nightcap.

KEN MacKENZIE: I've gone over this with people again and again. We were often very competitive and we weren't as bad as we looked. If you go back and study the box scores, you'll see we had 39 one-run losses, and a lot of those occurred in the late innings. Had we won just half of those one-run losses, we would have lost only 103 games. Granted, that's still not good, but it wouldn't be a historic total.

FRANK THOMAS: We should have won another 10 or 12 games. Probably more than that if we had had a long man and a closer like they have today. We scored a lot of runs, we just didn't have the pitching.

KEN MacKENZIE: We were shut out only six times.

JAY HOOK: They were bad. *We* were bad. I include myself in that.

The team did blow late leads in 17 games. That's not counting as double the four games in which they blew a lead then retied it, or took the lead again and blew it a second time. This double whammy happened in both games of a September 8 doubleheader against the Colt .45s.

The Mets had two 20-game losers in the persons of Roger Craig (10– 24) and Al Jackson (8–20) and could have easily had a third in Jay Hook (8–19) except that the season ended before his next turn came up. Yet it was another team's 20-game loser that provided one of the great moments in the annals of losing pitcher history. On September 29, the penultimate day of the season, the Mets started Bob L. Miller against Dick Ellsworth of the Cubs at Wrigley Field. At the time, Miller was 0–12 and Ellsworth was 9–19. If Ellsworth prevailed, Miller would have fallen to 0–13, which would have given him a share of the record for most losses without a victory in a single season. If Miller prevailed, Ellsworth would lose his 20th game of the season. In the end, the Mets and Cubs (a team that finished six games behind the expansion Colt .45s) managed just 13 hits off the two pitchers and Miller got his only win of the season, 2–1. Ironically, the other Bob Miller on the '62 Mets—reliever Bob G. Miller, acquired in a May trade that sent Zimmer to the Reds—pitched only 20⅓ innings for New York but won two games.

THE LEGACY

When Shea Stadium opened in 1964, the Mets began to outdraw the Yankees at the gate. For the decade of the '60s—even giving the Yankees the one-year head start of 1961—the Mets outdrew the Bronx Bombers by more than 20 percent. By 1969 and '70 they were doubling Yankee attendance.

ROBERT LIPSYTE: One really great side effect of the Mets was that this fringe journalist named Jimmy Breslin wrote this slipshod, not-very-good book called *Can't Anybody Here Play This Game?,* which John Hay "Jock" Whitney, the brother of Mets owner Joan Whitney Payson, read and must have liked very much because he gave Breslin a job at his paper, the *New York Herald Tribune,* and launched one of the most significant careers in American journalism.

KEN MacKENZIE: I always felt I was one ticket away from Syracuse. So I was living on the edge all the time. You had no security. If you're eligible every day to lose your job, you feel the pressure even when you're not pitching. You know that if someone else loses, they're apt to start making moves and who knows what will come of that. So it wasn't easy, but you hope you come away having learned how to deal with pressure. I'm not sure I did, but I tried.

JIM HICKMAN: You know, at the time we didn't like it too well. I think it did make me stronger as a player and better at handling adversity. Yeah, I think it did make everybody a little bit stronger.

THE LATINO WAVE

Featuring

JIM KAAT: Former pitcher, broadcaster, and Minnesota Twins teammate of 1965 MVP Zoilo Versalles and many other Latino greats, including Tony Oliva.

HARMON KILLEBREW: Hall of Famer and Senators/Twins teammate of many of the Latino players who were so prevalent in that organization in the 1960s.

DAVID MARANISS: A Pulitzer Prize—winning reporter, he is the author of *Clemente: The Passion and Grace of Baseball's Last Hero.*

MINNIE MINOSO: The man who broke the color line for Hispanic ballplayers when he made the Indians in 1949; the Cuban Minoso was a seven-time All-Star and retired with a career .389 on-base percentage.

TONY OLIVA: The Cuban-born Oliva burst on the scene with the Twins in 1964 and won the American League Rookie of the Year Award. He would make eight All-Star Game appearances and win three batting titles.

TONY PÉREZ: A native of Cuba and a Hall of Fame first baseman with the Big Red Machine of the 1970s and later the Expos, Red Sox, and Phillies.

LUIS TIANT: A four-time 20-game winner who pitched primarily for the Indians, Red Sox, and Yankees in a career that began in 1964 and spanned 19 seasons. Born in Cuba, he was the son of pitching legend Luis Tiant Sr.

TIM WENDEL: Award-winning author of *The New Face of Baseball: The 100-Year Rise and Triumph of Latinos in America's Favorite Sport,* as well as the novel *Castro's Curveball.*

WHILE THE LATINO PRESENCE in baseball is more pervasive than ever before and continues to grow every day, it would probably surprise most people to know that a Latin American player was present at the game's creation. Players from the Caribbean did not really begin to show up in numbers until the 1950s and '60s, but there was a Cuban player in the lineup for the fifth major-league game ever played. On May 9, 1871, Fordham University graduate Esteban Bellán was the Troy Haymakers' third baseman in their National Association debut. He stayed with the club for another year and played a handful of games with the New York Mutuals in 1873 before returning to Cuba, where he became one of the founding fathers of the famed Almendares club.

"One of the things that U.S. fans just don't understand," says author Tim Wendel, "is that there's no other game, including the NBA, that's more international than baseball. If you go outside our borders, baseball is considered as radical as the X Games. People hear me say that and tell me I'm nuts, but whereas here baseball is Mom; apple pie; red, white, and blue; and the 4th of July, in places like Cuba, baseball has always been this radical game of an independent nation. So much so that when the Spanish controlled the island they were very uptight about baseball—it was too radical. You go around the world and baseball is much more cutting-edge than people give it credit for in this country."

Many still debate the legitimacy and/or necessity of the Spanish-American War of 1898, but it would probably be less controversial if the United States had intervened in Cuba in 1869 as a result of the Spanish rulers banning baseball. For a few years the ban halted the development of the game on the island, but by the late 1870s it was growing again, becoming a part of the culture in much the way it was in the United States. The difference, though, was that in the intervening years, no other sport ever came along to distract Cubans from the game, unlike in the United States, where the national pastime was eventually crowded on all sides by basketball, hockey, and, most importantly, football.

Even the tumult of revolution did not shake baseball's hold on Cuban society. When Fidel Castro seized power in 1959 he made many breaks with the past, but he did not make the mistake of declaring baseball a bourgeois luxury. Instead he embraced it and made it a symbol of his revolution, a stick to shake at the game's originators and his archenemy, the United States.

Says Wendel, "I wrote a novel based on the question of what might have happened if Castro had pursued baseball a little bit more than revolution. It is one of the big what-ifs. If he had been locked up to a contract by [Washington Senators scout] Papa Joe Cambria or somebody else, the world as we know it would be much, much different. What we do know for sure is that he is a huge baseball fan, and he pretty much was the manager of that great national team that they had in the early '90s. That is still one of the best infields I have ever seen anywhere, with Omar Linares and Orestes Kindelán and all those guys. Castro called the shots on who was on that roster and who was going to travel.

"What we also know about Castro is that coming out of high school he was a very good athlete. He would be what we would call in this day and age, 'a blue-chip prospect.' He played basketball, he played baseball, and he was also a champion Ping-Pong player.

When he came to Havana he had to take a year of prep school because he had come from the eastern end of the island and was considered somewhat a hick, and his grades had to come up a little bit. I've actually been to this Jesuit prep school and one of the weirdest moments was when a Jesuit priest took us around back to this stone wall and it was full of these indents. And we're looking at this wall thinking, 'Why are we looking at this?'

"And the priest says, 'This is where Castro would throw the ball against the wall when he ran out of people to play catch with.' So maybe he had the arm, and I've got old pictures of him throwing and he had kind of a funky delivery, but I'm not going to sell a guy short who had most of his meager revolutionary army wiped out within days and then within three years took over the country. I'm not going to say a guy like that couldn't have made it in baseball. As to whether Cambria ever scouted him, some people get very indignant about this and say, 'He was never a good enough prospect for that type of serious look.' There was never any contract. But *Harper's Magazine* mentioned a couple of years ago that the New York Giants were interested in him, and the Washington Senators were interested in him. How true that is, we aren't sure. But there are enough stories I've heard from people living in Cuba: 'Yeah, Castro pitched batting practice for my grandfather,' or 'Yeah, Castro used to show up at the games with my uncle,' so who knows? It's lost in legend. Could he pitch at the major-league level? Who knows?"

BREAKING THE ICE: BASEBALL'S FIRST LATIN AMERICANS

COUNTRY	PLAYER	DEBUT
Cuba	Esteban Bellán	May 9, 1871
Mexico	Mel Almada	Sept. 8, 1933
Puerto Rico	Hiram Bithorn	April 15, 1942
Venezuela	Chucho Ramos	May 7, 1944
Panama	Humberto Robinson	April 20, 1955
Dominican Republic	Ozzie Virgil	Sept. 23, 1956
Nicaragua	Dennis Martínez	Sept. 14, 1976

THE 20TH-CENTURY INTEGRATION

Ask the average baseball fan today about the game's Latino lineage, and one of the first names to spring to mind is likely that of Juan Marichal, who won 243 games from 1960 to '75 (with a 2.89 ERA and 244 complete games) and is the only Latin-born pitcher enshrined in the Hall of Fame. Known for his high leg kick and his deceptive array of release points and pitches—fastball, curveball, slider, changeup, and screwball— Marichal, a.k.a "the Dominican Dandy," was the ace of the great San Francisco Giants teams of the '60s that featured countrymen Felipe and Matty Alou and José Pagán as well as Puerto Rican–born slugger Orlando Cepeda. Those players paved the way for the current crop of Dominican-born stars that includes Vladimir Guerrero, Manny Ramírez, José Reyes, Bartolo Colón, and Pedro Martínez (who grew up idolizing Marichal).

Dominicans were among the last Latino players to break into the major leagues, however. Cubans had a larger impact in the first half of the 20th century, though after Bellán it would be another four decades before the next Cubans showed up on big-league rosters. Because of baseball's strictly enforced color line, these players—Rafael Almeida, Armando Marsans, and Mike Gonzalez among them—were listed as being of European descent. While they were sometimes the target of racism from fans and the press because of confusion over just what constituted a Hispanic, as long as they were truly white, they were welcome in organized baseball. Gonzalez even did two stints as an interim manager with the Cardinals in the 1930s. The biggest-name Cuban export of the prewar era was Dolf Luque, a pitcher who had a cup of coffee with the Miracle Boston Braves of 1914 and later went on to fame with the Reds.

LUIS TIANT: The white Cubans played in the big leagues. Adolfo Luque was a great pitcher [194 career wins]. He played for the Cincinnati Reds. He won 27 games one year [1923]. A lot of guys played. The black Spanish couldn't play. And that's one of the problems. They were in the big leagues before we were. They were white and we're not. I guess that's in the past. You can't complain and hate anybody because of that. Because if that's what people want to do—it's not supposed to be that way, but that's the way it was. Can you get angry with anybody? I don't think so, because it ain't going to do any good anyway. What are you going to do, go and beat up every white person you see? It's stupid. Most of my best friends are white. I grew up in Cuba with white people around me. I didn't have a problem. I teach my kids—I can live with anybody. I can get along with anybody. I don't care. You respect me, I respect you. You show me love, I show you love.

In the 1940s, the Washington Senators—and especially their owner, Clark Griffith—began to look way south for talent.

TIM WENDEL: Joe Cambria [who died in 1962] established a cottage industry scouting in the Latin countries. His major claim to fame was in Cuba. There he was known as Papa Joe, and it's funny because from what I understand, he didn't really speak Spanish all that well. But he got the idea to scout down there when he was working for the Griffith family and the Senators. The Senators had noticed that there were quality ballplayers coming out of the Caribbean, especially Cuba. This is back in the '30s and '40s. And they could get them on the cheap. It was an economic situation to go into Cuba.

JIM KAAT: That is why the organization not only targeted Latino players but Cubanos, players from a poor country. Papa Joe Cambria was Clark Griffith's chief Latin American scout, and he had a virtual pipeline bringing in talent from Cuba. Now keep in mind, the conditions back in the 1950s, with Cuba still in revolution, millions of people living in poverty with no chance of improving their conditions, and over here in this country, no baseball players' union to stand up for players' rights. I'm convinced, although I don't have any hard evidence, just my own observation, that many of those players came here and played for less than the minimum, something a club couldn't get away with doing today. So they were a form of inexpensive talent for the team.

TIM WENDEL: Papa Joe Cambria was the guy who did it. He would pretty much just beat the bushes. He'd drive around in his car, in Havana and outside the city. When you travel in Cuba, you might go to some of these places way off the track. And yet, if you talk to some old-timer, he might end up telling you about the day that Joe Cambria was there looking at players. He seemed to have gone everywhere on the island!

HARMON KILLEBREW: Camilo Pascual, Pedro Ramos, Julio Becquer, José Valdivielso, Carlos Paula—Carlos had a good year my first season with the club, but he didn't hit much after that. They were the first wave. The Senators weren't the Yankees or the Dodgers, with all that money to sign all that talent, so they had to dig a little deeper to find ballplayers. And they kept finding talent in Latin America, only it improved. Camilo Pascual was a tremendous pitcher; that curveball of his could be unhittable. He was unlucky to play with a lot of poor clubs, and just as we got good he got hurt and then we traded him. And Pedro had some good seasons.

TONY OLIVA: Camilo Pascual and Pete Ramos—these were the big names I remember as I grew up, because they used to play for the Washington Senators. Pete Ramos was from Pinar del Rio, my province. I wanted to play in Cuba for the Cienfuegos ball club because Pete Ramos played for that club.

TIM WENDEL: It's funny how things work, because what started as an economic decision—hey, we can get quality players cheaper than we can in the States—really opened people's eyes about the quality of play coming out of Cuba. This is what laid the groundwork for Minoso and guys like Luis Tiant,

Tony Oliva, and José Cardenal. By the time those guys all came along, Cuban baseball had a great deal of respect.

The Senators of the '50s suffered mightily. This was, after all, the team that inspired Douglass Wallop to create the character Joe Hardy in the novel The Year the Yankees Lost the Pennant, *which was turned into the play and movie* Damn Yankees. *The franchise was slowly acquiring talent, though, and by the time it moved to Minnesota in 1961, it was definitely on the rise. That improvement culminated in an American League championship in 1965 and continued good play throughout the rest of the '60s. An example of the team's fortunes in that period can be found in the win-loss record of Cuban import Camilo Pascual. From 1954 to '58 he went 28–66. Yet he retired in 1971 with a winning record (174–170). Pascual was famous for his curveball.*

JIM KAAT: Going back to when I was a kid, we used to call that overhand curve a "drop." It almost came off your fingertips and had a definite 12-to-6 break. That's what Camilo's did. You had pitchers down there like Connie Marrero, the veteran Cuban pitcher, who also had a drop. You don't see many like that. And the slider you see today is, if you'll excuse the expression, sort of a half-assed slurve, it's really not a sharp breaking ball, which is why there are so many home runs hit nowadays, too, because that's really a mediocre breaking ball. The true slider is what Mariano Rivera throws, except now they call it a cutter. Back when Ted Williams said the slider was the toughest pitch to hit, that was the pitch Mo throws now: 95 percent fastball, 5 percent breaking ball. What they pass off as a slider today is 55 percent fastball, 45 percent breaking ball. When we'd give up homers years ago, we'd come back and someone would ask, "What did he hit that off of?" And most of the time you'd say, "A hanging slider." Meaning, you didn't throw it the way you wanted to. Now that's what 90 percent of the sliders that pitchers call sliders today are throwing. So they get hit a long way. The overhand curve that Pascual had, and later Bert Blyleven came along with it, dropped straight down. Every year, Camilo would go through a two- or three-week period where he just had to shut it down because his elbow was barking at him, but then he'd come back and be effective. Pitchers don't even develop that pitch anymore. Camilo started developing it, like most Latino pitchers, at an early age, and it was more "over-the-top" than any of us could throw it. We all tried to throw over the top, 12-to-6, but it usually came out 11-to-5. His ball came right off his fingertips. Can you picture yourself spinning a yo-yo? That's sort of the way the ball came off his fingertips.

If the major leagues were truly going to get the most out of the talent the Caribbean had to offer, they were going to have to erase the color line that Tiant described. While Dolf Luque was welcome, his dark-skinned countryman Martín Dihigo—probably the one man in baseball history who can challenge Babe Ruth in terms of excelling at both pitching and hitting—was not. (Dihigo played in the Negro Leagues from 1923 to '36 and again briefly in '45, and was posthumously inducted into the Hall of Fame in '77.)

TIM WENDEL: From what I've been told, imagine a Vlad Guerrero who is able to play any position and play it well *and* he can also pitch and pitch well. That was Martín Dihigo. And supposedly the pitching matchups he had with Satchel Paige are legendary in the Negro Leagues. They would just go toe-to-toe. And we had guys in more recent years—Bert Campaneris comes to mind—who could play all the positions, but that was maybe somewhat of a publicity stunt. Martín Dihigo could really play them all and play them well. He started as a shortstop—a fearsome hitter. We're looking into records here that are sketchy at best but he averaged well over .300 and he could really pitch. Unfortunately, he came before Jackie Robinson, before the color barrier was broken. So in many ways he's the best player that people don't know about. He's made four Halls of Fame: He's in Cooperstown, the Venezuela Hall of Fame, the Cuban Hall of Fame, and the Mexican Hall of Fame. And I think that's very indicative of the type of player he was. He was about 6'2", 6'3", he was ripped, and he knew the game so well that he went on to a pretty good second career as a manager.

MINNIE MINOSO: When I was coming up he was on his way out. After that, he was a manager. He was my idol and I used to hit him. I'd feel so badly. I hit a triple with the bases loaded off of him.

MINNIE'S MOMENT ARRIVES

Once Jackie Robinson broke the color line in 1947, it was simply a matter of time before the first dark-skinned Latino would make his major-league debut. As the last years of all-white baseball were unfolding in the States, a young Cuban was learning the ropes in his native country and for the New York Cubans in the Negro Leagues.

MINNIE MINOSO: *"Chicito [Little One], go over there and play third base."* We were playing Almendares, I came [into the game] in the 9th inning, got my first hit, and we won it. Then the second day I got a base hit off a guy who pitched in the Negro Leagues, Raymond Brown. He was inducted into the Negro Hall of Fame a few years ago. I was a happy man to make a professional team in Cuba. You have to be very good and very lucky. They only have four ball clubs. To become a professional there is like trying to make the big leagues here.

TIM WENDEL: Minnie Minoso in my mind is the Latino Jackie Robinson. He is the one who follows Jackie two years after and he is the first black superstar in Chicago, a major metropolitan center. So he had to put up with a great many of the things that Roberto Clemente or Orlando Cepeda did, but he had to do it in a larger setting. And I think Cepeda would agree. You had Latino players beforehand, but, of course, they were light-skinned. But this is a dark-skinned Latino player in a very large setting with a memorable team with Nellie Fox and Chico Carrasquel and those guys.

MINNIE MINOSO: Why did I want to go to the United States? You fall in love with what people say. I wanted to come

even though I didn't know how to speak English. I didn't have
a friend over there, but sometimes you have a dream, from a
long, long time, long way back, to visit some country just because you fall in love with what people say [about the country].
[The New York Cubans] had a few guys who had been playing
here for a little while, and they spoke pretty good English. In
New York they used to have a big Cuban population. Along
Lennox Avenue, a lot of people used to speak Spanish. There
was a Puerto Rican woman, Nancy Rosado, she used to be a
good friend of [the famous salsa singer] Celia Cruz, and she
used to help any ballplayer. She lived at 116th and Broadway.
She raised one of my boys over there.

*Seventy-eight years after Esteban Bellán, Minoso's entry into the bigs
marked the beginning of the true Latino wave—one that was open to everyone from the Caribbean. He was signed by the Indians and played his
first game for them on April 19, 1949. His first full season in the majors
was 1951 when, after being traded to the White Sox, he finished second in
the Rookie of the Year voting in a tight scrape with Gil McDougald of the
Yankees, who got 13 votes to Minoso's 11. (Minoso did receive one first-
place vote for MVP, while McDougald did not. Minoso finished fourth in
the MVP voting; McDougald finished ninth.)*

TONY OLIVA. I grew up on the farm, in Cuba. The only
baseball I listened to over there was the Cuban winter baseball league. I listened to Habana Almendares. My goal was
to play for one of those teams someday. But I never had the
opportunity to watch one of those teams play in person.
Minnie Minoso was the king of Cuba. He was the king of
Cuban ballplayers. With the way we followed him, his dream
of baseball, he was the big man in Cuba when I grew up.

TIM WENDEL: Minoso was aggressive both on the base
paths and in the field. He was willing to take the extra base. In
a sense, Clemente really followed in the footsteps of Minoso in
terms of the style of play. It's funny, I remember being with Ken
Burns when he was doing the final edits on his PBS series, *Baseball*. And we were looking at some outtakes. It was a ball game, I

believe, between the New York Giants and the Brooklyn Dodgers at the Polo Grounds. And it was just fast. Any time the ball is put in play, guys are going first to third. You had a lot of inside pitches. You had guys in the outfield really running to cut off balls in the gap. And I remember Ken at one point saying, "Well, it's too bad we don't see that style of play much anymore." And I almost had to laugh. I said, "Ken, you see that style of play. But it's going on in Havana and Santo Domingo." And I think it's that style of play that Minoso brought to the forefront. And also the guys who came along very soon after that, like Felipe Alou. This is the type of play that those guys brought back to the U.S. sensibility.

LUIS TIANT: Minnie Minoso was my idol. A lot of other guys played in Cuba that played in the United States in the big leagues. And I listened and I heard all about it. My dream when I was a kid was to pitch in a game against Minnie Minoso and Mickey Mantle—and it happened!

TONY PÉREZ: I grew up in a small town with a sugar factory, and the factory made a lot of noise with the machines. I didn't like that. It used to bother me. I'd tell my mother and my father I didn't want to grow up and work there. I wanted to play professional baseball. They used to kid around with me, "Oh, you're not that big. You're too skinny." I told them, "No, I'm going to be like Minnie Minoso." Minnie was a hero in Cuba. Everybody was talking about Minoso. Someone even wrote a song—a cha cha—about Minnie. I told [my parents], "I'm going to be like Minnie. I want to play baseball." And they were laughing at me. But I made it. After I made it they said, "You were right." I got bigger and stronger and when I got back to Cuba in 1972—I was out 10 years before I saw my family again—I came back because [my father] got sick. When they [last saw me], I was a skinny guy. When I came back at 200-some pounds, they were surprised. Then they said, "I know how you made it. You're big and strong now."

MINNIE MINOSO: I don't know who changed my name. When I first came here, I was Saturnino Orestes [based on the

Latino tradition of naming kids according to the saints of the day], then the second day [his second day with the White Sox] they called out my name, "Number 9, Minnie Minoso." I said, "What?" I didn't know any Minnie. Now I'm Minnie. But I'm glad they did it.

PRIDE AND PREJUDICE

Although organized baseball had opened its doors to Latinos, parts of the United States did not follow suit. And so the dark-skinned Latinos found themselves in the bizarre world of Jim Crow.

In a 2000 interview with Bob Ryan of the Boston Globe, *Marichal recalled his experience in Michigan City, Indiana, in 1958, as a minor leaguer for the Giants. "There were two of us Dominicans on the team," Marichal says. "Myself and José Tartabull. We didn't even know how to say 'glass of water.' We would go to a restaurant and look to see what was on people's plates. If we saw something we liked we would point to it and ask for the same thing." That, of course, assumes that the Latino players would even be served: Cepeda and Felipe Alou once entered a restaurant in Pittsburgh and were simply told that the establishment did not need any more dishwashers. The ballpark was not always a safe haven, either. Legend has it that at one point in the early 1960s Giants manager Alvin Dark banned his players from speaking Spanish in the clubhouse.*

> **TIM WENDEL:** Roberto Clemente said it best: "We're double minorities." He meant that he was being singled out for his skin color and also being singled out because maybe he didn't talk the language as eloquently as a native speaker.

> **LUIS TIANT:** When I came here and we went on a road trip, the white players used to have to bring the food to us so we could eat. Because we couldn't go in the restaurant; they didn't serve us. We had to stay in different hotels. And the people in the ballpark? Forget it. They called you all kinds of things. Made you feel like a little ant, like you weren't a human being.

TONY OLIVA: There was a lot of prejudice, but it didn't bother me that much. We had prejudice in my own country. Every country has its own rules. The only thing, when I came here there was a big, big difference: Where I grew up we play together, we sleep together, we eat together. There were only a few things that you weren't able to do. Like sometimes if you go to a dance, sometimes you have a club only for whites. Things like that, you know what I mean? Dances for whites only. Blacks didn't go. Or nightclubs for blacks only or whites only. That used to happen in Cuba, too. But, not the same way it happened here. Here it was a little bit more rough. White people stay in one place. Black people stay in another place.

LUIS TIANT: People don't know where you come from. Nothing comes easy in life, not just in baseball. Everything's tough. You have to deal with all kinds of people; some like you, some don't. And that's the way it is. You have to stick to your guns and do what you have to do. Show people who you are and what you can do. That's why I thank God that He made me strong in that particular way. I can fight back, not with my hands or punching somebody or anything like that. I know I can go to the mound and show people, "Hey, I can pitch as good as this guy. I can pitch better than this guy." And that's how you prove yourself. You don't have to fight with people and punch people. That's crazy. You can do it with your brains. You can do it a lot of different ways. That's what I tried to prove: The other guy is no different than me, no matter where I come from, no matter if I speak the language or not. To me baseball is a God-given talent, no matter the color of your skin, no matter if you're a genius or not, or if you go to college or not. It's all a God-given talent to us. That's what people some-times do not understand.

TONY OLIVA: I was in spring training in the big leagues in Orlando, Florida. We stayed in separate hotels for my first five years. Black people stayed in the black hotel. White people stayed in the white hotel. That was in Orlando. All over Florida, it was like that when we played. When we played in the rookie league, my first year, back in '61, in Tennessee, Georgia, and Virginia, it was the same way. I didn't think the same thing would happen when you went to the big leagues. You go to spring training, in Orlando. You had to stay in different hotels because of the color [of your skin]. But that stuff really didn't bother me. I think every country has its own rules and they can dictate what they want to do. But I was very, very happy, very glad that the system changed 500 percent for the best; that blacks and whites can be together. They can play ball together, go to a nightclub, eat, with no problem at all. This is beautiful. I think now, this country had a big change for the best.

MINNIE MINOSO: I was a lucky guy. My dad always told me, "Never look back and don't let worry bother you. Yes, prepare for whatever you have to face, but if you do good, you don't have to think about it. Do good to everybody and don't worry about it. You defend yourself, but you never try to hurt anybody." They called me names, they called me black, nigger, everything they could . . . then it stopped. If you're black, you're black. If I went to Puerto Rico, I was black. In Cuba, I was black. The country doesn't change your color.

LUIS TIANT: You have to deal with those people. You have to deal with all kinds of people. And, as I said, God made me strong to do that, not just sit back and feel sorry, "Why don't they like me?" I don't care. One thing I have all my life is I don't care who likes me or not. Only thing is, don't disrespect me. I expect to be respected. That's what my father taught me.

TONY OLIVA: I was lucky, too. In '61, '62 I was in the south; '63 I played in Dallas. I played all over and we didn't have that much discrimination. But, in '64 I went to Minnesota. I think Minnesota is super. I never saw any problem in Minnesota between whites and blacks or anything. I think Minnesota was the top of the line for me in the United States for that situation. There was no hue at all. I never saw discrimination, when I went there in '64.

LUIS TIANT: It's a hard journey; you have to fight against those things, against sick people. A lot of people were like that in that time. I know a lot of people are still like that, and they don't want to change. Because that's the way they grew up and that's how they are in their thinking. You have to let them think that way and you have to live your way.

DAVID MARANISS: In 1960 Roberto Clemente helped lead the Pirates to the world championship. He led the team in RBIs, he was brilliant in right field, he got a hit in all seven games of the amazing, unexpected World Series win over the New York Yankees. He came home to Puerto Rico after the seventh game and was literally carried off the airplane and treated as the prince of the island all winter. After that incredible season and the way he was treated in Puerto Rico, he reported to spring training in Fort Myers, Florida, and the city of Fort Myers held a celebration in honor of the world champions. Clemente couldn't attend—it was in a hotel that didn't allow blacks. The team itself held an annual spring golf outing where Clemente couldn't play. That's what he had to endure in 1961. That was really a turning-point year both in the civil rights movement and in the civil rights movement of baseball, where a lot of players—Clemente for the Pirates, Bill White for the Cardinals—and many others started to really speak out on the whole issue of their being American citizens, many of them veterans of the military service, and yet treated as second-class citizens.

TONY PÉREZ: I played in the South. I just followed the rules and then I was happy when everything opened up—when you could go to the same hotel and stay with the rest of the team downtown. I had to accept it. It was a rule.

TIM WENDEL: Anybody who came up in that era had to put up with a lot of BS. And I think a lot of them were surprised that here was this country they had put on a pedestal and it had segregated drinking fountains and different places to eat based on the color of your skin, things like that. Nothing really prepared them for the shock of encountering that. Orlando Cepeda's dad had heard enough of these stories and could have gone north before his son did but decided he didn't want to put up with that. So the ones that did had to have a pretty strong inner core.

LUIS TIANT: People used to tell me, "You're in America. Speak English." I used to tell them, "You know what? This is a free country, bro. I can speak any language I want." What happened? You have the Japanese coming here and now you look at the difference. Everybody wants to learn Japanese. Everybody wants to make it easy for them. That's crazy how things change. When I was here they used to tell me, "You have to speak English." Now, they have guys here that want to take a course to learn Japanese so that they can communicate with Daisuke Matsuzaka. Times change. People think different now than 40 or 50 years ago when I came here. And that's how the world evolves. Everything changes. People change. People have a different mentality. Young people find out that color don't mean anything. He's a person like me. They go to college together. They play together . . . they're better than they used to be. They are much better.

DAVID MARANISS: Clemente was a lot like Jackie Robinson—after Branch Rickey took the muzzle off Robinson. I think they both played with what I call a beautiful fury. They were mad. And they both channeled it into the way they played baseball. You could see it in the way that Jackie Robinson ran, some of the way Clemente ran. They were sort of on the attack in the way they played baseball. And I think that that's a major way that Clemente dealt with it. He was also very outspoken. In the early years in Florida, when the team would travel by bus to another spring training site and they'd stop on the way for lunch or dinner, the white guys would get off and the black guys would have to stay on the bus; that infuriated Clemente. And he told Joe L. Brown, the general manager, that he wasn't going to tolerate that anymore and until Florida changed its ways, he demanded that the black players be allowed to drive in their own cars and stop where they wanted to. He was pretty outspoken about all that. Eventually, that did happen. And then eventually, in the mid-'60s, after the civil rights laws, things started to change. And many of the teams moved to Arizona or bought their own hotels and did a lot of things to try to ease the problems that came along with Jim Crow segregation in the South.

TIM WENDEL: Vic Power [who died in 2005] was ahead of his time, both from a baseball standpoint, in the way he played the game, and probably ahead of his time because he was willing to socialize with people of all colors. You look at any first baseman playing the game today, they should just raise a toast or bow down to Vic Power. He was the first one really to have one-handed snatches out there. The first one to really apply the big stretch for errant throws. And when people in the United States first saw him when he was trying to break in with the Yankees, the immediate reaction was, "Gosh, he's so flashy. What a hot dog. What a show-off." The same criticism that was leveled at Clemente or in more recent times at Roberto Alomar, or even Andruw Jones. Somehow somebody comes up and plays a position differently, the reaction of U.S. organizations and managers sometimes is "They're showing off." But if you look at the way Vic Power would stretch and make these one-handed snatches to catch throws, it saved time. It made for more outs. It made more sense to do it that way. The same way with Clemente, the way he would turn and pirouette to get more power on the throw. And the way Alomar became the first one to do that slide thing to get to a grounder so he could pop up quicker and get the throw off. All these things are kind of flashy but they also make sense for trying to get outs.

A typical Vic Power story—and this is the type of thing that got him into trouble with the Yankees—he's someplace in the South at spring training. And what a lot of people forget is that a lot of these guys—Clemente, Power, Minoso, Cepeda—they're all coming to a country where they have to come face-to-face with the Jim Crow laws. They're facing legal segregation and they found it mind-boggling. You don't have that in Cuba and Puerto Rico. Suddenly they have to put up with eating in a separate place from their teammates, because a lot of places won't serve them. And Power one day comes into a diner, sits down at the counter, and asks for a menu. And the person behind the counter tells him, "We don't serve Negroes." And his response was, "That's great. I don't eat them."

THE VOTERS TAKE NOTE

In the 1960s Juan Marichal won an eye-popping 191 games—54 more than Sandy Koufax and 27 more than Bob Gibson—but he did not win a single Cy Young Award, a slight that he has attributed to discrimination.

In 1960 Roberto Clemente was a member of the world-champion Pittsburgh Pirates. Only Pirates got first-place MVP votes that year. Shortstop Dick Groat got 16, third baseman Don Hoak got five, and Clemente got one. It was a confusing time to be an MVP candidate. While the voters in 1960 went for members of the pennant-winning team, they had given the award the previous two years to the Cubs' African American shortstop, Ernie Banks—in spite of the fact that Chicago finished below .500 both years.

DAVID MARANISS: One sign of the prejudice [Clemente] faced, he felt, was that when the voting came out for the Most Valuable Player of the National League, he finished eighth in the voting (behind three guys on his own team!). And he knew that a couple of the sportswriters in Pittsburgh had actively campaigned against him. That left a pretty bitter taste in his mouth. Part of it was that they liked Dick Groat and Don Hoak. Part of it was a lingering stereotype that still persists in sports, where black players are described as athletic or talented but it's the hardworking white guys who really "get it done." Of course, anybody who's ever played sports knows that that's just a stereotype, it's not the way it is. It doesn't matter what color you are. There are lazy players of all colors and incredible players of all colors. But that attitude was more prevalent then, and that's what it was about.

TIM WENDEL: They won the championship that year and Clemente still felt like an outsider. He's wandering around Puerto Rico that off-season thinking, "Am I really a part of this?"

Just how much of an impact Latino players were making at the upper end of the sport really became apparent in 1965 and '66, when players from that part of the world won the Most Valuable Player Award in the American and National leagues, respectively. Oliva had been Rookie of the Year in '64 and Aparacio had won the award in '56, but it was Zoilo Versalles, the Twins' Cuban-born shortstop, who first took home an award in competition with the whole league, not just its freshman class. Roberto Clemente followed the next year with the Pirates, a National League team that was becoming increasingly Latino-friendly.

DAVID MARANISS: In 1966 [Clemente] first felt a measure of vindication. He wouldn't acknowledge being surprised because he was such a proud guy. He would have said, "I deserved it." And he was particularly happy to win it over Sandy Koufax. Clemente was a true competitor in the old-school way and he had a fierce competition with Koufax. It was no different than his competition with Bob Gibson. Gibson and Clemente hated each other. Not because they knew each other personally, just because they were such fierce players. But getting back to '66, Clemente wouldn't express surprise because he thought he deserved [the MVP Award] earlier.

Versalles [who died in 1995] had been a good player in the three years leading up to 1965. He had made the All-Star team two years before. But in '65 he played at a Hall of Fame level for the one time in his career and the voters rewarded him for it.

HARMON KILLEBREW: You have to remember I was hurt that year and missed nearly 50 games, and Zoilo did score 126 runs and started rallies and stole bases while hardly ever getting thrown out. So you can't discount what he did. All of that goes back to Billy Martin. He was a coach with our club and he decided to take Zoilo under his wing. He stayed on top of him all season, working with him in the infield, reminding him of what he had to do to help the club, challenging him to be better.

Killebrew and Kaat have differing opinions about the impact that Martin had on Versalles that year.

JIM KAAT: I came up in the minors with Zoilo. He was in Charleston in 1960 when I was there. Not to take anything away from Billy's ability to motivate guys as a great coach or manager, but Zoilo's season in 1965 was just the result of a natural maturation process, I think. Billy was probably more of an influence on Rod Carew. It was pretty apparent that Zoilo would become a terrific player, but what made Zoilo stand out that year wasn't just his offense, it was his fielding. I can tell you from having him play behind me that he saved us a lot of runs and a lot of wins with his glove. Just a fantastic year in the field. You know the way Derek Jeter can go down the left-field line after those fly balls? Zoilo could go way down in the corner. He could cover a lot of ground. Zoilo also generated unusual power for a shortstop, especially for someone his size. He hit a lot of home runs (19) and doubles (45), which wasn't common back then. In those days, shortstops were mostly "good glove, no-hit" types, so Zoilo stood out from that standpoint. And he had speed. Zoilo covered a lot of ground and he played with flash and dash; not intentionally, he was just an exciting player. In retrospect, the MVP was probably the worst thing that ever happened to him.

TONY OLIVA: Zoilo, he was great. He played great the whole year. He hit in the clutch. He hit 19 home runs. Many times on a base hit he'd make it all the way to second. He'd make a base hit into a double. He did a lot of stuff. Plus, he played every day. They were happy for us to be there the whole year. We had a few people who had a great year that year. But Zoilo was the key man in the run for the pennant that year.

TONY PÉREZ: I was proud because he was Cuban. He was small and you don't see the small guys become the MVP. You don't see too many infielders become MVP.

TONY OLIVA: But you feel when somebody from Latin America—Cuba, Puerto Rico, Dominica, or Venezuela—when somebody wins something, for us it's more. America is so big. We think, in our mind, that we'll never have a chance to compete, to win anything with somebody here in America. America has to have the best. You feel America is so big that you have the best players, the best pitchers, everything. In Cuba there's 11 million people. In Puerto Rico it's 4 million. Dominica it's only 7 million. Venezuela is big. Or Mexico or any Latin American country. It's not that many people. To be able to win is unbelievable.

Whereas Clemente's reputation only grew after his MVP, peaking five years later in his greatest moment in the 1971 World Series, Versalles's went downhill fast after his. Though he was only 25 during his MVP season, Versalles never again batted above .250, hit double-digit home runs, or drove in more than 50 runs, and he was out of the majors by age 31.

JIM KAAT: The year after, Zoilo took it upon himself to do more than he was capable of and his career went downhill after that. I think in 1965 you could have just as well made a case for Tony [Oliva] as the MVP. Zoilo was trying to get his family over here from Cuba, he just had a lot of personal issues going. Tony could have handled the MVP, but I think Zoilo was just overwhelmed by it.

TONY OLIVA: I know he was the MVP and everything, but he really didn't make much money. He had a big family. He had six daughters. He had some family in Cuba he helped. By the time he finished playing baseball he had to keep working. He was broke. Like all the old ballplayers, they're broke. Not too many of the old ballplayers have money. They have to keep working for survival. After that, he wasn't able to get a job in baseball. Baseball was different. He worked in a restaurant. He worked in the airport. He was a chef, because he loved to cook. He did a lot of things. It's not the same to make a little money [doing that] than it was to make a little money in baseball, in those days. We only made about 30, 40 thousand dollars [per year]. It was a lot of money compared to 8 or 10 thousand when you work in a restaurant. He went through tough times, not because it was his choice. He played baseball for a living. When he was done, nobody gave him a shot [at coaching]. I don't know if he tried. But he didn't work anymore in baseball.

DAVID MARANISS: The Clemente MVP was very significant, more in retrospect when you look back at that period. If you looked at the All-Star Games every year, there were more and more Latinos. And it was in that period, in the second half of the '60s, that the rise of Latinos started and became the incredible tidal wave that it is today. Roberto had a strong sense of history, of geography, of culture, of who he was and where he was from. He was very proud that he was a Puerto Rican first, that was his main sense of identity. He knew about the history of baseball in Puerto Rico, and when he got to the major leagues he was constantly talking to the other Caribbean/Latino players about what their responsibilities were in the major leagues, helping younger players. He had that sensibility. He wanted to get as many Latinos into baseball as were good enough to play. And one of the great legacies of Clemente is the extraordinary number of Latinos in the major leagues today. He also wanted to overcome the stereotypes and not fall into them. Clemente himself had that interesting contradiction of not wanting to be called a hypochondriac—even though he probably was one; he was constantly complaining about some ailment or thinking he was dying of something—but he played more games for the Pittsburgh Pirates than any player in history. And every game he played, he played hard. He resented the stereotype of being a lazy player, which he certainly was not in any respect. And that's where the contradiction between the reality of Clemente and the stereotype of Latino players was interesting.

BIRTHPLACE OF LATINOS IN THE MAJOR LEAGUES

Dominican Republic	452
Puerto Rico	220
Venezuela	205
Cuba	153
Mexico	100
Panama	48
Nicaragua	9

THE LEGACY AND THE FUTURE

Today, as many fans know, more than a fourth of the players in the big leagues are of Latino descent. Cuba, however, which got the early jump on the majors and which did so much to spread baseball around the region, has long since been passed as the top producer of major-league talent. A census of all the players born in the seven Spanish-speaking nations who have spent time in the majors shows the ascendancy of the Dominican Republic.

The numbers above are through the middle of the 2007 season and do not include players who may have been born in the States but who were raised elsewhere, such as Edgar Martinez, who grew up in Puerto Rico after being born in New York. When Castro closed the doors a few years after the revolution, he slowed the export of Cuban ballplayers to a trickle. In today's political climate, Cuban stars such as Orlando Hernandez and José Contreras have to defect from their homeland in order to play in the United States.

TIM WENDEL: The Cubans couldn't go back home. They were closed off. It's a situation that a lot of us probably can't quite comprehend. Okay, you're going to choose baseball and you're going to try to play in the biggest setting in the world, but that means you're not going to see your family. What is driving them to make that decision? A lot of Americans' knee-jerk reaction would be to say it's the big bucks. And yeah, that's probably a part of it. But a lot of the Cuban guys I've talked to—El Duque, José Contreras—it's also the fact that they want to play against the best. We're so blessed in this country. You want to be a stockbroker? Go to Wall Street. You want to write scripts? Okay, go to Hollywood and go against the best. I don't think anything right now could be more frustrating than to be a Cuban ballplayer. Guys like me go down there and say, "Maybe you could play in the major leagues," but they never get a chance to prove it.

Conversely, many of the Cubans already in the States when the curtain went down have never been back.

LUIS TIANT: I don't go to my country for 46 years. I want to go before I die to see my country, to see some of my family, if they're still alive. I haven't had contact with them for a long time. My aunts—I think, I know I have a couple of aunts still alive. One time I was on a cruise ship over there in Key West. You can see Cuba right there. It was so close you could see the cars and the people. It makes you sad. You're that close and you can't go to your country. Forty-six years here is a long time. You say the number easy, but it's a long time, a lot of days and nights. A lot of Latino players from the other countries, like two weeks before the season was over they all talk and laugh, "I'm going to go back to my country and go to Christmas and eat and party every day." And, I sit down there and listen to them, and they're happy. All of these lucky guys. They can go back to their countries, and I don't know when I'm going to go. It's amazing. It's a real bad feeling. You have to do what you have to do.

The sacrifices that so many have made in the past have laid the groundwork for much easier passage into the American professional game. It's difficult for a young fan today to imagine a time when Latino players weren't welcome in MLB. What does the future hold?

TIM WENDEL: I'm not sure where we go from here. I think in some ways we probably would have even more players from the Dominican Republic in the majors and minors today if it weren't for the visa situation. Most clubs are restricted to 20-some visas and then a little bit more on the minor-league level. I think what we're going to see is that the game will just continue to grow internationally.

BALL FOUR

Featuring

GARY BELL: Jim Bouton's roommate with the Seattle Pilots. He would be dealt to the Chicago White Sox after 11 starts.

JIM BOUTON: Pitcher and the author of *Ball Four*.

BOB COSTAS: Popular broadcaster who was a teenager when *Ball Four* was published.

TOMMY DAVIS: A former All-Star who had managed to hit .300 several times in a pitchers' era playing mostly in pitchers' parks. Not only was Davis Bouton's teammate with the Seattle Pilots, but he was also traded to the Houston Astros a week after Bouton.

LARRY DIERKER: The ace of the staff of Bouton's second team in 1969, the Astros.

FRED GLADDING: Astros stopper who led the team with 29 saves in 1969.

GREG GOOSSEN: Given up on by the New York Mets at a very young age, Goossen would have 104 plate appearances at Seattle's Sicks' Stadium for the Pilots and produce a punishing 1.122 OPS (on-base plus-slugging percentage) there.

MIKE MARSHALL: Miscast as a starter and misunderstood by the Pilots, he would go on to some of the more prolific relief seasons in baseball history.

JERRY McNERTNEY: A refugee from the White Sox system who caught 128 games for the Pilots and had the best year of his career for them.

NORM MILLER: Astros outfielder and Bouton's wry roommate after he was traded to Houston.

BILL SCHONELY: The voice of the Pilots for their lone year in Seattle. Longtime broadcaster for the NBA's Portland Trailblazers.

PICTURE A WORLD where secrets were safe, even among the people who would have the most to gain by revealing them. That was essentially the baseball landscape before the publication of *Ball Four,* written by Jim Bouton, in 1970.

The confluence of the right idea at the right time in the hands of the right man in the right place, *Ball Four* is one of the four or five most influential sports books ever published. In that baseball books are written for fans, it allowed them a glimpse into the reality of something that had been propagandized or glossed over for the better part of a century, namely, the everyday lives of professional ballplayers. What also set the book apart from other baseball books is that the majority go uncommented upon within the professional community. The impact of *Ball Four* in his profession was such that Bouton was able to publish a sequel—*I'm Glad You Didn't Take It Personally*—based almost solely on the reaction to the book among his peers.

THE BOOK TAKES SHAPE

Bouton was, in many ways, an outsider who happened to be on the inside. He did not party like most of the other players and, by his own admission, he struggled to be one of the boys. He was more well-read than many other players and not only stayed abreast of current events but actually partook in them. For instance, in 1968, he had participated in antiapartheid activities at the Olympics in Mexico City. Even the main pitch in his repertoire set him apart. The knuckleball can be as puzzling to managers, coaches, and catchers as it can to opposing hitters (when it's working right).

> **JIM BOUTON:** The reason I kept the diary was that I
> had this feeling I wasn't going to be around much longer and
> I wanted to write down the things I thought the fans would

enjoy. Ever since I was a rookie I would always come back home at the end of the season and tell people stories about what it was like to travel around the country with these guys who had nothing in common other than the fact they could play baseball. Most of them were just high school–educated and raw, partially developed people. So, I finally decided to write it down. The instigation came from Leonard Shecter, who was a friend of mine and a former writer with the *New York Post*. He was the editor of *Look* magazine, and he said, "Why don't you keep a diary this year?" It had always been in the back of my mind but the instigation came from Shecter.

BILL SCHONELY: I was doing Pacific Coast League baseball for the Seattle Angels, a Triple-A affiliate of the then California Angels. Jim Bouton had just come down from the big leagues. He was a member of our Seattle baseball team. Through spring training and all our games, we were flying around and busing it all over the place. We were on a flight to Hawaii. The Hawaii Islanders were in the league in those days. Jim and I were in the back of the plane. We had talked a number of times. We were horsing around and he always had this little pad in the back pocket of his uniform or his pants. This is a true story . . . and I said, "Jim, what the heck are you going to do? Write a book?" He said, "Schones, as a matter of fact, I am. I'm taking notes." And the rest is history.

JIM BOUTON: I had read Jim Brosnan's book [*The Long Season*] when it came out and I really liked it, and what excited me most about the book was when he had the players and managers talking to each other. What they said in the bull pens and the locker rooms was what excited me. The second I saw those quote marks, the page came alive for me. I would think, "This is actually what Brooks Lawrence said in the bull pen! This is what they say to each other?" I remembered that when I started the diary. My notes are basically the quotes. I found that if I didn't write a quote down right away, I would forget 10 minutes later. I would forget exactly how somebody said something. There's a way in which people speak that's very unique, that you can't make up. It just spills out. You don't even think about how idiosyncratic it is until you write them all down and see how the personalities emerge based on how they say things.

So I was very careful to get the quotes right because I knew that was what excited me about Brosnan's book and I wanted fans to see what the conversations were really like. With my notes of the day, I would then go back to my room and spread them out on the bed and talk them into a tape recorder. The notes would remind me of the story. I could remember the events well enough, but having those quotes is what really helped. So Brosnan's book was a big influence on me because of the quotes, and *Ball Four* is filled with quotes. You can't make up that stuff. I'm not that funny.

GARY BELL: Jim was my roommate and he told me pretty much from the start, "Look, I'm writing a book and I'd appreciate it if you didn't say anything." I'd sit on the bus and snicker while he made notes about all the crazy stuff that happened.

NORM MILLER: I lived with him when he wrote it. I listened to him record every night. It was the first thing he told me. I didn't know exactly what the book would be, but I knew it was about baseball and the players. I used to sit there every night when he called it in to his editor.

FRED GLADDING: He was always taking notes of stuff people were saying and jokes. One day I confronted him on the bus and said, "What are you doing, writing a book?"

JERRY McNERTNEY: I really didn't know he was writing a book. He was always taking notes and stuff. Fortunately for me, "hunting and fishing" was my big deal. When the guys had to answer to their wives where they were, they'd say, "I was with McNertney."

MIKE MARSHALL: Jim wrote the book with Lenny Shecter, who was credited on the cover, but he gave me the manuscript to go over. I knew, and I think everyone knew as early as spring training, that Jim was writing a book. And at various times he showed me some of what he had written. And I told him, "Jim, you're coming off a little bit too smart-assed. Just tell the story. This story carries itself. Let the people come to their own opinions, stop editorializing. Don't put that smart-ass wisecrack at the end of every story. And don't keep repeating the same idea over and over again for emphasis. Readers will get it." He ended up sending me the entire manuscript and I actually sat down and edited it. I took out all the smart-ass remarks; it was funny and intriguing enough on its own. And I tried to make Jim more of an impartial observer just reporting what was going on.

TOMMY DAVIS: I knew nothing about it at first, then I heard some rumors near the end of the season, and then it got around. Didn't faze me at all, although it was unusual to have a player writing a book about a season; I think only a few players had done it up to then. But it's not unusual anymore. Jim started something.

MIKE MARSHALL: The beauty of *Ball Four* is that people got to see that ballplayers were lesser-quality human beings than most, in situations in which they could do just about anything they wanted and no one would say anything about it. And you saw that. I mean, my God, the stories about a player going out and getting drunk and they make a hero out of him because he hits a home run. I don't think that's a hero. That's someone with no respect for the game of baseball or himself.

JIM BOUTON: I really just wanted to share the fun and tell the story. I was not an angry guy. I loved baseball. I loved being a player. I loved working out. I was a hard worker and always gave 100 percent. The only complaint management ever had from me was that I wanted to pitch more often than they wanted me to. Sure, I was outspoken and would sign a petition, but I also wore a crew cut and would work my ass off. I was not the kind of person you would associate with being a communist. There was this contradiction between my image and what the coaches and managers saw out on the field. I was an extremely competitive commie! I wasn't angry at anybody. I thought the Yankees shouldn't have sold me, but I understand why they did it.

THE RIGHT CAST

Fortunately for Bouton, there was no shortage of material on the Pilots (or the Astros, his second team in 1969).

JERRY McNERTNEY: Jim picked out the characters—the guys that were characters. If you were a normal guy, that went by him. If you didn't make any waves, you weren't the guy he cared about. He did a pretty good job of hitting the characters.

GARY BELL: The funny thing is what happened with Seattle wasn't all that unusual when compared to other teams I've been on. One of the things Jim got in that book was what it was like to be on a major-league ball club. We are a bunch of grown men and baseball is our business, but it's also a game and that brings out the boy in you. The season is long with a lot of travel time, so guys do things just to break the monotony and ease the pressure. Every club I ever played on, we screwed around and joked, so it wasn't anything new to me. It just happened that on our club a lot of characters all landed in the same clubhouse. Our club was like a big Frankenstein monster, assembled from parts grabbed from everywhere.

GREG GOOSSEN: I needed the Pilots a lot more than they needed me. But I had this reputation as a guy who liked to go out and party. I don't know where that came from, but I think it hurt me. And things would happen: Like one time in the minors I was in the airport bar with the team and we were all drinking and having a good time. Suddenly I looked up and everyone was gone. They had just vanished. When I looked out the window I could see the plane the team was flying out, taxiing down the runway. So I ran like hell out of the place and kept going until I caught up to the damned thing. I'm running alongside it and pounding on the door until the pilot finally stopped to let me in.

TOMMY DAVIS: Steve Hovley was a highly intelligent guy from Stanford, but he would do some odd things. Steve would go on a road trip carrying one brown paper bag with a toothbrush, one pair of underwear, deodorant, a shirt, and a pair of khakis. That was it. He was a good player who should have played more. Swung a good bat, fast in the outfield, could play all three positions. Made contact and knew how to get on base. But it was during that time, Haight-Ashbury time, and Steve was part of that.

GREG GOOSSEN: Of all the characters in *Ball Four,* the one player who didn't get as much ink as perhaps his personality deserved was John Kennedy. Only I don't think of him by that name. Ask Steve Whitaker, he'll tell you it's John *Kenn-a-deee!* Oh, man, he was crazy, but Jim didn't write all that much about him. He just had this subtle, wacky sense of humor and you never knew what he might do. For instance, this happened before he played in Seattle, but it tells you a lot about the type of guy he was. John was a good-fielding third baseman who couldn't hit much, and when he was with the Dodgers they would pinch-hit a lot for him. Now no player wants to get pinch-hit for, but in this game, Dodgers manager Walter Alston waits for Kennedy to get in the batter's box before he calls him back. In the third inning! Now *that's* humiliating. Taking him out that early and doing it in front of the whole stadium. At least don't let the guy out of the dugout, you know what I mean?

So John's in the batter's box and Danny Ozark, the Dodgers' third-base coach, is motioning for him to go back to the dugout, and Kenn-a-deee doesn't even move a muscle. He doesn't turn his head, doesn't move his feet—doesn't even blink. He just stands there. The umpire has called time, the pitcher's waiting for the new hitter to come up, but Kennedy's not budging. Finally, Alston and some players had to go out on the field to get him, and Kennedy didn't cooperate at all. He stayed in his hitting pose, with his bat cocked off his shoulder. They had to pick him up like a statue and carry him back into the dugout. And when they placed him down in the dugout, he still didn't move. Just stood there in front of the bench with his bat ready, like he was waiting for a pitch. God I loved him. I don't think Jim knows that story.

TOMMY DAVIS: Gene Brabender [who died in 1996] was called "Lurch." That name fit him. Oh my God, what was he—six-foot-six, maybe 260? Massive. This guy would make blowguns. Real blowguns. Then he'd take wire hangers and make darts out of them. With sharp metal points. You'd be sitting at your locker and suddenly hear *zwing!* shoot past your ear. You'd look around and there would be this dart embedded maybe a foot from your head. I would jump up yelling, "Who the hell . . ." and as soon as I saw it was Gene my voice would get soft and friendly. I'd just say, "Could you please stop it, Gene?" Big man.

Gene could take a bent base-spike in his bare hands and straighten it out perfectly. Try that sometime. And I saw some of the bent spikes. That's when Jim said, "I guess we should call him Mr. Brabender." One day we were in a plane and hit some weather, a lot of turbulence, and Bouton was joking, saying, "We're going down now." Then Jim and another teammate started praying, but in a very funny way and loud. I think they sang the Lord's Prayer. Brabender got up in front of them and said, "Jim, if you don't stop that I'm going to break your arm." And believe me they did. It got real quiet on board. But after the flight I think Gene apologized to Jim and told him he was just afraid the plane was really going to go down. Gene could be intimidating, but he got along with people. One day the radio was on and it was playing these hillbilly songs. You know, country and western. So I wanted to put on a little soul and changed the channel. One minute later I hear it changed back to hillbilly. There's Brabender standing near the radio. He said, "I like this kind of music, Tommy." And I said, "You know, I'm beginning to like it too, Gene."

NORM MILLER: He got most of the weirdos and characters in there. About once a year someone comes up to me and says, "You were in *Ball Four*—you're a real pervert." I tell them I was trying to get an endorsement deal with Black & Decker.

TOMMY DAVIS: Another outfielder we had was Wayne Comer. He could be a character. We were in spring training, playing the Triple-A team for the Angels. Ed Runge's son was just starting out as an umpire. Wayne was getting on him the whole game, "You can't see, you're just as bad as your father . . ." That kind of thing. Later, we're playing in Boston and Ed comes over to me on the bench. It was a Friday night and he was umpiring at second. Ed said to me, "Tommy, I'm behind the plate on Sunday. If Wayne's playing, you better tell him to swing at anything that comes up there because I heard what he said to my son during spring training." As it happens, Wayne is playing on Sunday and he's swinging at pitches over his head, near his feet, behind his back. And he got two hits that day!

JIM BOUTON: Sometime in July I began to see the players' words on the page. I could see them set in type. I was getting so tuned in to what the players were saying and doing and how it would play in the story. I could really see the finished book by that time. My favorite entry came in August when we were sitting in the bull pen and Fred Talbot and Merritt Ranew got into an argument about which part of the South is dumber. Talbot lived in Virginia and Ranew lived in Georgia. As they were talking it was like they were writing. I was two seats away and I could barely write fast enough, but as I was scribbling I could see it on the page.

THE KNUCKLER

What is Ball Four *about? Many different things, really—which is one of its charms. One of its more intriguing storylines is Bouton's ongoing struggle to reestablish himself as a major leaguer on the strength of a recently learned knuckleball. Bouton's arm, once as powerful as any pitcher's in the game, was shot after facing more than 2,000 batters in 1963 and '64. He had not been effective in the past four seasons and at age 30 he was count-ing on the knuckler to keep him viable.*

The vagaries of the pitch are intriguing. Throughout the course of the book Bouton's mood is governed somewhat by what the knuckler is doing on any given day, which makes sense when you consider that the continu-ation of his professional existence was contingent on the notoriously fickle offering. It's a pitch that vexes the mind, especially those of people like Pilots pitching coach Sal Maglie, a man who used "traditional" pitches in his day. Bouton explains that the pitch is hard enough for its practitioners, let alone a less-than-progressive thinker like Maglie. Their exchange in the May 17 entry is especially telling, as Maglie conjures excuses as to why Bouton wouldn't be an effective starter with just one pitch while Bouton counters with examples of men who were.

It is, in part anyway, a book about pitching and the nasty realities of that line of work. Apart from showing ballplayers as human beings and not cardboard-cutout heroes, Ball Four *illustrates the incredible uncertainty that haunts the lives of professional athletes. Many of the players in the book operate with a high degree of paranoia—well-justified paranoia. For those on the fringes, and as an expansion team the Pilots had more than their fair share of those, careers seem to hang in the balance every day. While the modern player is better compensated for hanging on the fringe than those in Bouton's time were, that part of the story remains relevant. The glamour that accompanies being a big-league ballplayer is built on a foundation of the fear that it could all end in an instant.*

TOMMY DAVIS: Bouton seemed to throw his knuckler a little harder than most knuckleball pitchers. It got up to the plate quicker and started doing its thing.

LARRY DIERKER: That's what Alan Ashby said about Joe Niekro's knuckler. Joe could come in with a fastball at 86 or 87; he threw a lot harder than his brother Phil and that was the difference. Ashby said he didn't think it would be hard to catch Phil, but it was a nightmare trying to catch Joe because if he got ahead in the count, he threw that knuckleball so hard. Jim probably did, too. It was a good pitch.

JERRY McNERTNEY: Jim still had a good knuckleball, and I think Jim was harder to catch than even Hoyt Wilhelm. I caught them both and Wilhelm probably had the best knuckleball of them all.

NORM MILLER: I never had to face it. It must have not been very good. He wasn't around too long.

TOMMY DAVIS: On the mound he gave you everything and he was a cheerleader on the bench. I thought they should have used him more with that knuckleball. He hadn't been throwing it all that long and it was already outstanding. A little slow sometimes and then you could pick it up more easily and hit it. But he threw a lot that would just dive on you and drop down. Great pitch.

LARRY DIERKER: When you remake yourself as a knuckleballer and you're not capable of competing without this one pitch, you almost feel like you're on the verge of getting released all the time. I think there is this mentality that if you ever lose that, you've got nothing. How can we coach you back into winning if the knuckleball doesn't knuckle?

JIM BOUTON: There aren't too many guys who struck out 10 players with a fastball and curveball early in their careers and then went on to do it again with a knuckleball [as Bouton did in his only start for the Astros, five days after coming to the team]. You're either a knuckleball pitcher or you're not.

LARRY DIERKER: You think of him and Joe Niekro both as guys who came up as conventional pitchers and then converted to knuckleball pitchers. That's not easy to do. I almost feel like most knuckleball pitchers—Hoyt Wilhelm, Steve Sparks, or Tim Wakefield—they give up their career to the knuckleball right away. They know their conventional stuff won't be successful at the major-league level. But Jim had been successful, and not just successful. He probably had better-than-average stuff when he was young and before his arm was hurt.

After he hurt his arm, he didn't have any way to pitch the way he did before. He had enough gumption and confidence and everything else to remake himself into another kind of pitcher.

NORM MILLER: When he was making his comeback he was on *The Tonight Show* talking about his knuckleball with Johnny Carson like he was God. He was talking to [George] Vecsey one time after he came back—I think it was Vecsey— and he was mad that people weren't making a bigger deal of it. He wasn't [Phil] Niekro or Wilhelm. I faced those guys. They left you wondering what way was up.

JERRY McNERTNEY: It was harder to catch Jim because it wasn't predictable. Bouton would throw you one where you'd say, "Where did that one go?"

JOE SCHULTZ

With a lesser personality than Joe Schultz at the helm of the Pilots, Ball Four *could not have possibly been as entertaining as it was. Handed the un- enviable task of cobbling together a ball club from the spare parts of other teams, Schultz, who died in 1996, went about his business with an opti- mism that belied the truth about his club. He was 51 that year and had cut his teeth as a player in a part-time catcher role with the St. Louis Browns of the 1940s. He had learned the game in a different era, and the men who ran baseball clung to the basic tenets of that period with determination.*

TOMMY DAVIS: A good guy. A great coach.

BILL SCHONELY: It was tough shaking hands with Joe. His hands were all gnarled up from catching all those years with the Browns.

TOMMY DAVIS: We were playing the Orioles. Mike Cuel- lar was pitching the next day [for the Orioles] so he was chart- ing pitches in the dugout. I drove in two to put us ahead late in the game and Cuellar realized I was hitting out of turn. Soon as I reach base, out comes Earl Weaver from the Orioles dugout. I lost that hit and those RBIs and it cost us the game. Schultz apologized to me later. He had given the umpires one lineup and posted a different one in our dugout. . . . But I loved him.

BILL SCHONELY: Joe was a good ol' boy. But I'll tell you he was a good, old, faithful guy. Everybody loved Joe. Sometimes they thought he was a fool. He knew the game. At the end of the games Jimmy Dudley and I were doing the games. We shared the entire broadcast together. For the most part I had to leave 'cause Jimmy always liked to do the final inning. So I'd go down to the dugout to get ready for the postgame interview. I'd be standing in the alleyway. If the ball club was winning the game, Joe knew I was there. I couldn't get in the dugout. You weren't allowed. But actually I was. Joe would say, "Hey Schones, the Bud's gonna taste good tonight!" He was a good ol' Budweiser guy.

TOMMY DAVIS: He made me laugh. In spring we had Gus Gil, a utility infielder, trying to make our lineup. He was sitting at his locker drinking out of a cup and when Joe asked him what he was drinking, Gus said, "Coke." And that was the first time I heard Schultz say, "You're not going to make this damned team drinking that stuff. You've got to pound that Bud."

GREG GOOSSEN: How could anyone resent Joe Schultz? Pound that Bud. He was such a great guy. I think he took a page from Casey Stengel's book. You know what Casey Stengel said about me? "We have this young man Ed Kranepool. He's only 21 and in 10 years he has a good chance to have a great career. And we have this other young man Greg Goossen. He's only 20 and in 10 years he has a good chance to be 30." We weren't as bad as those first Mets teams, but Joe knew we didn't have a good club and that we'd lose a lot of ball games, so he went out of his way to keep everyone entertained, take the heat off the players. And even though he didn't play me, he was a good game manager. Joe knew what was going on.

GARY BELL: Super guy. Wished he had been my manager years before. Joe was a fun-loving guy, liked to pound that Bud and have a good time, so he didn't get in the way. Yes, he had bed checks because the front office insisted, but we knew when they were coming for the most part and all you had to do was wait for the phone call, check in, and then you were free to go out. The curfews weren't that bad anyway. You had three or four hours after the game to enjoy yourself. If you can't get in trouble during that much time, you're not trying hard enough. And for the players who were chasing women, they understood the philosophy of "go ugly early." They know if you wait too long until near the end, there's nothing left.

JERRY McNERTNEY: I really enjoyed Joe. There was no high pressure. He was down to earth. He had a really relaxed atmosphere. For a team like ours, I thought he did a great job. We didn't have clubhouse meetings or those types of things. You know, he was a "write down your name and play" guy. He didn't expect us to win the division.

MIKE MARSHALL: Joe didn't know what I was doing but he didn't care. It was a lark. He knew the ball club wasn't going to win much, so he was going to have fun and he did. He rarely got angry over losses and he wouldn't try to teach anything. I don't think he said a word to me one way or the other—unlike Gene Mauch after I joined the Expos. Gene wanted to know everything, he was just hungry for knowledge. For instance, everybody thinks that a leadoff walk is the worst thing in the world for a pitcher to surrender. Gene came to me one day and said, "You know, I think you intentionally walk the leadoff batter sometimes." I said, "I don't, but I don't care. If I'm in, the game is probably close in the late innings, which means the next batter will bunt the runner over and give me an out. If I could walk over and kiss him full on the lips I would. Because now I only need two outs and he just made the inning very easy. I can go right to my toughest pitches without worrying about walking anyone else because I can still put two more men on." No one thought that way back then, but when I explained my thinking, Gene grasped it and accepted it. Joe was the opposite of that. Nowhere to be seen on the intellectual scale.

GARY BELL: He didn't get results because the team wasn't very good. I thought he won as many games as he could with the roster he had, maybe more. You want a manager who understands the game, and hell, Joe had been in baseball for nearly 50 years so he knew his way around the ball field. I think he'd been a minor-league manager in the Texas League when I was growing up. I thought it was unfair when Seattle fired him. What was he supposed to do, win the pennant with an expansion team filled with castoffs? You check the record and you'll see the Pilots were competitive in a lot of games they lost.

MIKE MARSHALL: But he knew his job was to keep us loose during all the losses, so he was running around the clubhouse with that "Pound that Budweiser" line of his. Usually on a losing team, things go to hell in a hurry and then they get worse. Joe wouldn't let that happen. I thought he did a good job keeping the club on an even keel.

GARY BELL: He wanted to win every game, but he understood that we weren't as talented as most of the other teams and that we were going to lose a lot, but he kept the clubhouse loose. It wasn't life and death in there. One of the funniest things I ever saw him do—Jim and I still laugh over this—came after a win. I'm sitting at my locker and Jim had been out in the bull pen working on his knuckleball. He comes into the clubhouse real excited. Apparently, the knuckler had been going good that day even though he didn't get into the game. He and Joe end up standing practically nose to nose in front of my locker and I'm listening. Jim says, "Skip, my knuckleball was really moving tonight, it was really great." And Joe says, very serious, "You really had the feel for it, huh, Jim?" Bouton nods and Joe grabs his crotch and says, "Well, feel this," and then he turns around and walks away. I fell back in my freaking locker, screaming with laughter, and Jim is laughing so hard, I think he had tears in his eyes. That Schultz was a beauty, man. He kept us loose. But we were pretty loose to begin with.

SAL MAGLIE

The one man who comes across especially poorly in Ball Four *is Sal Maglie, the pitching coach of the Pilots, who died in 1992. While Maglie had other talents as a pitcher, namely the ability to throw three different curveballs effectively, he was most famous for his proclivity to throw inside (hence his nickname: the Barber). Of course, he threw inside to make those three curveballs that much more workable. In his career he faced 7,182 batters and hit only 44 of them. As a comparison, that ratio is about the same as Greg Maddux, a pitcher famous for his control, and far less than that of another latter-day pitcher also known for being able to put the ball where he wants to: Pedro Martínez. There is no record of how many men Maglie brushed back in his career, however. It was clearly enough to give him the nasty reputation that kept hitters off-balance.*

Hitters not only expected to be brushed back in the '50s and '60s, they accepted it as part of the game. In these more sensitive times it seems incongruous that a man could accept that his own success would breed retaliation. Maglie's brand of pitching would not work today, although with his curve he would have no doubt found a way to succeed.

Regardless, he rarely imparted much practical knowledge. In the book, Bouton is amazed when, well into the season, Maglie finally shows him how Hoyt Wilhelm held his knuckleball. Maglie was not new to the job, either. He had previously been a coach with the Red Sox, including their Impossible Dream season of 1967.

GARY BELL: I got along with Sal, really; but one of the problems with great pitchers like Sal or Early Wynn—who I also liked a lot—is that when they become pitching coaches they don't realize the rest of us just aren't as talented as they were. They can't understand it when a pitcher can't execute something they tell him and they don't know how to explain it. Sal didn't throw all that hard when he was a player, maybe average, maybe a little better than that. But he had good control with this great curveball, one of the best ever. He could talk to me about it all day [but] with my horseshit curve, I still couldn't throw his curveball.

MIKE MARSHALL: I loved Sal Maglie because I believe in players' rights and unions in every industry and Sal stood up for himself. He left the major leagues and went to Mexico for a higher wage and fought that battle. So we got along well. Except when he tried to talk to me about pitching. He knew absolutely nothing. His idea was to throw it high and tight and low and away and that was it.

TOMMY DAVIS: We had this meeting one time when we were about to face the Washington Senators. And Sal was talking about how to go at them. And he said, "Whatever you do, don't give Frank Howard anything good to hit. I don't want him beating us. Pitch around him." And I raised my hand and said, "But Sal, the last time you said that Mike Epstein beat up on us." And everyone cracked up because it was true. Howard was the home-run champion at the time, so every coach would say, "Don't let him beat you." But Frank was right-handed and we had mostly right-handers on our staff and there were spots you could pitch him. Up and in, low and away. You could get him. I knew Frank from having played with him. Strong. I saw him once hit a ball one-handed, a pitch he was fooled on. He hit it to dead center field clear out of the ballpark. Epstein, though, was left-handed and for a few years there he could really hit. He hit so well against us, I think we made him a star.

MIKE MARSHALL: But back then Sal probably knew as much as, if not more than, the average pitching coach. The only pitching coach I ran into while I was playing who had any semblance of an idea was Red Adams with the Dodgers. Basically, Red would come ask me questions and we'd talk until he understood what I was doing. I got along fabulously with him. He respected knowledge and that was rare back then. And Walter Alston actually had taken kinesiology in a college course. My first day with Los Angeles, he came up to me and said, "I think I understand what you're doing and it's all fine with me. Let's deal with it this way: When you don't feel like you can pitch on a certain day, let me know and I won't use you. Otherwise, I'll consider you ready to go." I said, "Walter, you've got a deal," and I pitched 208 innings in 106 games for him. And I was still irritated. I thought I could have pitched more. Walter would get a little timid on me. After I appeared in 13 games in a row, Walter said, "I feel like I'm pushing this." And I'd say, "Walt, I'm getting better. I'm finding my release points quicker." He understood that but he was getting a lot of heat from a lot of people, mainly because Jim Brewer wasn't pitching at all. But hell, I was getting everyone out, every day, and our starters could go seven almost every day out.

JERRY McNERTNEY: A coach's role wasn't as defined as today. With films and videos, good pitching coaches can see things.

GARY BELL: Current coaches, with everything they have available, like computers and charts, I think are much better than what we had in our day. But I never paid much attention to that stuff. I just did what people told me when we worked on something and then I went out and pitched my game. Today's players are friskier. They can be demanding—or their agents can. But we were locked in with teams for life and had to mind our manners a bit more.

MIKE MARSHALL: The biggest problem there was Maglie. He kept calling my pitches and that meant slider, slider, slider and he wouldn't let me throw my screwball—my main pitch of any value. I mean, I had a nice slider, but the slider is overrated in and of itself. I don't care how good you can throw it, you're going to get hit if batters are looking for it. The movement is horizontal, so it stays in the hitting zone longer. If you have a dummy up there who will chase balls out of the strike zone, it can be meaningful, but essentially it's 10 miles an hour slower than your fastball, moves more laterally than it does down. If you throw it in to a left-hander, he can open up and take you deep. Throw it away from a right-hander who goes the other way, it's a triple down the right-field line. I just don't see the upside. If the batter is looking fastball and you throw a slider, fine. But throw it on a breaking-ball count, it's not a very good pitch. You need something that moves more dramatically. And if you don't know what you're doing with it, you can easily hurt your arm. Pitchers who try to crank sliders at you day after day don't last very long. I had a true sinker with a down break and I also eventually threw a four-seam screwball. I broke that pitch out around '74. Most people thought my sinker was a screwball. Sal couldn't understand balls that moved that way and he didn't think the screwball was worth working on. He didn't like me throwing it that much.

THE PILOTS

For its second wave of expansion, baseball headed to some fairly small markets, several of which, with time, proved to be successful, at least in the short term. Kansas City became a model franchise in its infancy, only to flounder in later years. Montreal was finally abandoned after moving to one of the worst stadiums of modern times and seeing its attendance bottom out for a variety of reasons. San Diego struggled early but has become a solid franchise. That leaves the Seattle Pilots, the worst-conceived of the four in that they were underfunded and played in a decidedly minor-league facility. They survived just one year before moving to Milwaukee, although their failure was pivotal in getting the city of Seattle to build a ballpark that would allow for the creation of another major-league team, the Mariners, eight years later.

GARY BELL: I was surprised to be on the Pilots. I had a couple of good years with the Red Sox in '67 and '68 after coming over from the Indians. My record was only .500, but I had a low ERA, especially for pitching in Fenway. But I was 33 and making a huge salary of $40,000, so they figured if they could dump my ass and get $175,000 back in the expansion draft, they'd be smelling like a rose. One year later I was out of baseball so they did the right thing, obviously.

BILL SCHONELY: They just enveloped that team all over the Pacific Northwest. We had a tremendous radio network that covered everywhere. All over the West Coast, Canada, Alaska, Montana, Wyoming. Everything was going; but they didn't have a stadium. It was on the drawing board at the time. I've often told the story this way: Yes, that franchise would have been embraced by the baseball public. No doubt about it. But that little bandbox of a ballpark did not seat very many people.

JERRY McNERTNEY: It was a beautiful country out there. That's what I remember; it was beautiful out there in Seattle. The fans were great. It was a wonderful bunch of guys. It was a Triple-A stadium that they fixed up for the major leagues—they added a bunch of seats and there it was. It wasn't the nicest ballpark, but the field was fine. It wasn't Yankee Stadium or one of those places.

GARY BELL: At Sicks' Stadium a pitcher could scrape his nails on the outfield wall in the middle of his windup. Oh, man, those fences were close. Not a good place to pitch, especially when your stuff had deteriorated as mine had. Ray Oyler could pick it but he couldn't hit at all. Even *he* was a threat in that park.

BILL SCHONELY: It was a Triple A–level facility. Not the playing surface—the field itself was terrific. But they could only get maybe 15,000 people in there. Then they had to expand the outfield and put plank boards out there so they could get maybe 25,000 people max.

JERRY McNERTNEY: The owner and the GM tried to put together a team that would win. They tried to go after older players with more experience, not like they were doing in KC with younger players. They tried to get older, more competitive players and we were doing all right until they traded our best player, Tommy Davis. I don't know why they traded him, but after that we went downhill.

BILL SCHONELY: The current commissioner of baseball, Bud Selig, had lost his Milwaukee Braves to Atlanta a little while before that. So County Stadium was available. Lo and behold Mr. Selig got together with the American League owners at the time. Joe Cronin was the president of the American

League and he got them all together. He said, "Hey, if they don't have a new stadium on the drawing board, I have my stadium." To make a long story short, the Seattle city fathers tried to save that franchise, but it didn't work. So the American League owners and Bud Selig took the team away from the city of Seattle. It was only a few months after that, had they waited and we were able to play that second year, that the Kingdome came into existence—at least, on paper. Then, it was finally built. It's such a sad story that the franchise didn't stay. But the city of Seattle finally got major-league baseball.

JERRY McNERTNEY: I don't know why they made the move so quick. I think the fan support was there. We played a lot of our July games at home in Seattle and we didn't have a lot of rainouts. There were a lot of damp, drizzly days, but not many rainouts.

HOUSTON

On August 24, 1969, Bouton was traded to the Houston Astros for his old Yankee teammate Dooley Womack and minor-league pitcher Roric Harrison. Like the Pilots, the Astros were in fifth place, but unlike Seattle, Houston was just 2½ games out of first and in the midst of a very tight pennant race in the National League West.

LARRY DIERKER: The Astros started the season 4–20, which is about as big a hole as a team can fall into. Our 20th loss was against the Reds. Jim Maloney pitched a no-hitter against us. But the very next day Don Wilson pitched a no-hitter against them. Shortly thereafter, we had a 10-game winning streak and then, not too long after that, we had another 10-game winning streak and suddenly the franchise was in a pennant race for the first time in its history. During that second half of the season each game meant so much—at one point we had five teams fighting for the division lead—I had an extra motivation. I just think my focus was better than at any other time in my career. I like to think I could have done similar things for more than that one season had I been with better teams, because being in that race was as much a factor as anything.

JIM BOUTON: From a writer's point of view you couldn't ask for more. Start out in the majors, get sent down, get called back up, and then, as the season is about to peter out and I'm spending most of my time on the bench and the book is starting to get flat . . . Boom! I get traded and meet a whole new cast of characters. Harry Walker, Larry Dierker, Jimmy Wynn, Doug Rader, and those maniacs over there. The first night I was on the team Larry Dierker sings the team song in the back of the bus, *Proud to be an Astro:*

> *Oh Harry Walker is the one who manages this crew*
> *He doesn't like it when we drink and fight and smoke and screw*
> *But when we win our game each day then*
> *what the fuck can Harry say?*
> *It makes a fellow proud to be an Astro.*

This is with Harry sitting right at the front of the bus!

LARRY DIERKER: I knew Bouton was writing a book and was fascinated by it. You know he didn't keep it a secret. If something unusual happened or someone said something funny, Jim would jot it down. He always had a notepad with him and a pen, even when he was in uniform. We all knew he was going to write a book. A lot of guys stayed away from him because of that, but that caused me to get closer to him. I went to college during the off-season and my major was English, so I was interested in writing. The idea intrigued me, plus I thought he had a terrific sense of humor and personality. He was much more fun to hang around with than most of the other guys on the team.

JIM BOUTON: It was marvelous when I got traded to Houston. First of all, they wanted me. As soon as I joined the team they were going to start me against Pittsburgh in a pennant race. Here the Pilots are in last place and they can't give me a start or put me in a meaningful game. I join the Houston Astros and they're starting me in a pennant race against the Pirates with Willie Stargell. I pitched the game of my life. I lost 4–2 but I went 10 innings and struck out 11 with a knuckleball.

LARRY DIERKER: In the second half of the season, I think I went 13 or 14 starts in a row where I didn't give up more than two earned runs. The game where I was trying to get my 20th win—my first attempt at it—we were playing the Braves. They were in first place and we were only two games behind them. I was pitching against Phil Niekro. There was no score and I had a no-hitter going into the ninth when Félix Millán got a hit with one out. It was an infield hit in the hole at short, but they didn't score. Then we got a few hits off Niekro, but couldn't score either. He came out after 11 innings. I pitched the 12th and then in the bottom of that inning they pinch-hit for me and we scored two runs. So I was going to win my 20th after pitching 12 shutout innings against the first-place team. Unfortunately, Fred Gladding came in and gave up three runs in the bottom of the 13th and lost the game. From that point on we went into a tailspin and the Braves rarely lost. It was the closest thing I've seen to a turning point for both teams.

I tend not to believe in clutch hitting and things like that. But it sure felt like a turning point. We were using a four-man rotation and the next game I pitched was in San Francisco. They asked me if I wanted to take an extra day off after pitching 12. I said, "No, we still have a chance. I'm taking my turn." I ran out of gas after seven innings, gave up a run or two. Bouton came in for the last two innings and saved my 20th win.

But then I went downhill. I had hoped to pitch 300 innings. It was so different back then. I put a lot of value on pitching complete games and now guys don't care if they go nine; they come out of shutouts. I was hoping to pitch 300 innings and I just about had to pitch complete games the rest of the way to do that and I pretty much did. I think my last two starts were complete-game losses. But I was giving up three or four runs in those games after giving up only one or two per start for what seemed like forever. I lost my last three starts while the team spiraled down.

NORM MILLER: We had a good team, a tight bunch of guys. They must have not minded [Bouton] too much because there were some guys on that team that would have moved his locker into the hallway, or castrated him, or electrocuted him in the hot tub or something. They didn't do any of that, so they must have been all right with him.

LARRY DIERKER: I never postured myself so he wouldn't say anything bad about me. I didn't see [the book] as a threat, so it was easy to be natural around him. There were probably a couple of things he included that, had I been the writer, I wouldn't have written about, like the deal with [Mike] Hegan being asked, "What's the toughest thing about playing baseball?" And he said, "Telling your wife she has to get a penicillin shot for *your* kidney infection." Stuff like that. There was something else that I think caused a player to be traded. I felt like, if you're going to say something that would affect someone's family, or their marriage, or their job, I'd try to stay away from it. I tried to stay away from it in my own book, but I still had people tell me I told too much.

JIM BOUTON: By the time I got to Houston I knew it was going to be a pretty good book. My other question was if anybody else was going to think it was going to be as funny as I did. I was afraid people were not going to get it. Some of it was, "Why is this funny?" Like the time Greg Goossen walked into the clubhouse and said, "Does anybody have any Aqua Velva?" and Fred Talbot said, "No, but I've got to take a shit if that will help you."

Why is that funny? What is the logic of that? Fortunately, fans have a great sense of humor and they got it right away and it turned out these guys really were funny. The stuff we laugh at in the bull pen is funny.

LARRY DIERKER: Jim wasn't much of a drinker. Most of the guys would go out drinking beer after the game. But he— I don't know if he had indigestion or what—his drink would be scotch and milk. He probably didn't drink many of them. I don't see how he could drink one. Someone else would never do that because he'd be embarrassed, but Jim didn't really care that much about what anyone else thought.

When he was with the Yankees his nickname was Bulldog. He was as competitive as anybody that I've ever been on a team with. When he got on the mound, it was serious business; he didn't want to give up anything. So as a teammate you notice that. I think guys on our team respected the way he competed and the things he said as we went through August and September with our first chance to win anything. He was good for the team in terms of leading by example and with his competitiveness. He'd been in pennant races and could speak with authority and credibility, telling guys to relax and not to try to do too much. Like coming down from the bull pen during that game against Atlanta to calm me down. I think Jim did that because I was a young kid and he was a veteran who had been through pennant races with the Yankees. He got down to the dugout, heard me singing "Rocky Raccoon," and just turned around and went back to the bull pen.

FRED GLADDING: He was a great competitor. I tell you that. Aside from that book and everything everybody talks about, he was a great competitor.

LARRY DIERKER: He was into it big-time and everyone knew that. He was a pretty important guy to our team during that second half. The bull pen wasn't that great and it got a lot better with him in it. I think there were some guys who thought he was weird and were suspicious of his writing, but everyone respected what he did when he got out on the mound.

1970: PUBLICATION—AND REACTION

Ball Four *was published on June 19, 1970. The initial outcry was fierce, at least inside the game. Baseball commissioner Bowie Kuhn suggested that Bouton sign a statement claiming that the book was a lie. (Bouton, not surprisingly, would decline.) Less than two months after the book was published, Bouton was released by the Astros. He went on to work as a sportscaster for WABC-TV in New York for three years, and made a brief comeback with the Atlanta Braves in 1978 at age 39 before retiring for good. It would be 20 more years, however, before Bouton would finally be allowed to return to Yankee Stadium for Old-Timers' Day. (Bouton's exile ended after his son Michael wrote a letter to the* New York Times *on Father's Day, asking the Yankees to reconsider their position.)*

JIM BOUTON: I thought they would get upset but it wouldn't last long and I thought that it would get lost in the book—it would be part of the tapestry of the whole thing and not jump out. Of course, it did, particularly when *Look* magazine published the excerpts and all people had to talk about for a long time was the excerpts. The book was late in coming. It wasn't available until June. World Publishing did a poor job of getting them printed and getting them out there. The excerpts appeared in March, so that gave the sportswriters about three months to beat me over the head. It created what is known in the business as "pent-up demand." The excerpt contained random stuff from throughout the book like the bits on [Mickey] Mantle and the two guys kissing on the bus. I almost didn't write that down because it made no sense to me. Yes, the guys were laughing and it was funny and as they were kissing each other on the bus I said to myself, "How can I explain this?" But I figured I would write it down and see how it came out. Later I said to Shecter, "What about the kissing stuff?" and he said that it had to be in there.

The *Look* excerpt was the first inclination I had that there was going to be a lot of reaction to the book. Early on, Dick Young of the New York *Daily News* wrote three columns in two weeks about what a terrible book this was and how awful

Shecter and I were. He called us "social lepers" and that we
didn't have any friends and that we would write these things
in our bitter moments. He was outraged that I would write
what goes on in the clubhouse. Now, mind you, the title of his
column was "Clubhouse Confidential." I guess he felt that if
anyone was going to reveal something confidential going on in
the clubhouse, it should have been him. This amused me. When
he came into the clubhouse after writing these columns he came
over to me and I stuck out my hand and said, "Hey Dick, how
are you doing?"

He said, "I'm glad you didn't take it personally." Of course,
that became the title of my next book.

NORM MILLER: Plenty of reporters showed up the morning it came out. Howard Cosell was first. We were in New
York. I remember they timed the release of the book so that we
were in New York at the time. It was 7 a.m. and Bouton was
giving a radio interview on the phone. There was this bang on
the door. *Bang, bang, bang.* Jim pointed at me to get the door,
and I heard, "This is Howard Cosell. Open up the door!" There
was Howard, in his trench coat and hat. I was standing there
naked, and he walked up to Jim and said, "This interview is
terminated," and hung up the phone and proceeded to interview Jim himself. I went back to bed.

JIM BOUTON: The lowest moment was when the Astros
came to New York to play the Mets in late May 1970. My mom
and dad lived in New Jersey and came to the Sunday-afternoon
doubleheader. We were going to go out to dinner afterward. I
came in to pitch and when they announced my name, everyone
in the stadium stood up and booed me because they hadn't read
the book, they had just read *about* the book from Young and
Jimmy Cannon, who called it a terrible book, and Red Smith.
They booed me unmercifully. As I described in my next book,
it felt like garbage washing over me. After the games I met them
at the players' entrance and my mother was crying and she said,
"Maybe you shouldn't have written that book."

I said, "Mom, this is just temporary. Don't worry about it. The book is not out yet. When people read the book they're going to realize it's not as bad as they're saying. They're going to like the book. It's mostly funny. This will pass." It was very hard to comfort my mom. She thought I had done the worst thing in the world, that I was going to go through life as a pariah, and that they would be the parents of a pariah.

Then Christopher Lehmann-Haupt of the *New York Times* and David Halberstam wrote positive reviews. The book started to get reviewed by people who reviewed books about subjects other than sports and didn't feel like they had turf to protect. They were looking at it from a different point of view and they liked the look at the game. It said a lot of things about sports that they all suspected anyway, and here was a guy who was confirming it from the inside. I had no intention of writing a piece of sociology, but sometimes you set out to do one thing and it turns out you did a completely different thing.

There was very little positive reaction in the baseball community. My Astros teammates were pretty good about it, and my roommate Norm Miller was really good about screening all the calls I got on the road—requests for interviews. Norm would get on the phone and pretend to be me sometimes and he would say, "Yeah, I'll tell you about the book—what do you want to know?"

BOB COSTAS: A lot of people overreacted to what they thought was an assault on the cathedral of baseball and it caused them not to appreciate, at least not initially, how well written it was, how groundbreaking it was, and at its core how affectionate it was.

GREG GOOSSEN: Funnier than hell, wasn't it? I thought this was good for baseball, the way it made all these personalities seem humorous and human. I told you how I felt not getting into the lineup, and I think Jim had some of that in his book, that things aren't always great when you're in the majors.

There's pressure to perform and when you're on the edge like so many of us on that team were, including Jim, you worry a lot whether you're going to have a job the next day. So you do crazy things. No one had ever done that before in a book, I don't think. A lot of guys were pissed off about his revealing so much. Some still are.

FRED GLADDING: I didn't think he was right, but he wrote it. He made money off of it. You don't write about people who are your teammates to make money. Of course, they do it all the time now.

MIKE MARSHALL: It was a frank telling of the day-to-day story of major-league baseball players and the life they lead. I had written a paper in a sociology-in-sport class called "Baseball is an Ass," because I couldn't and can't imagine any major industry that has more dumb people in charge. They have absolutely no idea what they're talking about on any level. They have no idea about exercise physiology, kinesiology. And psychology is beyond them. Leadership abilities . . . I've never met anyone in professional baseball that had any reason behind what he did except it seemed like it felt good.

NORM MILLER: I kind of enjoyed being in it. When you spend as much time sitting on the bench as I did, any recognition is good.

GARY BELL: It was funnier than hell, even though a lot of guys were offended by it.

TOMMY DAVIS: I was one of the few guys he said only good things about. So I was chastised by some. When I saw Joe Schultz the next season, during spring training I think it was, he said, "Here comes Bouton's Bobo." And some players asked me if I had helped to write the book, but it was all in fun. I loved it, thought it was funny. And [Seattle] was a good team for that because there were a lot of funny situations on the Pilots.

LARRY DIERKER: I can remember the signs in the clubhouse: "What you see here, what you say here, let it stay here, when you leave here." So it wasn't just part of an unspoken, unwritten oral tradition, it was right up front. And yet, at the same time, I remember we had some rowdy guys on some of those teams who were involved in incidents that would have made great copy had some writer revealed them and the writers were around. They saw what was happening, but they chose not to write it. There wasn't the same mentality as you have now.

NORM MILLER: It was kind of breaking the code. Nobody was talking about this stuff. We all knew about it. Everyone in baseball knew about it. Jim broke the code. It was like the Mafia: Break the code and you get killed. Jim didn't get killed, though.

BOB COSTAS: I read it when it first came out. I thought it was hilarious. I understood the sense of violation that some players might have felt about the "What happens here stays here" baseball clubhouse code. Although when you look back now, it all seems rather mild.

GREG GOOSSEN: You can ask them but a lot of it was just that old-school approach to the clubhouse and not discussing anything that goes on in there. I didn't think Jim revealed anything that hurt anyone. He was a good guy. Mantle hated what he wrote. I heard he and Jim patched things up before [Mantle] died, but Mickey wouldn't talk to him for years. And yet later books about Mantle were much more revealing, more damaging—like that book by Joe Pepitone. Pepi was a piece of work. He had Mantle partying with him big-time. I thought a lot of what Jim wrote about Mantle was good and that somehow got overlooked. You got the idea from Jim that Mickey was a great teammate. But people didn't focus on that.

BOB COSTAS: As a kid who grew up loving Mickey Mantle, I wasn't shocked or disappointed about some of the things in the book, which now come across not so much as horrible but as extended adolescent high jinks. That came as a little bit of a jolt, but I didn't have a problem reconciling that with Mantle the heroic baseball player. I was never one of those people who thought that if you like a baseball player you have to assume that he's a one-dimensional guy from a Wheaties box. The reason you like them is the way they play the game and the way they carry themselves on the field. Bouton also went out of his way to highlight the sense of humor Mantle had and his kindness toward the scrubs and the rookies on the team. It really came across what a good teammate he was.

GARY BELL: The old-timers lived by that rule, you know, whatever you hear or say in the clubhouse, stays in the clubhouse. So they thought he violated that. And there are a lot of guys still pissed off at him even though far worse books and stories have come out since. I was a little more progressive, felt like I moved ahead with the times. No royalties, though. I keep asking Jim if my checks were lost in the mail and he says, "Maybe." I keep joking with him that if it weren't for me playing such a major role in the story, he couldn't have written the book.

JERRY McNERTNEY: I didn't have anything to hide. It didn't bother me.

FRED GLADDING: It was, you know, something to write about your teammates. That's the way some people are. You just take it in stride. I was in *Ball Four*. It didn't bother me. When I was in sports, we never said nothing about one another.

LARRY DIERKER: It was good for the game. My opinion is not the majority opinion. One, because it was entertaining and it got people interested in baseball that may not have been otherwise interested. You know there is something in baseball now that I think is analogous. When guys start making 50 or 100 million dollars it goes beyond the sports page and gets onto the front page. People want to know who was seen at such-and-such restaurant and it creates a movie-star or rock-star persona for the athlete. I think, in that sense, the stuff in *Ball Four* took baseball beyond where it had been and created a more . . . I don't want to say tabloid because what Jim wrote was true. He documented and took notes and he didn't make things up. But he opened eyes and got people interested in baseball who might not have been interested in the game but became interested in the culture.

BOB COSTAS: And what I thought even then and I believe this even more strongly now was that what came through with Bouton was his true affection for the game, and his affection for many of the people who played the game. When he talks about the hold that the game has on him, and how you spend your whole life gripping a baseball but then you realize in the end that it's the other way around. Far from something that was designed to damage baseball, it was an authentic appreciation of the game, just from a different perspective than we were used to.

BILL SCHONELY: I've been saying this for a long time: It's all true. I thought it was a terrific book. I know it was very controversial at the time. It's not so controversial now. But then it was, when it came out, because he told stories on people. They weren't serious stories. You know, baseball players are fun guys to be around. They were having a good time. Then when they got between the lines, they played the game. He told all these little stories, and that upset a lot of folks. That, I realize. I often pull it out when I want to get a little laugh. I have it in my little office at home. I'll grab it and flip open to a page and there's history for me. It was fun.

JIM BOUTON: When the book finally came out it immediately jumped onto the bestseller list because everyone had been waiting for it, and they wanted to read it and get their anger out against me. They were surprised when they read it. I started to get mail, the tone of which was, "I just read *Ball Four* and I can't believe it—it's nothing like they've written about. Sure Mickey Mantle hit a home run with a hangover, but who cares?

I like him even more now. It makes him more of a real person." I got some that read, "I was laughing so much my wife wanted to know what I was reading so she insisted on reading it too, and now she wants me to take her to a ball game."

NORM MILLER: I've done some writing too. I wrote 50 pages about baseball once and a publisher in New York called and said: "I really like this. Can you throw in some screwing?"

BOB COSTAS: It was at or near the forefront of a change in tone in the way the game is covered, of a move toward greater irreverence, and something that was a little grittier than what we had been used to. It was part of that change in tone and sensibility.

LARRY DIERKER: Do I think Jim's book contributed to the more candid baseball reporting we read today? It probably did. It's run-around-and-get-quotes now. I've done quite a bit of research for other things I've written, and if you read the newspapers from the first 40 years of the 20th century, you see hardly any quotes in the baseball stories. And the writers embellished everything with grandiose language. It was almost as if their purpose was to entertain. I think many of them just sat in the press box and typed that stuff up and didn't go down to ask questions or quote players and managers. It was like a writing contest. It's fun to read. It's not like anything you read in the paper now, which is, "Let's get behind the scenes and get some quotes, we'll string them together with a few sentences and you've got a story." There was much more of a flourish, much more creativity in the writing back then.

BILL SCHONELY: The publication of *Ball Four* probably changed the way the game was covered by the print and broadcast media community. It was very instrumental. Of course with the advent of ESPN and all the cable TV and the reporters, television folks, and extra radio people now, you get all that stuff firsthand immediately. It was a breakthrough, though. I'm quite sure.

LARRY DIERKER: It was a landmark book. Perhaps not seminal—I think *The Glory of Their Times* was that—but it was a culture-changing event when that book came out.

NORM MILLER: If *Ball Four* came out now, no one would publish it. Come on. Mantle drank? Who would care about that now? I drilled a hole to look up a girl's skirt? The real commentary now is mental illness and depression and what leads to these types of things. Mantle was a sweet guy. It was a first and whenever you're a first you have to buckle up your seatbelt and be prepared.

JERRY McNERTNEY: I still get notes from people who send for autographs and stuff and mention me in *Ball Four,* so I think people are still reading it.

GREG GOOSSEN: It gave fans something to identify with, something to root for. You know I always thought it was too bad that the Pilots moved to Milwaukee the next season and became the Brewers, because I'm positive that book would have helped us draw fans in Seattle and maybe have made the franchise a success.

THE BIRTH OF THE PLAYERS' UNION

Featuring

JIM BOUTON: Early outspoken critic of the inequities in baseball's labor situation. Writing in *Ball Four,* he poked fun at himself for his failed player rep bid.

BOB COSTAS: Popular broadcaster and host of HBO's *CostasNOW.*

DENNIS ECKERSLEY: Hall of Fame pitcher with the Indians, Red Sox, Cubs, A's, and Cardinals.

BOB FRIEND: Three-time All-Star and Pirates player rep, whose career spanned 1951 to 1966.

BILL GILES: Owner of the Philadelphia Phillies and son of National League president Warren Giles.

BOBBY GRICH: A six-time All-Star second baseman and a member of the famous first class of free agents in the winter of 1976.

JIM KAAT: 283-game winner and alternate player rep while with the Minnesota Twins, he pitched in the major leagues from 1959 to 1983.

MARVIN MILLER: Executive director of the MLBPA from 1966 to 1982.

RICHARD MOSS: Chief counsel to the players' union until 1977, when he left to become an agent.

TONY OLIVA: The Cuban-born Oliva burst on the scene with the Twins in 1964 and won the American League Rookie of the Year Award. He would make eight All-Star Game appearances and win three batting titles.

MILT PAPPAS: 200-game winner who served as the Reds' player representative. His career spanned 1957 to 1973.

JOE RUDI: Starting left fielder for the dynastic A's of the early '70s, he later became a member of the first free-agent class.

BUD SELIG: Owner of the Milwaukee Brewers during some of baseball's most tumultuous labor negotiations and current commissioner of baseball.

KEN SINGLETON: Three-time All-Star who spent his 15-year career with the Mets, Expos, and Orioles and moved into broadcasting in 1984 when his playing days were over.

JOE TORRE: Nine-time All-Star and union rep who went on to become a highly successful big-league manager.

IF NOT FOR A LACK of action at a precise moment in history, the entire course of labor relations in baseball would have been entirely different. Had the players of 1890 taken more decisive action, then none of what you are about to read would have ever taken place. Having formed their own league and played a full schedule in the 1890 season, the renegade players had the owners of the existing National League and American Association on the ropes, but did not fully grasp the advantage they held. Instead, they folded their league after one season and returned to the ranks of the indentured.

If the players had had a bit more resolve, what would have occurred instead? Profit sharing? True worker ownership? Would these things have even proven viable in the unique marketplace that is major-league baseball? As the players who revolted in 1890 got older and moved out of the playing ranks, would they have clamored to become owners in the traditional sense themselves, undoing all the gains that the players would have made to that point?

We'll never know, of course, because they did back down, keeping in place an owner-dominated patriarchy that would take nearly a century to undo.

Baseball's labor history in the ensuing years has run almost counter to that of the prevailing labor current in the nation at large. As workers were getting organized in the early part of the 20th century, baseball players were toiling in indentured servitude at the whims of owners who held the holy writ of the reserve clause. When unions were reaching new heights in membership in mid-century, ballplayers remained the chattel of their employers. When unions like the United Auto Workers were negotiating lucrative contracts for their rank and file in the 1960s, ballplayers were still operating under the strictures of an earlier time. For instance, a ballplayer's minimum salary had barely risen since the end of World War II. The $6,000 minimum of 1946 should have been more than $10,000 by the mid-'60s with simple cost-of-living increases, but it was not.

THE START OF THE PLAYERS ASSOCIATION

While there were attempts to create guilds and players associations in the decades since the Players League back-down, it wasn't until the mid-1960s that a body was in place that could get some real traction. It was then that the players' representatives began to look for a real professional to take them to the next level of negotiating viability.

> **BOB FRIEND:** You really couldn't call [the organization we had] a union by any means. What we had were player representatives from each team and the two leagues. Ralph Kiner was the player representative for the Pirates, and then in 1953 he became the National League player representative. I was voted to take his place as the Pirates representative. We did have meetings several times a year and we'd discuss whatever grievances concerned the players on our teams. You know, things like getting more meal money or better travel conditions and accommodations. And then we'd meet as a group with the owners and discuss these matters. We'd usually come to some resolution as long as we didn't ask for too much and as long as we didn't bring up changing the pension. That, they [the owners] wouldn't discuss.

Harvey Kuenn had this good friend, Judge Cannon in New York, and the judge offered to act as a go-between with the players and the union. And he did a good job, for the most part, in the [limited] role he had. But we still didn't have any leverage and we were not a union. So we moved on through the late '50s and '60s. And then we heard [about] a union that a firm in New York wanted to organize all sports under, one union for football, hockey, baseball—everything. We got wind of that and said, "We don't want anything to do with it. We'll stand on our own." We got together—we were meeting three or four times a year. And Robin Roberts called me and said we needed a more experienced representative who could work full-time. The judge was part-time.

BILL GILES: Up to that time, the Players Association had been run by Judge Robert Cannon almost as a house union.

BOB FRIEND: So we put together a search committee and I appointed Roberts and Jim Bunning to go out and see if we could line up someone. Roberts had heard about Marvin Miller, who had worked with the steelworkers' union. Some of the players were concerned about Miller's background with labor, because we really weren't interested in having any strikes. Finally, Roberts comes in and says, "I think [Miller] is the man we want, and I'd like us to talk to him."

MARVIN MILLER: I was with the Steelworkers Union and had been for 15 or 16 years to that point. I was involved with a committee study with Kaiser Steel Corporation and the steelworkers union. The committee consisted of nine people, three from the company, three from the union, and three impartial participants, the chairman of which was the dean of the Wharton School, George W. Taylor. He had been a labor advisor to every U.S. president from Roosevelt to Lyndon Johnson, and he also had been the chairman of the National War Labor Board during World War II, which is where I met him.

Now it's 1965, toward the end of the year. We were in San Francisco, it was just after breakfast, and I was heading for the conference room. I got in the elevator and George Taylor was already there. Just in the time that it took to descend to the conference floor, he said, "Do you know Robin Roberts?" And I said, "No, but I know who he is." And in no time at all he said something to the effect that the major-league players feel they have a problem. They've never had any standing to say anything and they're worried about their pension plan being attacked.

Taylor said, "I don't know Roberts, either, but he telephoned me cold and said he had seen my name in the paper in regards to various labor-management matters. He asked if I could help him and recommend somebody who could help the players." With that brief explanation, Taylor said, "Are you interested?" And I said, "I don't know, George. I certainly would be willing to talk to them." He said, "Good enough. I recommended you but I didn't know if you'd be interested. I'll make a call and we'll arrange an appointment for you to meet with the search committee."

BOB FRIEND: We met and Miller was very honest. He said we had to organize, that right now we had absolutely no leverage.

MARVIN MILLER: Ballplayers were not like other employees in the sense that they had no bargaining power. They were really pieces of property that were owned and that the owner could do with whatever he wanted. And that was the source of any problems the players might have.

BOB FRIEND: [Marvin] didn't mention union, but we got the point. He left the room and we took a vote and decided to go with him. Everybody was excited. He came back and we were prepared to offer him a nice, big salary, but he said, "Just a minute. I don't know if I want this and I don't know if the players will want me. So don't throw any money at me just yet until we find out what's going on." A lot of the players really liked that. He was an up-front guy and that impressed everyone.

RICHARD MOSS: Marvin was very good at that. One of his great talents is he can make fairly complicated issues simple to understand. It reminds me of that wonderful quote from Albert Einstein, "Make everything as simple as possible but not simpler." Marvin could clearly explain and demonstrate to players that individually they had no power at all, but collectively they could wield enormous power. They *were* baseball, not just the players but also the product, and the whole idea was to stick together and function collectively in regard to negotiations. They quickly came to trust Marvin because he talked sense to them.

MARVIN MILLER: Really, I was kind of amazed by the whole thing. They talked about almost nothing else but their pension plan. What surprised me so much about it was not just that they talked only about that, but that while they were all veteran players, these were still very young people. And in industry, when you deal with matters relating to pension, it was hard to keep the workers you were representing interested. Except for those at the upper age end of the workforce who might be approaching retirement, almost no one was ever interested.

Not that the pension wasn't a problem, but I wanted to know about their workaday lives . . . they'd always get back to the pension plan. At one point, I think, Robin Roberts . . . was trying to sum up, get something done. He said, "I want to explain to you what we have in mind." And I thought, Good, because I still didn't know what that was. He said, "We visualize an organization that would have more muscle than we have now, that would be in the interest of the players and of the game and so on.

"We don't really mean a union as such, but we do want somebody like you who has had vast experience with unions and negotiations and pension plans. But we're just a search committee and we're out to make a recommendation of somebody to the elected player representatives from all the ball clubs. I don't want to offend you, but you have to realize that players are basically conservative people without work experience outside of baseball and, therefore, without union experience. In order for you to lead the organization, you'll have to be elected by them. We have a plan . . ."—he should have said, *I* have a plan because he was really doing it all—"for the vote we think we'd like to have a ticket, composed of you for director and then a person with a conservative background as general counsel. It will be a balanced ticket that we'll present to the players to vote on."

So I asked the obvious question. "Who do you have in mind for this conservative person?"

And Roberts said, "Well, it's not just that we have him in mind, we've already been to see him. And he's agreed that he would serve not as an individual but as a member of the firm he's with. It's Richard Nixon."

I swallowed hard three or four times and said, "That will not work." Roberts, whom I think by this time had decided he wanted me, was crestfallen by my reaction. I said, "Would you like to know why? You've talked about the pension plan, for example, as being your most important concern. It's about the only thing that the old company union had anything to do with, about their only accomplishment. Richard Nixon wouldn't know a pension plan from the Empire State Building. He'll be absolutely no help in what you're describing as your greatest problem. And furthermore, he's a pal of at least half of the owners in baseball. He's on the wrong side of the fence. His whole voting record when he was a congressman and a senator was anti-working people."

I then told them that Nixon wouldn't be able to devote much attention to the job anyway, because it was obvious that he was planning to run for president again. Bunning, who'd been quiet up to then, said, "Well, how do you know that?" and I said,

"I don't really know it, but you have to remember that ever since he came to New York to be a partner in his law firm, he has spent his entire time not in New York, but traveling around the country fund-raising for Republican candidates for all kinds of office. He's obviously piling up political capital . . ." This was all greeted with profound silence. And shortly thereafter the meeting appeared to be coming to an ungraceful conclusion. I got up to go. Shook hands all around and wished them luck.

I got to the door, but I came back and said, "Look, I'm now going to do something I never do. I'm going to give advice when it hasn't been asked for. I don't usually do this. But don't do what you are on the road to doing. When you get a candidate to be a director for your organization, let him pick his own counsel. Don't foist somebody on him."

And I left. Went back to Pittsburgh where I was living when I was with the steelworkers, and told my family, "I blew it and we're not going back to New York." I was wrong. They thought about what I had said and they came after me within two weeks or so. Roberts told me, "We're going to accept the idea that the director will pick his own counsel." That's how it started. I asked Dick Moss to act as chief counsel.

THE OWNERS REACT

While baseball was not generating anything like the money it does today— even adjusting for inflation—the players began to realize that they were not getting their fair share of the take. Furthermore, they had no control over their own destinies. Their realization that things could be done a different way brought about a semi-organized campaign on the part of ownership to keep things status quo for as long as possible.

BOB FRIEND: When Marvin studied our business, he said, "These owners are making more money than you think. You're not getting anywhere near the share you should be getting from the All-Star Game and World Series. You guys are shortchanging yourself." That opened our eyes. And he was right. The retirement fund was terrible. We had an unfunded liability, which was unbelievable. It wasn't sound at all. But Marvin changed all that right away. And we were pleased with what he did, even after I left baseball. Robin and I weren't pleased with the strikes that came in [1972 and '81], but I would have to say it turned out fine.

MILT PAPPAS: Before [Miller] officially took over as head of the union, the owners were spreading stories about him. They called him a hired gun and said we shouldn't believe anything he said. *[Laughs]* They made it sound like he was this outsider who was going to break up this big happy family of ours. Right!

RICHARD MOSS: [The owners] went on the attack from the start. Absolutely. Sportswriters participated in that, too. Dick Young in New York City was one of the leaders of that, writing things that suggested these outside guys, these union guys, were going to come in and ruin baseball. When Marvin was touring the baseball camps before the vote to ratify his selection, there was an all-out campaign . . . they were saying, "This is a union guy. You're not steelworkers, you're not coal miners. You're professionals. Why do you need a union?"

BOB FRIEND: He made that tour of the camps to introduce himself to the players, and the owners said, "My goodness, what are you guys doing? He's going to kill the game." I remember we had players coming in and saying, "Why are we doing this? He's going to kill baseball. We don't want this guy." There's no question the owners got to those players. The owners knew who Marvin was, knew he was always prepared and a terrific negotiator from his reputation with the steelworkers, so they saw what was coming and wanted no part of it. We signed on with Marvin anyway, and he opened the office in New York and that was the start of it.

MARVIN MILLER: They were buttonholing players. They sent people from the commissioner's office and the two league presidents, who were then Warren Giles and Joe Cronin, actually went around to all the training camps before I got there. The arrangement I had made with the search committee was that before there could be any vote I wanted an opportunity to meet and talk with all the players.

And so management had their cohorts going around to all the training camps, meeting with players in Arizona, California, and Florida and telling them all kinds of things, like, "We have this great thing going here. If this union man comes in you'll have strikes and gangsters. We understand he's from the Teamsters." I'd never had anything to do with the Teamsters in my life, but that didn't matter to them.

MILT PAPPAS: My first impression when I heard him speak was, this guy really knows his stuff but I don't know if he has a fire in the belly.

JIM KAAT: It was the spring of 1966 when Marvin made his first tour of spring training and was introduced to the players and we learned about his background. Of course, that's also when we immediately felt the heat from the front office about how this guy was no good for baseball, we players were doing the wrong thing. It created a little division within ball clubs. You had some guys who were more loyal to the front office than others. I always fell in that category of being a bit of a rebel and maverick. I went to war with [Minnesota Twins owner] Calvin Griffith every year over my contract. You always had a squabble of some kind with Griffith. So I was in favor of Marvin and the union right from the start.

That was my first memory of Marvin and then I point to a meeting we had, I believe it was the winter of 1967. Bob Allison was our team player rep and I was the alternate. That's when Marvin invited all of us to New York. There was a move under way that we had to band together and not sign contracts to show solidarity. Marvin was riveting. He never raised his voice or did anything dramatic, but he pointed out in his soft-spoken manner what we had to do.

JIM BOUTON: I was waiting for a wild-eyed labor leader type. I was waiting for John L. Lewis, Walther Reuther, a real hard-nosed union guy. Someone to come in and pound the table. And here's this college professor talking to us. Soft-spoken, congenial, very calm, very understated. So it was a completely different demeanor from what I had expected. We were told that Marvin Miller would lead to strikes and picket lines and bicycle chains and all of that. The owners went all out. Joe Reichler, who was the assistant to the commissioner, pulled me aside and said, "Jimmy, you know this Marvin Miller, this union guy? He's going to be very, very, very, very bad for baseball." This was supposed to scare me off. And [general manager] Paul Richards of the Braves called Marvin a "mustachioed four-flusher."

MARVIN MILLER: You know Roberts took that one seriously. He called me in Pittsburgh and hesitantly came around to saying, "You know players don't wear mustaches." So I said, "Well, I know that, but they used to [laughing] before they were told they had to shave." And I even reminded him that Frenchy Bordagaray [a player from the '30s and '40s] was the last one with a mustache. But it was strange.

BILL GILES: Miller was an experienced labor economist, and he was both shrewd and very smart. He worked patiently and diligently with the players on issues such as the minimum salary, the pension fund, and a grievance procedure. I can't say he was motivated by a love of the game. I think he just wanted the players to get their fair share of revenues.

JIM BOUTON: Ironically, it was the owners' extreme reaction against Marvin that convinced the players that we needed him. As I understand it, the St. Louis team was on the fence over Marvin. [Cardinals owner] Augie Busch got the players together in spring training and told them that Marvin would be the worst thing that ever happened in baseball. The Cardinals voted unanimously in favor of Marvin.

JIM KAAT: Marvin, in his soft-spoken way, made it clear that we had to band together, and the only way anything we would do could work is if the big guys don't fold. In other words, he knew that ownership would target the Yastrzemskis, the Aarons, the Gibsons, and the Killebrews. If they could get the stars to crack, we'd have a house of cards. So I never will forget that meeting at the Biltmore Hotel. He left the microphone open for anyone who wanted to speak, for or against what he was suggesting. He wanted everyone to speak their minds. We had [Willie] Stargell, [Hank] Aaron, and [Willie] Mays there. One by one, they took their turns and said, "We're going to stick together 100 percent, whether you're the best player on the team or the 25th player."

MARVIN MILLER: The higher-priced players, with rare exceptions, were the backbone of the effort to create a different kind of organization. Absolutely. A lot of people at the time were surprised by that. The general feeling of people who haven't made a study of this is that the least skilled, the lowest paid, are the ones most in need of a union. Therefore the logic goes that they're the ones who back it. Actually, it's quite the reverse. In the beginning, the problems you have in organizing often revolve around intimidation tactics by the owners. The employees who are least intimidated are the most skilled and most valuable.

JIM KAAT: That was really the day that made the union what it has been since [then]. Marvin early on convinced us that we could only make progress if we projected a united front. And, of course, the owners did capitulate. We won our increase in minimum salary, and that had an impact all the way up the scale, plus we got the share of the television [revenues] that we wanted in the pension plan. And that proved early on that if we just stuck together we could get things done.

JIM BOUTON: The owners said that Marvin would have to go around and collect the dues from the players himself. He said, "That's fine." And then he went to the Topps Chewing Gum Company and said something like, "Right now, you've got the players on your baseball cards and all you're paying for that is a gift from an S&H Green Stamp catalog worth $100. And that's the retail price, the wholesale is about $50 and I think the players are worth more than just a barbecue grill."

Topps said, "Well, that's nice, but we already have lifetime contracts with these guys." Marvin said, "Yes, but you don't have any of the new players coming along and we'll make sure none of them will sign your contract. In a few years, you'll start having holes in your collections and soon you'll be offering one half of a team but not the other half."

The upshot was Marvin negotiated a whole new deal on behalf of the Players Association that brought in hundreds of thousands of dollars. The players saw some money right away and the rest of it went to fund the office. That happened pretty soon, so we realized we had a pretty savvy guy working for us. We were in Marvin's corner. Wherever this guy wanted to take us, we were on board.

MILT PAPPAS: There were repercussions. Oh, you better believe it. If you were a player rep, you better be an All-Star or there was a good chance you'd get traded, and even if you were an All-Star that might not be enough. Go back and look at the percentage of player reps who got traded in their prime. There were a lot of them. Player reps were the most hated people in the world by the general managers and owners. It was a tough job. They would harass you, go behind your back to your teammates and other ballplayers to tell them falsehoods about the negotiations. I had two big confrontations when I was with the Reds.

JOE TORRE: There was a lot of tension. Before the union came along, player reps used to ask about things like broken showerheads in certain clubhouses or getting more towels. Now we were going in there asking about money and pensions and the reserve clause. There were a lot of hard feelings.

MILT PAPPAS: On road trips, we would fly to the next town with the press and media occupying the first-class seats and the players would be stuck in coach, cramped three across. So when I went to [Cincinnati Reds general manager] Bob Howsam to complain, he said, "Well, the writers and broadcasters reimburse the club for travel. We're not paying for their tickets." I said, "Fine. Then tell them to take another flight so we can sit in their first-class seats. Put them on another plane."

We were supposed to have a meeting to resolve the situation. It was going to be, or so we were told, Marvin representing our side and some representatives of the media. The deal was the player rep wouldn't go and neither would anyone from the Reds front office. So I stayed home. Howsam went to the meeting and when I found out, I was livid. I let him have it over the phone for lying to me. So there was bad blood between us.

The second incident came when Robert Kennedy was killed. St. Louis was in Cincinnati to play us and the players had agreed that we wouldn't take the field until Kennedy's body had arrived in Washington. Something delayed the arrival of his body, but we voted, 15–11, to delay the game. I went out to talk to the umpires and they said, "As long as neither team takes the field, we don't have any problem with waiting."

While I'm out discussing this with the umpires, Howsam and Dick Wagner are in the clubhouse threatening the players with punishment if they don't take the field for the scheduled start of the game. I walked in and told them to get the hell out of the clubhouse. Three days later, Howsam traded me to Atlanta. That happened to a lot of player reps.

FIRST NEGOTIATIONS: THE PENSION

A major concern in an industry where careers are relatively short-lived has always been sustaining an income in one's post-playing years. By coincidence, this was the first item on the docket when Miller took over. It was here that the owners were determined to demonstrate that, regardless of how organized the players became, it was they who were going to continue dictating terms.

MARVIN MILLER: I began officially on the job July 1, 1966, and the benefit plan which contained both pensions and health insurance expired on March 31st of the following year, so it was the first order of business.

When we look at that, you have to go back and realize that the financing of the benefit plan which had been started on April 1, 1947, evolved to be what they called a "60/40" formula based on the radio and television money. A formula had been adopted to be applied to the national television [revenue], which was shared equally by all the teams, unlike local television; 60 percent of the radio and television proceeds from the World Series and the All-Star Game and 95 percent of the ticket proceeds from the All-Star Game provided the basis for the financing of the plan.

What had really started the whole business that led to the players changing their organization, and this was long before I got involved, was a rumor that the players had picked up that the owners were disturbed about this formula because television money was accelerating at a rate that nobody had anticipated other than Walter O'Malley. O'Malley had, and he had been lobbying for years to get rid of that way of financing the benefit plan.

The first act in all of this was the renegotiation of the new television contract between the owners and the networks. That summer they completed their negotiations with a substantial increase in what the networks were paying. I received a notice from the commissioner's office, it was Spike Eckert at the time, that the Executive Council of baseball, consisting of three or four owners plus the commissioner, would be meeting in Chicago just before the All-Star Game, which was being played in St. Louis, and inviting me. To my amazement, they had invited me to tell me that the council had made a decision. There hadn't been any negotiations yet, but they had made a decision.

This is the way they did things . . . they showed me great politeness, but they were telling me that the new pension plan that would go into effect the following April would have to be renegotiated and have to be funded in a different fashion, from a fixed sum of money rather than from a percentage of what the networks were paying.

After I got as much information as I could as to what the figures were, they kind of indicated the meeting was over—it was Eckert and one of his attorneys from Washington; Bowie Kuhn, who was assistant counsel to the National League; an American League attorney, the two league presidents, and one or two other people. Eckert informed me that they were going across the hall. They had scheduled a press conference and he was going to announce to the press the new television contract details and how this was going to be handled in relation to the players' benefit plan.

I said, "Mr. Commissioner, if you don't mind, I'd like to make a little statement before you go across there." Near as I can remember, I said, "I don't want to start our relationship with filing an unfair labor practice, because you're about to commit one and I'm trying to prevent you. Under the law, you have just announced a violation that you intend to commit. And since you have counsel present, several people here, you are not going to be able to say that it was done without knowledge of the law. So I am going to tell you what the law is. You have a collective bargaining responsibility under the Wagner Act as amended by Taft-Hartley. The Players Association is the collective bargaining agent recognized by you as the representative of all the players and, for benefit plan purposes, for the coaches, the trainers, and the managers as well. We've had no negotiations. We haven't even made a proposal to you. You've made no proposal before today and have given us no opportunity to respond with a counterproposal. I've rarely seen a more clear-cut violation."

So, they sat down again. They conferred and Eckert said, "So what is it you're saying we ought to do?" "Well, there's no reason why you can't go across there and give them the details of your new television contract with the networks, which is what you want to start with. But my advice to you is to stop right there. If anyone asks about the benefit plan, you have to tell them the truth; that the negotiations have not yet begun. That's all." So they went across the hall and I went with them. I was going to be witness to this and that's what he did.

MILT PAPPAS: [Those early negotiations] could get rough but, for the most part, they just treated us with friendly contempt. They were in the driver's seat, so why not? The first thing I noticed was that even though we were supposed to be negotiating with the owners, no owners ever showed up at the meetings. Marvin would be there with us [the player reps] and you'd have Warren Giles, the president of the National League, Joe Cronin from the American League, and the league counsel. Bowie Kuhn was the lawyer for the National League.

We had to fight them on every little thing, and then when we'd reach an impasse or some part of the negotiation that called for a decision, they'd call a recess so they could run into the hall or next door and phone whichever owner headed one of the committees. They couldn't make a decision on their own. We finally said, "Can't anybody here make a deal?" It was ridiculous.

JIM BOUTON: [The owners] gave no ground. They would not make any comments. They would gather information, but they would not say what they would be willing to do. It was always, "We'll give that some thought." I never saw any real

negotiation on their part. I remember once when I asked
if they would allow players to become free agents after a
certain number of years, say after five years. No. Ten years?
No. What about Social Security age? I really asked that, it's in
Marvin's book, I think. And they said, no not even then. I said,
"Okay, I just wanted to find out the level of absurdity here."
The owners saw us as meat.

RICHARD MOSS: The owners were hostile and patron-
izing at the same time. At an early negotiating meeting we had
the two league presidents and the two league counsels. Joe
Cronin was the American League president at the time and his
father had been a fireman and the president of the fireman's
union. So he came from a strong union background. But that
didn't matter. During one of our discussions, we raised the
subject of scheduling. And Cronin sputtered, "Scheduling?
You guys have no fucking business with that! That's for us to
decide. That's outrageous! You can't bring up things like that!"
And then he got up and left the room.

MILT PAPPAS: Right after the first day [Marvin Miller]
took the reins, we started negotiating with Giles and Cronin
and Kuhn. It got off to a friendly start. Everybody welcomed
each other, we introduced Marvin. Then we started talking.
Right away we tried to bring up free agency and they shot us
down. So then we focused on the pension plan and putting pro-
tective padding on the outfield wall. Finally, we're discussing
meal money, which back then was $12 a day, not an awful lot.

We go back and forth and finally both sides agree on $16 a day.
We signed off on it and so did the owners. The next morning
we walk in and the coffee and doughnuts are out. We barely sit
down when Bowie Kuhn says, "Marvin, you know that $16 we
talked about yesterday?"

Now remember, we didn't just "talk" about it, we had all
agreed on that figure. Marvin said, "Yes, what about it?" And

Kuhn says, "Well, we thought it over and we're taking it back. We have to keep it at $12." Marvin almost did a double take, he was so shocked. "Excuse me," he said, "this is a negotiation. You can't just agree to things one day and take them back the next." Kuhn said, "I'm sorry but we decided we just can't afford it." So we had to fight them all over again.

Later, we're downstairs with Marvin having a drink and I remember him scratching his head over Kuhn and saying, "I wonder if I made the right decision taking this job." And we all laughed. He was dumbfounded by the way the owners treated us. But Marvin learned quickly and he was a master negotiator, as they soon found out. The problem with the owners was that they didn't know how to negotiate. They never really had to do it before. It was, "What we say goes."

MARVIN MILLER: [The pension talks] got acrimonious. You see, they had done some things before I arrived. Some time before that they had violated the law by, in effect, taking money that had been promised to the benefit plan and returning it to the owners. By controlling everything. The benefit plan was administered out of the commissioner's office. The commissioner was their employee. The players were innocent lambs at that point. As long as nothing untoward seemed to happen, it was not considered unusual for them to have a joint benefit plan administered by one party. When the payments were made to the clubs by the networks [for the national rights including All-Star and World Series broadcasts], it first went into a fund in the commissioner's office before the clubs divided it.

From that fund, part of the money that fell under the 60/40 formula was instead divided by the owners. It's a little more complicated than that, but it's basically what they did. The reasoning behind that ran something like this: Under the law, money that is allocated and put into a pension plan cannot be withdrawn for any purpose except for the agreed-upon benefits and/or the administrative costs of the program. Under no circumstances can it be given back to the employer who put it in there in the first place.

But they thought they had an out. They argued that the plan was overfunded and that they were not going to be able to get a tax deduction unless they removed some of the money and that's why they did it.

There was one fly in the ointment. In New York State, where the plan was based, there is a State Insurance Administration and they have a responsibility to see that all health, welfare, and pension plans are properly administered. They were investigating the owners at the time we were negotiating. They came to the conclusion that the owners' taking out from that money was illegal, so they were in clear violation. The examiner for New York State, having read in the papers that players were now represented by a union, sent me a letter inviting me to the hearing.

The owners' lawyers were there, and he explained to them that this money had to be returned with interest. This was ammunition that I now had and used. We settled on a figure that was equal to the old 60/40 formula, plus the amount that they had to return, plus the interest on the money they had illegally removed. But we discarded the formula itself.

PLAYER SALARIES

When it came to salaries, owner control was absolute. Multiyear contracts were rare. Players were routinely offered contracts for less than they had made the year before, depending on a variety of factors such as performance, club attendance, and how much the general manager thought he could get away with offering. Since most salaries were unknown, raises-by-comparison to one's peers were out of the question.

MARVIN MILLER: When we were negotiating the first Basic Agreement, we certainly were going to be talking about the minimum salary, for example. It had risen $1,000 once in

the prior 20 years. That's *one* raise of one thousand in 20 years.
I explained to the players that we needed information about
salaries because raising the minimum significantly would have
an impact on quite a few other salaries above the minimum.
We anticipated that the owners would claim hardship, that it
cost too much to do this, etc., etc. Therefore, we would need
some hard facts to judge this. I knew about the general reluc-
tance of people who had been talked into hiding their salaries.
Since I didn't have to know who was earning what, I concocted
a plan to ask the players to write their salaries without their
names on a piece of paper and to pass it on to the player rep,
who would send them in.

Management knew what I was doing and they laughed. They
said, "No one is going to tell you and if they tell you it will be
wrong." As it turned out, with few exceptions, everyone told me
what they were earning, but anonymously, as I had asked. When
we met with management, I had made a bet with [the owners'
chief labor negotiator] John Gaherin. I said, "I'm going to bet
you, with rare exceptions, this data is correct." By this time,
I had worked out what the averages were, what the high was,
what the low was, what was the midpoint, and so on. So I gave
him the figures and he came back later and said, "You win."

JIM BOUTON: I realized right away that in baseball the
players were paid in a shockingly different way than I had
always imagined. You know, when you grow up you see the
Giants and the Dodgers in the '40s and I never tried to imagine
how much the guys made, I just assumed they all did pretty
well. They were major-league baseball players, they were stars.

My rookie year with the Yankees, they paid me the minimum
salary [$6,000]. Okay, the minimum, that was one year. But af-
ter that one year, I thought I'd get a $5,000 raise or something.
We won the World Series and I was a pretty good pitcher for
them down the stretch. No, they offered me a contract in the
spring that said I would make $9,000 *if I made the team* and
$7,000 if I didn't.

I said, "What do you mean *if* I make the team? I was with the team the whole year, why wouldn't I make it?" And I said, "Why would you even want to plant that kind of doubt in the mind of a rookie pitcher? Why would you want me thinking that I might not make the team?" It was demeaning. I thought they should have treated me better, I thought they should have had more respect. That's when I realized we're just pieces of meat here. They're going to treat us badly no matter what.

JIM KAAT: The minimum salary hadn't been changed, or rarely changed, over the years, but it wasn't just that. Meal money hadn't gone up with inflation. Owners weren't giving any ground and the TV revenues were about to become a huge factor.

JOE TORRE: [Atlanta Braves general manager Paul Richards] wanted to cut me to the limit because I had been hurt the year before, and I wouldn't agree to it. One of the owners invited me to Florida to talk to Paul, and when I walked in there, the offer didn't change. I was working for a municipal bond firm in New York and like an asshole I handed him a card and said, "This is where you can find me." He threw the card in the garbage. I think my union activities played a part in it. It was an uncomfortable time. You found yourself feeling the dislike.

TONY OLIVA: We didn't know different. Me, I didn't know different. I'd toss a figure out there. If [the general manager] came close, I signed. I don't think I ever signed when I thought it was really what I wanted. It was close enough. I said, I'll play and next year I'll make some more money. I never thought, hey, I have to make everything this year. First of all, I didn't want to argue too much for a little money. I wanted to get something that I could live with. Be a little fair. Go and enjoy myself and have a good time. This is the way it used to be. We didn't have any lawyers. Lawyers came in the '70s.

BOB FRIEND: All we wanted to do was play baseball, and we were getting paid for it and we thought that was great. We didn't know any better. Miller kept saying, "I know this is how it is but this is how it *shouldn't* be." And it took a strong personality like him, always educating us, someone who was just brilliant when it came to labor law, to finally make the point. And of course then we learned how many players were down and out after they left baseball. We had a lot of horror stories back then. You know we'd get meal money, say 8 or 10 dollars a day, on road trips. Some players would just pocket that money or spend very little of it; they actually skipped meals just to give themselves some extra cash.

First, you had no agent, no agents at all. The clubs wouldn't speak to you if you brought in an agent. Forget it. My first four years with the Pirates, I was still learning how to pitch and we weren't a good team most of those seasons. Branch Rickey was our general manager and when I'd go see him to discuss my contract. I wanted a $1,000 raise. I'd been with the club for three years at that point and I was still stuck on $5,000 a year, which was the minimum.

And there were a lot of people in my situation. There wasn't a lot of money being made. So I made my case for a raise and Mr. Rickey said, "I base a player's salary on three things." I asked him what they were. He said, "The club's attendance for the year, our position in the race, and your value to the team. Now, we drew 700,000 people, we finished last, 11 games out of seventh place, and you had a losing record. What do you think your value is?"

Well, by the time he finished with that, I felt lucky I had a contract at all, you know? He wasn't mean or anything. Mr. Rickey was a gentleman and he just explained it in business terms that made some sense. Didn't get me a raise, though. He was pretty much saying I had to prove myself a little bit more before he'd start handing the money out.

JIM BOUTON: They always tried to get the player for as little as they could possibly pay. They never said to themselves,

"Gee, this guy is making this much so we have to pay this player the same amount because he's as good or better." No, they said, "We can get that guy for less and it doesn't matter whether somebody who is not as good is making more money."

They ended up giving more money to the guys who bargained harder than the guys who didn't. You were paid for your willingness to take a tough stand and try to get more money rather than on what you did on the field. And then they would try to punish you if you did bargain hard. You were a bad guy if you held out. "Who's Bouton, holding out after his first year? Who does he think he is?" You finally ended up signing.

I remember that many players needed to make money during the off-season to make ends meet. You're not going to believe this: There was a basketball team with guys living in the New York area: Larry Bearnarth, Ed Kranepool, Dick McAuliffe, Phil Linz, Al Jackson, John Orsino, Frank Robinson, and me. We played against high school faculties in the area for $50 a man, and we needed that money. The high school faculty would use the games to sell out the gym and raise money for band uniforms and sports equipment and things like that. We never lost a game with that team, by the way. We had a foolproof system for winning. We'd double-team the gym teacher and let the biology teacher go free.

RICHARD MOSS: None of the players made that much money. The owners were always crying poverty and, to listen to them, they were performing a public service, losing all this money just so fans could have a ball club to root for. They acted as though they were doing a favor for that city. To be honest, it was not that profitable a business back then, not like today. It was a relatively small business, but the owners would have you believe they weren't making anything. Players were told not to reveal their salaries to each other, and most of them didn't. When it came time to negotiate, general managers could tell them anything they wanted. They could just make numbers up for the sake of comparison.

There's the classic story of [longtime baseball executive] Buzzie Bavasi. In a series of articles he wrote some time back, Buzzie told the story of a player who met to talk about his contract. The player mentioned the salary he had in mind and Buzzie said, "Oh no, I can't pay you that. No one on the team makes that kind of money, not even . . ." and he named the star of the club. Then a phone call comes in from the outer office and the secretary asks Bavasi if he could step outside for a moment. Buzzie excuses himself, goes to the outer office and closes the door behind him.

But he left on his desk a contract that was supposedly signed by the star player he had referred to, at a much lower salary figure than the player was actually earning. While the player sat there waiting for Buzzie to come back, he leaned over and read the terms of the contract. When Buzzie came back, they agreed to a contract on Buzzie's terms. And Buzzie's commentary was that there was nothing wrong with that because the player shouldn't have looked. Buzzie was great at stuff like that. He would issue credit cards to players and then he'd get copies of the bills. So he knew everything the players did.

THE RESERVE CLAUSE

It is interesting to speculate what would have happened if the owners hadn't used their position of absolute power as a bully pulpit. Had they thrown the players some crumbs now and again—an extra dollar of meal money, or a cost-of-living increase on the minimum salary—perhaps they would have placated the rank and file to the point that the players would have stopped thinking about the big picture. There was no bigger big-picture issue than the reserve clause, the legal binding of a player to his team for life, or until such time as the team chose to release him from his obligation.

MARVIN MILLER: It was my view that first, [abolishing the reserve clause] had to be done and that second, we had to consider the various avenues that would make this possible. One avenue, obviously, was litigation. You didn't have to be an antitrust lawyer to know that the reserve clause was in violation of the antitrust laws.

The problem was, however, that I saw—long before Curt Flood—the Supreme Court itself had declared that you couldn't attack the reserve clause because of the prior 1922 Supreme Court decision that baseball was not governed by the antitrust laws. One of the worst—well, we can't call it the worst decision the Court ever made. The Dred Scott decision was the worst decision, but this comes close.

BOB FRIEND: Marvin talked about attacking the reserve clause not too long after he came in. He talked about going after it all along. He said unless we got rid of it we would never have any leverage. We didn't think he had any chance there. It was such a part of baseball that we didn't even think about it. Once you signed with a team you were stuck, that was how it was. And some of us thought that this was not right, but that's how it always was.

JIM BOUTON: You end the reserve clause and it was the end of baseball. All the players believed it. All of them except for a handful of black players. They were the smartest guys. When I ran for player representative on the Yankees, my mini-platform was that we needed to change the economics of the game and that we needed to fight harder for a better deal. I got three votes.

One of them was my roommate, Fritz Peterson, one of them was Héctor López, and the third was Rubén Amaro. The black guys in baseball have always been the savviest guys, because they already came with this experience of being taken advantage of. Whereas the white guys all came from farms and mines, they were conservative guys who grew up in small towns in which *union* was a bad word.

I didn't see how the players could possibly change the reserve clause, so I just said they should use the reserve clause to show that the owners—because they had these lifetime contracts—should give the players the benefit of the doubt on the contracts.

MILT PAPPAS: We had a system that would have worked for both sides and made things just a bit more reasonable. The contract with the reserve clause was so one-sided. We proposed that if a player was in the majors for 10 years, five with the same team, and wanted to test the market, he could go out and get offers from other teams, but his original team had the right of first refusal. They had to match the offer. So some of our stars would have moved, but a lot of them would have stayed with their original clubs, but at better money.

The players this really would have helped were those good fourth outfielders or the utility infielder who could start for another club or the pitcher who was in the bull pen but could make the rotation of another team. This would give them the chance to move on to regular jobs or at least make more money for sticking with their original teams. All we wanted was just this little bit of freedom.

JIM BOUTON: If the owners had said to us somewhere between 1962 and '65, before we hired Marvin Miller, "Don't go searching for a new union leader. Here's what we'll do. We'll raise the minimum salary from $7,000 to $10,000. And we'll raise it $1,000 a year for the next 50 years." The players never, ever would have hired Marvin Miller or attempted any of those changes. Baseball would still be under the same reserve system because the owners would have said, "The minimum salary back in 1963 was $7,000 and here we are in 1983 and it's $27,000. That's tremendous." We never would have been able to break that.

MILT PAPPAS: But [the owners] told us, in so many words, to take a walk. We own you. And since the Supreme Court had upheld baseball as the only sport with antitrust protection, they figured they had all the leverage and anything they gave us was a gift. Take it or leave us. When we hollered, they wouldn't listen. They were owners and their job was to own you. And if you had a bad year they could automatically renew your contract by March 10th and cut you 20 percent. You had absolutely no recourse. You had no say. The only way you could leave a team was if the club traded or released you. [Even if you died] I think the owners would have kept you under reserve in case you came back in another life.

MARVIN MILLER: Certainly most fans didn't seem to care [about the reserve clause] and that was because most fans didn't seem to know what the reserve clause meant. My father knew and he would talk to me about it. You know, there's this whole business of revising history.

I'm thinking of that historian, Doris Kearns Goodwin. She has written on more occasions than one about how, in the old days, players were loyal and they stayed with one team and they didn't move around. And she cites a period when her father would take her to games when the Brooklyn Dodgers were a contender almost every year.

What nobody ever told her was that more players changed teams before free agency than after. It's just that she talked about a period when her team was a contender and it's true that a winning team did less trading of its players for obvious reasons. While a losing team, like the Dodgers of my earlier days, were always trying to trade to find a combination of players that would get them out of last place or seventh place or sixth place. And this belief that players now change teams and there's no stability as compared to before is crazy, just crazy.

BOBBY GRICH: To be honest, the reserve clause confused me. You heard both sides of the coin from the owners and the union, and of course I sided with the union. The players should be free to choose where they would play. But I have to admit

I had some sympathy for the owners. From a business stand-point, obviously without them you had no teams and no league and then where would we be?

You could see, just by looking in the stands, that some teams weren't drawing and they had to be losing money. The owners told us that if the reserve clause died, we'd have so much chaos that it would ruin the game. Players moving around, going to the highest bidder, the small-market teams left without any talent. Fan loyalty would be lost with all that movement. Sure, they exaggerated some of that out of their own interests, but there was some truth in their argument. But Marvin had the answer to that, when he said we could self-impose restrictions, limit free agency to players who had been in the major leagues for six years. That way the owners realized some return on their investment in the players and the players could go out and get what they were worth. But to be honest, there were times before we had that structure in place, before I heard about how it might work, that I thought the owners might be right. And without that structure, who knows, they might have been. Un-limited movement would have been chaos, and instead of root-ing for players, fans would have been rooting for uniforms.

RICHARD MOSS: There were congressional hearings in the early '60s on baseball's antitrust exemption, and various people testified, including Jackie Robinson. And Jackie testified that it was essential for baseball to retain the reserve system or the game couldn't function. Jackie later testified for us during the Flood case. We told him, "During the cross-examination, they are going to talk about your congressional testimony." And he said, "I'm prepared for that."

So indeed, on cross-examination, he was asked, "Now, Mr. Robinson, isn't it true that in your testimony before the United States Congress you said such and such?" And Jackie replied, "Yes, that's true, but I was very young and didn't know any better. I know better now." Jackie was a very bright, well-educated man, but he'd been brainwashed back then, too.

MARVIN MILLER: Litigation had to be considered, but I didn't think it had any real promise because of the way the courts had handled it [in the past] and it wasn't just the 1922 federal case. In 1953 a player named [George] Toolson in the New York Yankees' minor-league chain got himself a lawyer and sued under the antitrust laws. It went all the way to the Supreme Court, and the court ruled against him. Only this time they declared the earlier decision [from 1922] stands. Players were banned from baseball for going to the Mexican League—Sal Maglie, Hal Lanier, and others—and one of them, Danny Gardella, was a plaintiff in a third case. Given that whole history it seemed to me the courts were not the way to go.

A second possibility, of course, was to negotiate a change through collective bargaining. That didn't seem to be promising either. A strike, given the attitude and knowledge—or lack of knowledge—of the players, seemed to me to be something we had to put on the back burner, at least for quite a while.

And so in my own mind the best bet always was an arbitrator interpreting the contract. And I say that because the first time I read the players' contract and was told that the language in it was what formed the entire basis of the reserve system, I couldn't believe it. I just absolutely couldn't believe it.

You just had to read it. You can check it any time you want; it's in every player's contract and the major-league rules stipulated that no contract would be approved by the commissioner's office that didn't contain this language. And the owners' lawyers wrote it, because there was no organization negotiating with them [on the players' behalf] back in those days. It said [that if] at a certain date, when the season was over, I believe it was the March following [the just completed season], the owner and the player have not agreed upon a contract for the subsequent year, then the owner could *unilaterally* extend the contract—quote—for one additional year—unquote—without the player's signature.

I did a double take when I first read that. I said, "There's got to be more to it than this. They can't be relying on this!" Man, this is a paper tiger here. But the problem was, first, there was no grievance procedure. Second, after the first Basic Agreement, when there was a grievance procedure, there was no terminal point for arbitration. What it said was, the matter could be referred to the commissioner for his decision. So the bells went off. To my mind we had to get rid of the commissioner from the grievance and arbitration procedure.

RICHARD MOSS: We continually told the players where they were and what we wanted to do. We had read the clause and interpreted it as extending only for an additional year and not in perpetuity. But we needed a player who would play out the season without a contract to test that, and that was an enormous risk. You couldn't ask for volunteers for that. Ted Simmons was, I think, the first to come close to challenging it. Before Simmons, the owners simply wouldn't let an unsigned player play. But Simmons was such an important part of that team, the Cardinals made an exception. Ted's a very bright guy and we talked to him and he let us know he intended to play out the season and test it. But then the Cardinals gave in on everything he wanted and he signed.

CURT FLOOD GOES TO COURT

The late '60s and early '70s were a time when one seemingly couldn't turn a corner without running into a protest of some kind. In this atmosphere, Curt Flood, who died in 1997, might seem like just another American with an ax to grind. The difference between Flood—the St. Louis Cardinals center fielder who, in the 1969–70 off-season, took umbrage at being traded to the Phillies after a dozen years in a Cardinals uniform—and most of the rest of the disgruntled was that he was willing to give up a great deal for the betterment of his peers. Flood's disenchantment with having no say in his own destiny after so many years at the top of his profession was just the sort of test case that the players' union needed to see if an end could be brought to the reserve clause.

MARVIN MILLER: Unlike what people have written and thought, I didn't think the Flood case would be our salvation. I didn't look for the Flood case; it happened.

RICHARD MOSS: Our biggest concern was that Curt would come under enormous pressure from the owners and writers and we wanted to know if we were going to go out on the limb with him and finance this action and support it in every way possible, would he stick it out? Was he sincere or was this just some ploy? So first we warned him how he was going to be criticized, probably by some players, too, and how the owners would line up the media against him. We described the pressures.

MARVIN MILLER: Curt Flood was a very determined, very principled man. He was so unshakable. I felt obligated to explain all the downsides of pursuing a case like this. Given the fact that he was already 31 years old and there was no telling how long the case could take. He'd be out of baseball all that time and with the long memories of the owners, I doubt he'd be given a shot at managing or coaching or any other job in baseball.

And he was walking away from a significant amount of money. His new team, the Phillies, were offering what was for the time a big contract to join them. I was obliged to tell him that I didn't think we could win. I went even further, because I felt obligated. "It's a million-to-one shot that we're going to [win]. But even if we were to win, you're not going to get any damages." He asked why, and I said, "The court is not going to go back and say, 'During the period when we, the court, upheld the reserve clause . . .' You know?" I said the most that will happen is something for the future.

And he said, without taking any time to think about it, "But that will still benefit all the other players and the players to come in the future, right?" And I said yes. He said, "That's good enough for me." Now there's a man.

RICHARD MOSS: Curt was, among other things, eloquent and sincere. We invited him to an executive board meeting in Puerto Rico to speak directly to the players.

MILT PAPPAS: What an impressive man. Likable, soft-spoken. I was immediately moved by his sincerity and his passion for this cause. He wouldn't give in, no matter what they offered him. I thought, My God, this man has courage, to fight this thing that we've only been talking about fighting. You have to remember, Curt was in his prime then and he was a tremendous ballplayer. He turned his back on a lot of money. But he felt that we were all slaves, and that bothered him more than anything. Flood thought it was ridiculous that anybody could get treated like this in America.

JOE TORRE: I was going to sit out the 1969 season before I got traded to the Cardinals, so I was with Curt. Marvin Miller was the devil's advocate in those days. He didn't candy coat anything. I don't remember specifics other than Marvin telling everybody what was going to come of this. I remember Marvin being very strong. I thought we had to back Curt, and I spoke to people individually about that. But I didn't speak to the whole group.

MILT PAPPAS: When [Curt] finished speaking [in Puerto Rico], we all voted to back him 100 percent.

JIM BOUTON: I was happy but I didn't think [Flood] would get anywhere. I knew that baseball had pretty much locked up the government; that the owners had too many friends in Congress and that there was a close relationship between seats at the ballpark and schmoozing with athletes and all of that and that the Congressmen would always go with the owners, but it drew attention to the fact that the players were not being properly treated by the owners.

RICHARD MOSS: [The players] voted unanimously in [Flood's] favor. I have to say I thought the case was winnable. I was even confident heading into the Supreme Court case. And, in fact, had the court not changed from the time the case was filed to the time it was heard in the Supreme Court, I believe we would have won. But Richard Nixon had appointed three conservative members of the court who later voted against us and we lost, 5–3. If you read that decision, the opinion in the Flood case, it's a bit odd because it is packed with baseball lore, mentioning different players. It's all bullshit.

MILT PAPPAS: He lost, but he did wake some people up as to how unfair the reserve clause was. The fans were so gullible and the press was worse. After negotiations, we would walk out and the reporters would be there waiting for Marvin to speak. He'd present our side of things, but you barely heard about that the next day. I told some of the writers, "You guys are the biggest culprits. We walk out here, telling you about our plight and you hardly write anything about it [at] all. Then the owners come out here and tell you they're losing money and you print that like it's the gospel without doing anything to verify it. You're supposed to be journalists, but you don't even ask to see the books." So the owners used the press to sell their side of the story and the public came away looking at us as a bunch of greedy athletes.

MARVIN MILLER: When I explain that after the Flood case lost, the reserve rules were exactly the same as they were before the case started, [people] look at me as though I had just said that the world came to an end. Indirectly and almost inadvertently, the existence of that case brought about a change in the attitude toward arbitration, because in all of the cases before, that went to the court arguing that baseball should be under the antitrust laws, no one had ever exempted it before the courts did.

Congress never exempted the baseball industry from the Sherman Antitrust Act. There is no mention of baseball in there or in the Clayton Antitrust Act. No mention of the game. But what the industry's lawyers had always been able to argue was that this was a unique industry and it's a self-regulating industry. It has its own internal system with a commissioner of baseball who acts as a czar who is impartial. And there was never any union to argue the reverse of that. So it ran unopposed. Now shift fast-forward and the Curt Flood case has been filed.

Now the lawyers had to say, "What's our argument going to be now?" That we're a self-regulating industry with an impartial commissioner. You mean Marvin Miller is going to sit there and say nothing? And so, with the Flood case pending and the collective bargaining agreement open in negotiations, we pressed for impartial arbitration at the end of the grievance procedure. And with the Flood case coming down on their heads, they folded. I was never told [why] and obviously I was never in any of their private sessions. So I don't know that. If you want my guess . . . they took their eye off the ball.

EARLY GRIEVANCE CASES

In hindsight, the changes that Miller effected were rather rapid. After 75 years of the owners having things pretty much their way, Miller and the players' union had done much to make things more equal inside of a decade—and that was before they cracked the nut of the reserve clause.

BILL GILES: Miller was able to place the players on an even plane with the owners primarily by incorporating a grievance procedure into the basic labor agreement. It was this grievance procedure, and the hearing by an independent arbitrator, that brought about free agency in December 1975, as the [arbitrator Peter] Seitz ruling declared that the reserve clause did not bind a player to one team in perpetuity.

RICHARD MOSS: What you have to know about Charlie [Finley of the A's] is that he was one of the brightest owners around. Knew the game better than most. But he could do some crazy, stupid things. For example, we had an arbitration case with two of his players, Ken Holtzman, a starting pitcher, and the reliever Rollie Fingers. When it was Finley's turn to talk about Holtzman he said, "Yes, he's had an excellent record pitching for us. His numbers look pretty good, but all of our starters do well. But the reason is we have great relievers. Our starters know they can go all out until they run out of steam and then our relief pitchers will come in and take care of the game. That's how he assembled these numbers and you have to keep that in mind."

The next case was Fingers, and Charlie argued, "Yes, he had great numbers but that's because our starting pitchers are very good. They pitch long into the game and our relievers don't get overworked and that's how Fingers was able to put up such good numbers."

Now you think that's bad using two contradictory arguments? It's worse because he made both cases *in front of the same arbitrator!*

When Reggie Jackson appeared before the arbitrator, I represented the Players Association at that hearing, and we presented a strong case with statistics, and Reggie's statistics were pretty good, to say the least, compared to everybody else. When the arbitrator said, "All right, Mr. Finley, time for you to respond," Charlie said, "No goddamned baseball player is worth $100,000 a year."

The arbitrator looked at him and said, "Yes, I understand. Go on." And Finley said, "That's it." That was his entire case. Charlie lost all three of those decisions.

In the [Catfish] Hunter case [in 1974], Charlie didn't live up to the conditions of the contract. [Finley failed to make a $50,000 payment into an insurance annuity as called for in Hunter's contract.] We filed a default notice. Charlie, being Charlie, ignored it. Just being stubborn. Just like no player is worth $100,000, no player is going to tell him what to do. Winning that case created the first free agency for a player, and it proved to everyone, most importantly to all the other players, what the true market value was for their services. It was enormously important.

Hunter was making $100,000 a year, and now he signed a long-term contract for millions of dollars. That was the eye-opener. And it contributed to understanding free agency. Very significant and, people may forget this as well, that was a Peter Seitz decision, too.

We had another landmark decision, but few people remember it. Alex [Johnson] was a very talented hitter with the California Angels and in 1970 he led the league in batting, but no one really liked that he won that title. He hit .329. Alex was a different kind of guy. He would refuse to take batting practice or participate in pregame drills. Alex would hit a ground ball to the infield and he'd seldom run it out. He was paranoid. When he ran [warm-ups] in the outfield he would strap his bat under his belt to make sure no one tampered with it. He had numerous run-ins with reporters, and the Angels had disciplined him a few times.

Bottom line, Alex was very disturbed. But the culminating event was when he had a run-in with a reporter named Miller—I forget his first name—and he took the reporter's typewriter and threw it in a bucket of water. The Angels suspended him for a year without pay. We filed a grievance and right away people wrote, "A grievance? How can you defend a guy like that?" Alex was from Detroit. Through a friend of mine, we got him a black psychiatrist in Detroit. He analyzed what was going on. In the grievance, we essentially argued that this man was sick and he should be treated like any other player who is physically incapacitated. He should be placed on the disabled list, get treatment, and be paid. There were three days of hearings, but the bottom line was the arbitrator ruled in our favor. And that was groundbreaking, as significant a case as Catfish Hunter and the [Andy] Messersmith decision, in terms of the union.

There was one other, smaller, very early case, but I thought it was significant. It involved Buzzie Bavasi. At the time, players had to live at the club's hotel [in spring training or whenever the team was on the road]. If they were married, they could stay with their wives somewhere else and receive an allowance equal to the amount the clubs would save by not putting them up in the hotel. Buzzie was the general manager of San Diego at the time.

Several San Diego players got shortchanged on their allowance. Insignificant amounts, by the way, maybe 5 or 10 dollars a day. The whole case involved maybe three or four hundred dollars, but I thought it was significant because we had to hold the club to the contract. We tried the case and we won. The club was ordered to pay certain players various amounts. And Buzzie didn't honor the arbitration ruling. So we went back to arbitration and had another case to enforce the ruling. And we won on that. Buzzie finally had to pay these insignificant sums but I think in that case we established that we weren't going to be screwed around.

STRIKE: 1972

By 1972, baseball as a profession had existed for more than 100 years. Apart from the isolated incident of the Detroit Tigers sitting out a game in 1912 to protest the suspension of teammate Ty Cobb, there had never been a players' strike. But with the pension matter still pending, salary arbitration on the table, and the players' union possessing more solidarity than ever before, that was about to change.

The players' strike of '72 lasted 13 days, from April 1 until April 13. It ended when the owners and players agreed on a $500,000 increase in pension fund payments and when the owners agreed to add salary arbitration to the collective bargaining agreement. The 86 games that were lost to the strike were never made up, because the league refused to pay the players for the time they were on strike. Some teams therefore played only 153 games, nine fewer than normal. One significant result of this was that the Detroit Tigers played one more game than the Boston Red Sox, and wound up winning the American League East by half a game over the Red Sox.

RICHARD MOSS: We were involved in pension negotiations, and we had it down to one issue, the issue of how the excess contributions would be dispersed. The owners were proposing that they get the money back. It was a fairly simple issue, but it was symbolically important because the players understood it was a test to see if they would act like men or cave in and do whatever the owners said. At the end of spring training, April 1st, we called a meeting in Dallas with the player reps and their alternates. And the question was "Were these men prepared to strike?"

Marvin and I felt strongly that they were not. And at the meeting we explained that the owners had this great PR system through the commissioner's office and the league offices and the clubs and that the players would be made to look foolish and selfish and there would be enormous public criticism of their actions. We had no PR apparatus, we were not going to win a battle in the press and the public eye, and we didn't have a strike fund, so there would be a sacrifice.

MARVIN MILLER: I'll tell you exactly what happened there. Very revealing. It was in spring training and I was there with my wife Terry and Dick Moss, the general counsel. We had conducted a meeting with the players, explaining where things were and recommending a strike vote. As I always did, we left before they voted. I was playing Ping-Pong in the

Dodgers' Vero Beach lounge room and the player rep came in and told me about the 21–4 result in favor of the strike.

I no sooner got that news than a messenger arrives to tell me that since it was St. Patrick's Day, Mr. O'Malley was having his usual party with a planeload of season-ticket holders flown in from Los Angeles. He would like you and your wife and Mr. Moss to join them. I was concerned about the seeming lack of understanding on the part of the negotiators with whom we were trying to negotiate a new pension plan and I welcomed the opportunity to possibly talk with O'Malley. We stayed the rest of the afternoon and attended this great dinner. When the appointed time came, Mr. O'Malley and Peter O'Malley, Dick Moss, and I met in a private room off from the party.

I tried to explain to him that we were heading into a strike situation that shouldn't occur; it was absurd. There was enough money in the pension fund to accommodate what we were talking about in the way of benefits without increasing the costs by one cent. This made no sense at all. He kept tut-tutting me, saying, "Ah, you're a worrywart. It's not going to be, it's not going to be."

After a while I realized there were owners who were intent on putting the union in its place and it had nothing to do with the issues. I was right and he was wrong. He said, "Do you know the results of the strike vote today?" I said, "Yeah, it was 21–4 in favor of a strike." He said, "Who were the four?" I said, "You don't understand, Walter. First, I don't stay for the vote. Second of all, if I did know I wouldn't tell you." "Oh," he huffed, "Well, I'm going to find out." I asked, "Why are you so interested?"

He said, "Look, if there are other people who don't understand that this is a team game, I do. Make no mistake. I would have preferred that they had voted 25–0 against the strike. But with all of these players voting for a strike, I don't want that kind of a split on my team. We just can't have it and I'm going to get rid of them." I said, "Walter, let's go back a bit. I never heard you say that. Because you would be violating a law."

He said, "I don't understand." I tried to explain it to him, but he said, "No, you've got it wrong. Look, the four who voted against the strike were voting *for* management. If I penalize them, it's not because of union action." And he was right, absolutely right. I want to tell you that one year later, not one of those four players was still with the Dodgers. Walter could find out things. He was the brightest of the owners and the most industrious in terms of doing what should be required of all owners: learning what the hell was going on.

RICHARD MOSS: There was another owner, Gene Autry of the Angels. On the day the strike started, Autry went down to the clubhouse where the players were packing their bags. He was no friend of the union and was, in his broadcasting companies, very antilabor. But when the strike started, he made a speech and he said, "Now I don't agree with what you guys are doing, but one thing is very important. If you start this, you all have to stick together." He also understood the importance of remaining a team.

MILT PAPPAS: Marvin and Dick Moss weren't pushing a strike.

RICHARD MOSS: We made our pitch for caution and even said perhaps now was the time to see what we could do through the Congress.

MILT PAPPAS: Marvin thought we would get killed in the press and he believed we could still negotiate our way to a settlement. When it came time to talk, I stood up in front of those 300 players and I said, "Marvin, we've been trying for how many years to come to terms with these people and they're not negotiating in good faith." I felt a strike was the only thing that would make the owners understand.

RICHARD MOSS: But we told them this was going to be a tough situation and that we couldn't recommend it to them carte blanche. One by one, players stood up, it was very dramatic, and the bottom line was they voted to authorize a strike, not just at the beginning of the season but for the very next day, April 2nd. It was unanimous with one abstention, and that was Wes Parker, the player rep for the Dodgers. When Parker went back to his team, he was impeached. So that's how determined and united the players were, and it was a great and pleasant surprise.

MILT PAPPAS: We walked out for a little more than a week, and the owners quickly reached a settlement with us. It was the only way to get through to them.

McNALLY AND MESSERSMITH BREAK THE ICE

Curt Flood's June 1972 defeat in the Supreme Court did not extinguish the hope on the union side that the reserve clause could be abolished. And once again, owner hubris was about to play right into the hands of the players.

MARVIN MILLER: I talked to the players in spring training [in 1973] immediately [after arbitration was established]. And we had a number of possibilities [to challenge the reserve clause]. Bobby Tolan, who had been with the Cincinnati Reds and gotten traded to San Diego, had a contract problem and didn't sign a contract right away. We were in touch with him, told him what his rights might be. Ted Simmons was after the fact. Ted Simmons knew about this, I don't know how, through scuttlebutt with his teammates, through [St. Louis Cardinals union representative] Joe Torre, I don't know. Before that, there was Sparky Lyle. He went to the last day of the season in a contract dispute with the Yankees. They finally gave up and signed him for what he wanted. And I may be forgetting one or two others.

We told them what we knew, what we suspected, and what we didn't know. It enabled them to make judgments. And it was their judgment. When Sparky Lyle decided that the contract the Yankees offered him on the last day was fine with him, it was fine with us. When Bobby Tolan decided to take what Bavasi was offering him, that the loan the Padres were giving him to buy a house out there made the contract worthwhile, we said, Great. No pressure was applied on anyone.

All during [Andy Messersmith's] fateful season, when he played under a contract that had been unilaterally renewed, he kept in touch with me. At some point he said, "I just want to tell you the salary they are offering me is now acceptable. But they are refusing to give me a no-trade provision." This was so ironic, considering what the reserve clause meant, with the owners saying once you lost it the players would leave.

Here was a player saying, "All you have to do is give me a no-trade provision so I won't leave, and I'll sign," and they wouldn't do it. Andy was honest with me. He said, "If they now meet this request, having met my salary demands, I'm going to sign." I said okay. That's when I called Dave McNally. McNally was out of baseball, but he had played for a month or so with Montreal under a contract renewed without his signature. I explained to Dave where we were and that my gut instinct told me the Dodgers would give Messersmith what he wanted, just to get rid of this case. I was wrong, of course, but that was my gut instinct.

I explained all this to Dave and he said, "Okay, I understand it. What is it I can do?" I said, "Well, you could join the grievance so that it ensures that no matter what they do with Messersmith, the case goes forward." When I told him I needed his permission, he said, "You got it."

Dave was another principled man. He already had turned down an offer from the Expos to come to spring training with a guarantee of $25,000 if he didn't make the team. What people didn't understand was that Dave McNally had been a player representative. He understood what this was all about. One of the unsung heroes of the whole thing. He joined the case because he realized its importance. Not long after that, Andy Messersmith called and said O'Malley had now told him it was against baseball rules for the Dodgers to grant a no-trade clause. I said, that's a lie, and even if it were true, considering it's O'Malley, he writes the rules.

RICHARD MOSS: You have to understand that the lawyers for the owners were all security lawyers. They didn't know anything about labor relations or labor law. The owners' representative in Messersmith-McNally, John Gaherin, understood what Peter Seitz was signaling. At owners' meetings, he would raise the red flag. The owners' lawyers would dismiss him and the chief lawyer in that case, Lou Hoynes, would always reply, "Don't worry about it. We think we're going to win the case, and if we don't, we'll just go back to the courts and get it overturned." He didn't realize how difficult it is to get an arbitrator's ruling reversed. I think he was relying on the past court decisions that had gone in the owners' favor, but it was stupid, absolutely stupid.

MARVIN MILLER: And their lawyers must be blamed for that. There was no way to interpret that contract any other way. I don't care who the arbitrator was. They should have seen it coming. . . . If Peter Seitz wanted anything in this world, it was that [the owners] take the case away from him by coming to an accord with the union. But they didn't pay attention and were genuinely shocked when he ruled in favor of Messersmith and McNally.

RICHARD MOSS: First [the owners] tried to enjoin the case in Federal court in Missouri and lost there. Then after the decision, they did try to get it overturned. Lost at the district court level and I argued on our behalf in front of the Court of Appeals. They lost there, too. By that time, they had the good sense not to take this to the Supreme Court.

BILL GILES: When free agency became reality, [Charlie Finley's] idea was to "make 'em all free agents," because he understood that a large supply would serve to hold down prices. His fellow owners were aghast at such a notion and moved to place restrictions on free agency, which was exactly what Marvin Miller wanted.

MARVIN MILLER: Charlie knew what he was doing, and thank goodness they didn't listen to him. I would have had a difficult time explaining to the players why it wasn't in their best interest to accept a system that made every player a free agent at once.

DENNIS ECKERSLEY: At the end of '77 a lot of people were going to be free. But [the Cleveland Indians] had to sign me, so that's when I knew what was going down.

What happened to me was they signed [Baltimore Orioles pitcher] Wayne Garland to a 10-year, $2.2 million deal, which seemed like, "Holy shit!" But, when you think about it, it really wasn't that good of a deal. It was $200,000 a year. So here they are, I thought, "They just signed this guy and I'm the best pitcher on the staff." So I'm thinking, "Man, I'm holding the cards." So, for me . . . imagine being a free agent at 21, 22 years old. But Cleveland didn't have the money. They had a hard time getting me a $50,000 bonus. Their ownership was screwed up back then. I couldn't even tell you who the owners were. I went to a dentist once in Cleveland and he told me he was part owner. He probably had 25 grand in there.

JOE RUDI: [After hearing about the reserve-clause decision], I was like a lot of players. On one hand, we were scared to death because we had no idea what would happen. We didn't know if baseball would blackball anyone else who became a free agent, you know actually get together and say, "No one signs these guys." It was scary because we hadn't been through it before. No one knew what to expect. The good thing about it, though, was that we had so many guys on [the Oakland A's] who were eligible for free agency, we supported each other. You know, misery loves company, right?

BOBBY GRICH: I made $84,000 in 1975 and really enjoyed being part of the Orioles organization. My agent, Jerry Kapstein, negotiated with [Orioles general manager] Frank Cashen to keep me in Baltimore and Frank offered a five-year deal at, I believe, $125,000 a year. I was impressed with that. I knew [Orioles principal owner] Jerry Hoffberger didn't have the money of the big-market clubs and he and Frank were making an honest, concerted effort to keep me. I felt complimented, and might have signed. But Jerry [Kapstein] did have an idea what that A's deal meant and he said, "This is a good offer, but I think the market will be somewhere else if you become a free agent." And by somewhere else he meant there'd be more money. So we turned down the offer.

[New York Yankees owner George Steinbrenner] made an excellent offer, really impressed us with his generosity. I thanked him and said we needed time to think about it. The market for me, I thought, hadn't really gelled yet. The only other offer I had at that point was from the Angels. I kept hoping to hear that four or five other teams were interested. But really it was just California and Baltimore. I was surprised, especially that Boston didn't come after me.

I have to admit I liked hitting in Fenway and with that lineup, Yaz, Rice, Lynn, Dwight Evans, I would have hit somewhere near the top, I guess, first or second. That would have been fun. But they never called us, which mystified me. And, really, no one else made a serious offer. I left Baltimore the first week in November. My plan was to take a slow drive cross-country back to California. Just before I left, I heard that Joe Rudi had signed a five-year contract for over $2 million. He had been the

Angels' top priority, and they went right after him. Now, re-member, I expected Jerry would go back to the Angels with the Yankees offer and Harry [Dalton, California Angels General Manager] would raise his offer. So I'm already thinking when I hear the news that this is awesome. Joe Rudi is my teammate. He was the best left fielder in baseball, clutch hitter, hit to all fields, could bat anywhere from second to fifth in the lineup.

JOE RUDI: Going into 1976, I think I was making $85,000, and Finley cut all of us 20 percent when we didn't sign for the '76 season. Jerry and I did negotiate with Charlie. We made offers to him. Jerry sent Finley a contract offer, three years at something like $400,000, which turned out to be ridiculous when we look backward. I'm happy to say, Finley didn't even answer us. Jerry did that for each player he represented on the A's, but Finley wouldn't respond to any of the offers. After so many days, Jerry withdrew those offers.

Harry Dalton had always liked me. It was sort of funny in a way, because we didn't know what to expect, how it would all happen. Jerry Kapstein was just amazing, the way he handled it all. His foresight was invaluable and he knew how to keep our brains together. He never gave us any numbers. He kept assuring us that everything would work out, that no one would blackball us, and that we should keep playing hard and keep our mouth shut. He was very secretive during that time.

That was one thing about Jerry that I remember as much as anything, how cautious he was. A lot of times he would call me from a phone and give me a phone number to call him back. But he didn't want me to call from my home. I had to go to a pay phone downtown and call him. And then he'd give me the number for another pay phone to call and when I got him there, we could talk. As we got into those days and the offers came in, he wouldn't even tell us who was trying to sign us.

We had to take the red-eye express out of San Francisco to Boston and he would pick us up and drive to his office in Providence, Rhode Island, where he was from. He was still negotiating with several teams, and we didn't know who we would sign with or for how much until we sat at the table and he showed us the offers. California had the top bid, which was great because it meant I could stay in California, and that was another good park for me.

BOBBY GRICH: I get to Las Vegas and pull into a hotel and hear on a sports broadcast that the Angels had just signed Don Baylor [after signing Rudi]. I'm thinking, Wow, we're going to have a hell of a team. I called Jerry, and he was busy, but he got back to me in an hour. I said, "Those signings are awesome. I'm really excited. Let's strike a deal with California."

Jerry said, "I've got some bad news. I spoke to Harry about you and he told me Gene Autry told him there was no more money to sign anyone." Man, that was like a knife right through my heart. "You're kidding," I said—but he wasn't. "Well, I guess I'm going to New York." I was so convinced that I'd be a Yankee, I went and got a map of New York. I'm from Long Beach, California, and I saw this town not far from New York City called Long Beach, New York. I wanted to be near a beach so I figured I'd check the place out, see if I could live there. That's how resigned I was to playing for the Yankees.

Woke up the next morning, and took off. All the time I'm driving from Las Vegas to L.A., to be honest, I still couldn't believe the Angels wouldn't go for the three free agents they were entitled to. [A team was originally limited to two free-agent signees unless it had lost more than two players to free agency; then a team could sign as many free agents as it had lost. The Angels had lost three.] So I made a decision. I stopped in a gas station and called Jerry from a pay phone, literally in the middle of the desert. "Jerry, I want you to call Mr. Dalton right now and tell them I'll take their first offer of $1.5 million. They don't have to raise it at all. Let him know that the Yankees offered us $2.2 million and I'm turning down at least $700,000 to sign with them." He said, "Well, I'll tell him, but don't expect anything." I drive home to L.A. and two hours later Jerry calls me and says, "Mr. Dalton told Gene Autry what you said and Mr. Autry said, 'Well, if the kid wants to play for us that badly, you go on and sign him.'" And that's how I became an Angel.

MILLER'S LEGACY

Consider how far the players had come since 1965, when they had no agents, no mobility, and no leverage, to the fall of '76, when Bobby Grich, Joe Rudi, Don Baylor, Wayne Garland, Reggie Jackson, and others represented the first class of free agents. Consider also the strength and solidarity of baseball's players' union, which staged a lengthy mid-season strike in 1981 over the issue of free-agent compensation. (That strike resulted in a controversial split-season format and an extra round of play-offs—with the winners of each half-season meeting in a best-of-five series—and made for some oddities, such as the Cincinnati Reds and St. Louis Cardinals finishing with the two best overall records in the National League but missing the postseason.)

The players' union became powerful enough to charge the owners with collusion to hold down free-agent salaries in the mid-1980s (winning $280 million in damages) and to endure a 232-day strike from August 1994 until April '95—a work stoppage that wiped out the entire '94 postseason—in order to prevent the implementation of a salary cap.

Marvin Miller, the man who was greatly responsible for all that, stepped down as executive director of the players' union in 1982. While Miller has the eternal gratitude of all knowledgeable players past and present, does he deserve more? Has he earned recognition from baseball's Hall of Fame?

KEN SINGLETON: Oh, very much so. Damn right. Who changed the game more than Marvin Miller? But it may be harder for him to get in than some of those steroids guys, because none of the owners want him in. Everybody talked about how free agency would be bad for the game. But look at what happened: Owners had to come up with different revenue streams, and now you have new parks, more games on TV, the

Web sites, and everything else. It has been great for the game. It was forced on them and it worked out very well.

BUD SELIG: I have said he does. I know that surprised a lot of people. The criteria one uses for the Hall of Fame are, "What kind of impact did he make on baseball?" I don't think there's any doubt about it.

JOE TORRE: Very much so. He was a long shot, you know. In every photo of him, he looked like a B-movie actor and he was a baseball outsider. But he knew what had to be done and he had a way of talking to you. He was nothing like you expected him to be. A very smart man.

JIM KAAT: He should be in, with the others from the executives category. You look at people who have had a major influence on the game. You know, there are a couple of things, looking back in baseball history, that if they could have renamed them, would have made life a lot easier for voters. One is the Most Valuable Player Award and the other is the Hall of Fame. Because if it was a Hall of Achievement, it would be looked at differently.

But even as a Hall of Famer, Marvin is as famous a figure as anyone from the executive branch and can match anyone in what they've done and how they've influenced baseball. You look at Nolan Ryan and his record. It might not be that much more impressive than many other pitchers, but he's famous with all those no-hitters and strikeouts and creating all that attention, so he belongs in a Hall of Fame. And so does Marvin.

BOB COSTAS: With the possible exception of Branch Rickey, Marvin Miller is the most significant executive in baseball history. He's more significant than any commissioner. It's a crime and a joke that he's not in the Hall of Fame. He did brilliant and principled work for a long time. And then he, like his protégés, Don Fehr and Gene Orza, eventually became so rigidly ideological, that they couldn't make fair and commonsense concessions when circumstances dramatically changed. So I think that while Marvin was dead right about many, many things for a long time, he is dead wrong about a lot of things today whenever he speaks up.

And Fehr and Orza certainly have sacrificed the intellectual and principled high ground that they once commanded. Just because the players have historically been right and the owners have historically been wrong doesn't mean that it has to be that way forever, and that anything said on behalf of ownership has no merit. The players are not perpetually on the side of the angels. Just witness the whole steroid controversy. The players' union could not have been more wrong about that [to resist testing]. Not just wrong about what was good for the game, but wrong about what was good for the non-cheating portion of their membership. We have to assume that they were always the majority.

And just because free agency might have helped the game in the '70s, and the Players Association's positions were generally correct, doesn't mean that they still make sense once these enormous disparities in revenue streams began in the '90s and beyond and that [the union] should reject and resist commonsense reforms, not designed, as their propaganda would have it, to roll back the clock and take away essential rights from players, but designed to try to tweak a dysfunctional system. It just doesn't make sense.

Whether it's a salary cap or revenue sharing or a system of revenue sharing where there are salary minimums, there are various mechanisms that could be designed to make a league function closer to the way a league should, while still essentially protecting the freedom and earning power of the players. That was always do-able, and [the union was] so intractable.

JIM KAAT: There isn't any other sports union, maybe not any other union of any kind in history, that has had the solidarity that we had from day one, and that was all his work. I think of the strike of 1981, near the end of my career. I had warned [commissioner] Bowie Kuhn it was going to happen and advised him, under his so-called "best interests of baseball" authority, to step up and do something about it with the owners because there was no way the players were going to crack.

I told him, "I'll give you an example. I don't know how much money it's going to cost me in the end"—I was making $150,000—"and I will never get any of it back, because I won't play much longer. But I'm voting for it because that is how we have achieved what we've achieved. It's not about any one individual player, and we all know that. We're going to do it." I'm not sure he or the owners believed that, but they found out when we finally did strike with a third of the season gone. And once their strike insurance ran out, they came back to the table and made the concessions to get us back on the field. Marvin and the union had won again, because we never forgot the power of solidarity. He taught us that.

THE DESIGNATED HITTER

Featuring

RON BLOMBERG: The first DH in 1973 while playing for the Yankees, the left-handed swinger's eight-year career was cut short by shoulder and knee injuries. His autobiography, *Designated Hebrew,* was published in 2006, and he is currently the manager of the Bet Shemesh Blue Sox of the Israel Baseball League.

THOMAS BOSWELL: His baseball writing career began with the *Washington Post* in 1975, and he has gone on to author such books as *How Life Imitates the World Series* and *Why Time Begins on Opening Day.*

RICO CARTY: A perennial .300 hitter before injuries nearly ended his career in the early '70s, the Dominican-born slugger became the living embodiment of the second life that the DH could offer a player—especially in 1978, when he hit 31 home runs as a DH for the Toronto Blue Jays and Oakland A's.

BOB COSTAS: Popular broadcaster and longtime opponent of the designated hitter rule.

TOMMY DAVIS: Eighteen-year major leaguer who excelled as the Orioles' first DH under manager Earl Weaver.

DENNIS ECKERSLEY: Hall of Fame pitcher whose career began early in the DH era and who spent time in both leagues.

OSCAR GAMBLE: One of the most dangerous platoon hitters of his era, he served as DH with the Indians, White Sox, Rangers, and Yankees.

BILL GILES: Phillies executive who voted on the DH rule and later became owner of the club. His autobiography, *Pouring Six Beers at a Time and Other Stories from a Lifetime in Baseball,* was published in 2007.

WHITEY HERZOG: Longtime manager who won 1,281 games, mostly at the helm of the Kansas City Royals and St. Louis Cardinals. He won division titles in both leagues and the 1982 World Series with the Cardinals.

RALPH HOUK: Manager who won 1,619 games in 20 seasons. As skipper of the '73 Yankees, he was the first manager to ever send a designated hitter to the plate. He later managed the Boston Red Sox and Detroit Tigers.

JIM KAAT: Veteran starting pitcher and 283-game winner who was entering his 15th big-league season when the DH rule was introduced.

HARMON KILLEBREW: One of the most prolific home-run hitters in baseball history who served as designated hitter with the Twins and Royals in the last three years of his career.

EDGAR MARTINEZ: Considered by many to be the best designated hitter of them all. His career spanned from 1987 to 2004 with the Seattle Mariners, and he fashioned a .312 batting average in 18 big-league seasons.

GEORGE "DOC" MEDICH: A DH-era pitcher who was with the Yankees from 1972 to '75 and went on to pitch for six other teams in both leagues.

TONY OLIVA: Once the DH came into effect, Oliva—an eight-time All-Star outfielder with the Minnesota Twins who was hampered by knee injuries in the final years of his career—never played in the field again.

FRANK ROBINSON: Hall of Famer who got the majority of DH time with the California Angels in '73 and had the best season of the first crop of designated hitters.

BUD SELIG: Former Milwaukee Brewers owner (he purchased the team in 1970) and current commissioner of baseball.

LUIS TIANT: The right-hander won 229 games in a 19-year career with six big-league teams. Was with the Boston Red Sox in '73 and spent all but one season in the American League.

JOE TORRE: One of the 10 winningest managers ever, at the helm of the Mets, Braves, Cardinals, and Yankees, his career has been split fairly equally between having and not having the DH at his disposal.

P ITCHERS HAVE ALWAYS been a breed apart. Once baseball got organized at the professional level, it didn't take long before the necessities of their role began to take a toll on the quality of their hitting. By 1880, just the fifth year of the National League, the men for whom pitching was a primary responsibility posted a combined OPS of .516 while everyone else in the league was at .595. In the coming decades pitchers' hitting got worse and worse compared to the rest of the league, so much so that, soon after the turn of the next century, the concept of a permanent pinch hitter for the pitcher was already in existence.

Some sources suggest that it was Connie Mack, the manager of the Philadelphia Athletics, who first proposed the idea around 1906. It didn't catch on then, but from that point on it became a concept that could be discussed at league meetings when it seemed like a radical change was in order. By some accounts both leagues came very close to implementing it 45 years before the American League ultimately did. Retired Hall of Fame manager Joe McCarthy told the *Sporting News* in 1970 that he distinctly remembered National League President John Heydler advocating the DH years before. Not one to shy away from change, the then-82-year-old McCarthy said, "I was intrigued with the idea then and I think it still has possibilities."

So did the American League. In spring training of 1969 the league experimented with the DH in selected games, and the International League adopted the rule for full-time use during the regular season. (DHs were still referred to as "designated pinch hitters" then.) Two things were happening that were driving the junior circuit in this direction: The first was the dominance of pitchers throughout the decade, culminating in the time-machine trip back to the Deadball Era that was the 1968 season. That year Carl Yastrzemski, the American League batting champ, hit only .301, and in the NL Bob Gibson had 13 shutouts and one of the lowest ERAs in history: 1.12. (The following year, under new commissioner Bowie Kuhn, the mound was lowered from 15 inches to 10 in order to decrease the pitchers' advantage.) The American League was also being outdrawn by the National by no small amount. From 1968 to '72 nearly 24 million more fans attended National League games than American. To put it in a different context, for every fan visiting an American League park, there were one and a half going to see a National League game. In the 1972 season overall attendance dropped by two million fans, owing in part to lost games from the players' strike as well as the subsequent ill will from that work stoppage. People were no longer talking about baseball as the national pastime. Football had usurped the grand old game's position of prominence, and baseball owners were casting their eyes about for solutions.

THE IDEA GAINS MOMENTUM

Had Oakland A's owner Charles O. Finley conceived of the DH idea himself, instead of merely being one of its loudest proponents, there is a chance it never would have come into being. Finley, who died in 1996, was not a favorite among his fellow owners, to the extent that even his good ideas were often ignored simply because of their source. If he had his heart's desire, Finley would have gone to a complete platoon system with a separate offense and defense and special team players for pinch-running duties. He wanted to have designated hitters for any position, not just for the pitcher. Famously, Finley used sprinter Herb Washington solely as a pinch runner one season. And for five consecutive games in mid-September of 1972 the A's started Dal Maxvill at second base without his ever getting a chance to hit. He batted eighth in the order, playing a few innings of defense before his first turn to bat came up. Each time it did he was pinch-hit for by Don Mincher.

It was around this time that Howard Cosell made a guest appearance on NBC's Monday Night Baseball, *suggesting the very thing that Finley sought: the elimination of two-way players in baseball. Blasphemy though it was, it was an indication of the general mood that surrounded the game at that time—change of some sort was required.*

BUD SELIG: I'll tell you, and I'll be very blunt with you. I was in the American League. It was December of 1972. We met at the Plaza Hotel. There had been a lot of conversations. I was never before or after in favor of anything that Charley Finley wanted. If Charley was still alive he'd agree with that, even though we had a pleasant enough personal relationship. But the American League was struggling mightily for offense and a lot of people were pushing [the DH]. My mentor in baseball at that time was John Finch, who owned the Detroit Tigers. We always flew together to meetings and we talked about it on the way in. We were both "purists," call it whatever you want, but it seemed like this one time that we ought to try this. And so we did. But when I voted for it, I must say it's the only time I ever agreed with Charley.

WHITEY HERZOG: In 1973 the NL was the most competitive league. They expanded. They were drawing more fans.

BOB COSTAS: It was a gimmick. But it was a gimmick that at one time at least had a coherent rationale. In the early 1970s, when [the DH] came to the American League, baseball was just coming off a period where offense was as depressed as it had ever been in the modern era. The whole American League hit .237 in 1968, and about a fifth of all games in the major leagues—*a fifth*—were shutouts. Carl Yastrzemski led the American League in batting at .301, and three years before Tony Conigliaro led the American League with 32 homers. There was definitely a perceived need to juice offense. Plus, at that time the American League lagged behind the National League. The Yankee dynasty at that point was in ruins, so the Yankees couldn't carry the American League anymore. And the American League was still paying the price for being relatively slow compared to the National League in signing black and Hispanic players. So they had the less exciting league; what they had to sell was just less than what the National League had to sell. It made sense that they would try this thing and try to sell it as new and exciting. And in some respects it was.

HARMON KILLEBREW: Obviously the American League felt it had to do something. It was falling behind the National League in popularity and [AL owners] wanted to create some excitement in the game.

RON BLOMBERG: Baseball was trying a lot of things back then. You remember Charley Finley with his orange baseballs, and he tried to promote the designated runner with Herb Washington, but that all faded kind of quickly. The DH is still here.

DOC MEDICH: They did it to increase offense, which is always more interesting to watch than good pitching, but I had been exposed to it before in the Eastern League. In 1970 there was a DH in the Eastern League . . . and I liked it, I really liked it. It was the kind of thing that kept starting pitchers in the game, and it helped you keep your focus on pitching, so considering all of that, I thought it was a positive.

THOMAS BOSWELL: The late '60s and early '70s were a time of action in America. The country was really amped up and needed tons of stimulation. As Bill Veeck said, it was really a time for violent sports, not reflective sports, to catch the public's attention. It was a wonderful time for the NFL. Baseball at that point, in the late '60s, just didn't have enough offense and it was really getting boring. And talk about a bad time to be boring: 1968—when everybody's hair is really on fire over one tragedy or political event or controversy after another and here's baseball with one 2–1, 1–0 game after another. The need to add the DH seemed screamingly obvious at the time, unlike the recent changes with interleague play and the addition of the wild card that a lot of sensible people—like me—resisted, only to find out we were wrong.

ANTI-DH SENTIMENT

Not surprisingly, there was an undercurrent among traditionalist players and fans who didn't like the new rule. After all, it was a violation of the game as it had always been played. Others had a negative reaction at first but came around.

JIM KAAT: I wasn't in favor of it and never have been. Selfishly speaking, those of us who were starters back then when it came on the scene, we benefited because we got a chance to stay in games a lot longer and pick up four or five more wins a year than we may have gotten without the rule, but I was disappointed that it gave us two different leagues playing by two different sets of rules. That never made sense to me.

WHITEY HERZOG: No part of the DH is good! The original idea was to prolong the careers of fading stars like Harmon Killebrew. Now the DH is a bad defensive player, like the guy in Boston [David Ortiz]. I think it originally added .8 runs per game in the AL. And for that it takes the strategy out of the game. It changed the game too much.

RALPH HOUK: Honestly, I didn't like it, wanted no part of it. I wasn't sure it would be good for our club, whether it would put us at a disadvantage to teams that had more offense. Going into the season I really didn't know who the DH would be, or if we would go with one guy or move hitters in and out of that spot. But then, as I began to get into it, I thought this was very good for the game. Back when it was first proposed, we needed something. Attendance wasn't anything like you see today, not just in New York, but all over the American League, and fans like offense. Plus I thought it would keep the older stars, some of the biggest names in the league, in the game, and you had players like Orlando Cepeda and Frank Robinson prolonging their careers.

A CAREER EXTENDER

This idea Houk mentions was very important to proponents of the new rule: that the DH was potentially a great way to extend the careers of some of the game's biggest stars. Others, notably some pitchers, had their own selfish—and completely understandable—reasons to embrace the new rule.

BOB COSTAS: Some people may have felt, with justification, that whatever you lost with the DH was worth it for what you gained, not only in overall offense, but because you could take some exciting players who were near the ends of their careers and extend those careers.

RON BLOMBERG: I was 23 years old, and if you go back to the newspapers back then, I think most people thought of it as something that was for older players, you know like Tommy Davis, Orlando Cepeda, Al Kaline, or Tony Oliva, great hitters who had slowed down some in the field but could still help you with the bat.

TONY OLIVA: I first heard about the DH in '72, because I got hurt in '71. In '72, I didn't play. I missed the whole year. At the end of '72–73 [Twins owner] Calvin Griffith said, "I changed the rule, just for you. That way you'll have a chance to play."

RALPH HOUK: It's too bad it came five years too late or I could have used Mickey Mantle in that spot. Mickey would have been a perfect DH, and if that's all he had to do he might have reached 600 homers or more [his career ended at 536 when he was 36].

TONY OLIVA: In those days the superstars in the American League—we had Mickey Mantle, Harmon Killebrew—they were older, so [the DH] was good for the American League. I'm glad they kept it up, because it was a success for baseball. The people like to see hitting.

DENNIS ECKERSLEY: I like to see guys that can hit in their older days.

FRANK ROBINSON: I felt good about it because of the reason why they were putting it in. That was to kind of extend an outstanding veteran's playing career. He probably couldn't field as well—or a guy who probably wasn't as good a defensive player. He could still help the ball club with his bat. That type of thing. It was more for veteran players. I thought it was a good idea.

RICO CARTY: I wasn't prepared to be a DH. But as the days went by I realized that it would keep me in the game a couple of years longer. In 1973 I took over as DH and played the outfield part-time, and I went from '73 to '80. So that means that the DH gives me seven years more maybe—I'd say about five more of my playing years.

RON BLOMBERG: Players joked about it when it passed. They said it sounded like a glorified pinch hitter. I thought it would be good for baseball, keeping those big names in the game and putting in more offense. And it turned out to be true.

HARMON KILLEBREW: When it was first announced I was still a first baseman, and with Tony Oliva coming back but his knees still bothering him so he really couldn't take the field, he was set to DH for us. So it really didn't affect me at first. I know they thought it would be a good way to keep older hitters who couldn't take the field anymore. But I don't think it did to any great extent. Tony Oliva was an exception.

TONY OLIVA: I didn't have any idea how the people would react to it. The only thing I knew for sure was that rule was great for the American League. In those days the National League didn't want to make any change. [The AL] gave the opportunity to players like me. A lot of the guys who were the DH were old guys. I was only 30, but I was hurt and wasn't able to play in the outfield. But I was able to hit.

LUIS TIANT: The DH gives a lot of chances to a lot of players; maybe they can't run very good, they might not be able to play another position, but now they get to hit. And they can play maybe five or 10 more years. That's a good thing for a lot of hitters. And as a pitcher, maybe it's good for you. If your team has a good DH and the guy hits a long ball, he wins a game for you, hey, that's great.

DENNIS ECKERSLEY: I loved it. I didn't want to hit anyway.

DOC MEDICH: For starting pitchers, we played once every five days, and back then the idea was to stay on the field for as long as you possibly can, a little different than the attitude today, so, heck, we wanted to stay out there for the whole game no matter what. We liked the DH.

TOMMY DAVIS: The idea sure sounded good to me, but before I could worry about that I had to make the team. I finished the 1972 season with the Orioles and I hit okay with them, but nothing great because I didn't play that much. In 1973 Baltimore wanted me to come to spring training on a minor-league contract, but I wanted to come with the big club and prove I could make the team. Fortunately they let me, and I showed them I could still hit, and then [manager] Earl [Weaver] started using me as the DH, which made sense. I had played first and third base in the majors and put in most of my time in the outfield, mostly left. But I was never more than average defensively, and after I injured my ankle defense was not my strength. The idea of being able to hit and not play defense at all, that was heaven to me.

OSCAR GAMBLE: I understood the ramifications of the DH right away. I thought it would be a good thing for me.

I'd been in the majors for four years and I was scrapping for playing time, but it was hard to get. In my first year [1969], with the Cubs, the manager was Leo Durocher, and he liked to play veterans. During the off-season they traded me for Johnny Callison, and that was a compliment because he was an excellent player and I was still a prospect. I hit well with the Phillies that first year, but I didn't show much power. Then they brought up Roger Freed [in 1971] and they told me we would be in kind of a platoon and I would play against the right-handers that Roger couldn't hit. Great, except those right-handers he couldn't hit were named Bob Gibson, Tom Seaver, Ferguson Jenkins, Don Sutton—all Hall of Famers. I didn't do much that year or the next, which is why they traded me to the Indians.

DOC MEDICH: Like most pitchers I used to be a pretty good hitter, but as you move up in class your hitting skills don't keep pace with your pitching. We never got an opportunity to practice, so pitchers in general are overmatched by the time they get into the higher levels of professional ball. In the lower levels in many cases pitchers are some of the best athletes on teams and could always hit, but advancement outstrips that ability, so I was not at all displeased with the DH rule.

THOMAS BOSWELL: The DH always made people scream. There were people who said we need more offense and there were people who said the DH was a bastardization of the game. They would say that everything about baseball should be "nines." Nine players, nine innings, and, over the last century, an average of nine runs scored between the two teams in a game. That's when the game is in the best balance. It should not be a game with 10 players on a side with 10 runs a game or eight runs a game. But, when you get down to eight runs a game, in some cases, high sevens—maybe you have to add that 10th player to bring the game back into balance.

DENNIS ECKERSLEY: As a fan, I don't like 1–0 games; that's like soccer. I guess it comes down to being a traditionalist. But if they're going to put it through on both sides, that's fine too. Personally I'd rather not see a pitcher hit. You could talk about tradition all you want. And that's just my own personal feeling. I don't want to see the pitcher bunt. To me, it wastes three innings. It's like, "When's the pitcher coming up? He coming up this inning? I'll go somewhere else. I project the game's going to be brutal the next inning." Because if the pitcher gets a hit, how do you feel? "Oh my God, the pitcher got a hit."

LUIS TIANT: I liked to hit. I was a pretty good hitter. I was a good fastball hitter, but a breaking ball? Forget it. Fastball I was pretty good. I think most of the pitchers like to hit. Some guys don't like it because they can't hit nothing. You can throw 2 mph and they can't hit.

THE DESIGNATED HITTER'S DEBUT

Say this about the advent of the DH, it got people talking. Its merits and demerits made for a lively hot stove league in the 1972–73 off-season. Once it was passed, its debut was very much anticipated. On April 5, 1973, the NL's Reds hosted the then-traditional season opener, but it was the Red Sox's opener the next day that got everyone's attention. Boston and the visiting Yankees would be the first clubs to employ DHs. In this role, Ralph Houk had Ron Blomberg, a part-time first baseman and occasional outfielder who was nursing a hamstring injury, in the number-six spot and Boston manager Eddie Kasko had Orlando Cepeda batting fifth. Cepeda was more in the mold of what people thought DHs were going to be: a veteran player (he was 35) in the last leg of his career. Blomberg, however, was just 23. Another such polarity occurred in the A's-Twins game played later that same day. Minnesota used veteran Tony Oliva as its first DH, while Oakland went with rookie speedster Billy North and batted him leadoff.

It could have fallen to either Cepeda or Blomberg to be the first man to bat as a designated hitter, but a three-run first at the expense of Boston starter Luis Tiant meant that it was the Yankee who became the Neil Armstrong of this particular endeavor. (Though one observer that day remembers a funny twist to that piece of history, at least as it is recognized by the Baseball Hall of Fame.)

Tiant and the Red Sox would win the war that day, 15–5, but Blomberg won the first battle of the DHs, driving in a run with a walk in his first at bat and singling in his second. Cepeda, meanwhile, was hitless in six at bats. In spite of playing only about half the time, Blomberg was one of the Yankees' three most productive players in 1973, notching career highs in batting average (.329) and RBIs (57). Cepeda went on to have a solid season as well (.289, 20 homers, 86 RBIs) and was one of the mainstays of the Boston offense.

RON BLOMBERG: They already had me as a platoon player, so I rarely got to play against left-handers, and the Yankees back then faced a lot of left-handers. But what was I going to do, tell them to play me or trade me? Hold out? Where was I going to go, what was I going to do? [Yankees general manager] Gabe Paul would have laughed at me. So that limited how many games I had to learn the [first-base] position. So as far as I was concerned I was still learning first base, but I believed I could play the position once I had experience, and I played it through most of spring training in '73. It's simple: In order to be a good fielder, you have to play in game situations until the position becomes second nature for you. I didn't get much chance to do that. In 1973 I played first base early on but I made some mistakes like anyone learning a position would, and next thing I know, they brought in Mike Hegan to play first and he was one of the best defensive first basemen in the game. So I'm DH-ing, and you can't improve your defense doing that. A year later, Chris Chambliss came over in a trade, and I said to someone, "I could just give my glove to some charity."

RALPH HOUK: I was thinking of [Blomberg as a DH] but I hadn't decided, and I think it's true that his injury made up my mind. Honestly, I don't know who I would have used. If you look at my best hitters, Bobby Murcer, Roy White, and Graig Nettles, they were all excellent defensive players. Thurman Munson was another great hitter, but he was our catcher and he was too valuable behind the plate, although you could

DH him once in a while to give him a rest and keep his bat in the lineup.

RON BLOMBERG: I had hurt myself down in Fort Lauderdale, pulled a hamstring during spring training. After we broke camp and were coming up to Boston, Ralph Houk came up to me and said, "I'd really like to get you four or five ABs against Luis Tiant in that opener. Can you hit?" And I said, "Of course, I can hit." When we got up to Boston, I saw the Opening Day lineups in the paper, the *Boston Globe* or the *Boston Herald,* and there was my name next to DH. I go to the ballpark, I take some swings and it's like 25 degrees out and I'm thinking, You know, maybe this *is* a great position for me. After the AB I can go back in the clubhouse, stay warm, and grab a snack. I forgot that the clubhouse guy in Boston had the worst food in the American League. Just awful.

It was hard to stay loose. Bobby Murcer had two things I remember him for, besides being a great player. His rocking chair in the clubhouse and his hot-water bottle. On cold days he took that bottle everywhere with him. I didn't have that. Now I'm doing something I've not done my whole life, DH-ing, and all of a sudden you have to make this adjustment. I was very muscular and it took a long while for me to stretch, especially in cold weather. The runway from the dugout to the clubhouse in Boston was tiny, so there wasn't much room to run. I went to the clubhouse and listened to the game to follow it and I ran in there. Stretched a lot, too.

LUIS TIANT: It was like any game: You just go and do what you have to do. I didn't think about it. I just wanted to get him out and he was lucky enough to walk. But, it wasn't any different for me that he was the DH. We didn't have any meeting about it. I don't remember sitting down and talking about it with the manager at all.

RON BLOMBERG: I walked my first time up, and when we made the third out of the inning, I stood on first, waiting for someone to throw me my glove. [Coach] Ellie Howard finally came over and said, "Come back to the dugout, you can't stay out here." I didn't know what to do with myself. He said, "Just sit next to me and watch the game."

RALPH HOUK: You wanted someone who could hit well in that spot and Ronnie was the best choice from that aspect since he wasn't a polished first baseman.

RON BLOMBERG: People who wrote that I couldn't play first base forgot that I wasn't a first baseman, really. I beg to differ when they say I couldn't field. I came up to the Yankees as an outfielder, right field that first season [1971], when I came up toward the end of the year. That's where I was most comfortable. You know the Yankees didn't sign me number one in the draft just because I could hit. I ran well. I was a 9.6 in high school, I could get down to first in 3.7 and I could throw well until I hurt my shoulder. I didn't come up with a reputation as a bad fielder. But we were set in the outfield. Bobby Murcer was in center and he was one of the best players in baseball; he had an MVP-like season that first year I was up. Roy White was a fixture in left and he could do everything but throw. You had to see Roy play every day to appreciate just how good he was. Roy didn't have as much power as Jim Rice, but he could hit the ball a long way and would have hit more home runs playing his home games in a different park. He was always on base and he was one of the best defensive left fielders in the game. People don't realize that because he had an average or below-average throwing arm, but he covered as much ground as anyone and almost never made an error or mental mistake. I learned a lot watching him play. Anyway, we had Bobby and Roy and Felipe Alou, plus the club had picked up Johnny Callison, another terrific outfielder, during the off-season. But the biggest trade we made was with Boston. Danny Cater for Sparky Lyle. With Cater gone, the club needed a first baseman, and since I couldn't throw as well with my hurt shoulder, I was it.

RALPH HOUK: Well, you know Ronnie was Ronnie. I remember times with men on base, a spot where you would look to him to drive them in, and he'd unexpectedly bunt, so he had his own way of doing things. Whether he would have developed into a better first baseman, I'm not sure. But he fit in as a DH right away. He didn't play against left-handers, though, and we brought in Jim Ray Hart to platoon with him and that move worked out very well for us. Hart was a veteran with power who could hit left-handers, and he geared himself to being a DH right away. It really is a tough position from the mental standpoint.

RON BLOMBERG: Facing Tiant made it easier, believe it or not. If you couldn't concentrate with Luis on the mound, you might as well just crack the bat in two and leave it at the plate. You were dead. I didn't face him when he was younger; players told me he could throw 96, 98 miles an hour back then, with control. When he was with the Red Sox he was probably throwing 92, maybe 93. But he was a smart pitcher. He had those herky-jerky motions, sometimes he'd throw his arm up high, and kick his leg up over his head, sometimes the leg would go out to the side. Sometimes it was as if his arms, shoulders, and legs went in all different directions at once. If you paid attention to that, he had you. So with him on the mound, I focused on his release point. Forget the antics. Luis was a disciplined pitcher. He had one release point and I zoned in on that each time up. And then I looked for something in my zone, middle and in, until he had two strikes on me. Then you go with what the pitcher gives you. That's the time you can tell a good hitter: Can he adjust and hit the ball the other way with two strikes on him?

LUIS TIANT: I just wanted to get him out and he got away from me [Blomberg walked] and there's nothing I could do. I tip my hat to him, and good for him. If he's in the Hall of Fame for that, good for him.

RON BLOMBERG: I was not only the first DH, I was the first DH to get on base, the first to drive in a run, and the first to get a base hit. A few years back, Dick Schaap came up to me and said, "Bloomie, you have a record no one in baseball can ever break, being the first designated hitter." And you know, he's right. Think of it. You add up my career at bats and it comes to maybe three seasons' worth, but here it is 30 years later and people still know my name. They ask for autographs, I give speeches. And now I'm one of the first managers in the new Israeli baseball league. Why? Because I'm an outgoing guy and I was the first to do something that made baseball history.

DOC MEDICH: I read a blurb a couple weeks ago by Blomberg about how he got a base hit with this particular bat and it went to Cooperstown, but that's not what I remember. This was my first game after having made the team, so I remember what was going on. We were in Boston, two guys are standing in the runway behind the bench, two little guys from the Hall of Fame. Our manager was Ralph Houk and Ralph didn't like anyone in the dugout who wasn't part of the team. He didn't like these guys being around, and I could tell he was annoyed. So Blomberg comes up in the bottom of the first, and Luis Tiant is pitching, and these guys from the Hall of Fame are waiting to get the bat. Tiant pitches to Bloomie and Bloomie's bat just explodes into a million pieces, the kind of fracture that no doctor could put back together. These guys from the Hall of Fame have this look on their faces that's one of total dejection, like, What are we going to do now? We can't go back to the Hall empty-handed. Ralph turns around and grabs one of Blomberg's bats off the rack and says, "Now here's the bat, get the fuck out of here!" I can't forget that, I mean that was so funny, and I knew it was serious, but I was trying not to laugh, and later I saw a twinkle in Ralph's eye. So anyway that's what I remember. I talked to [Yankee pitchers] Mel [Stottlemyre] and Fritz [Peterson] about that and they don't remember it at all, but I do.

THE DESIGNATED LIFESTYLE

Players had varied reactions to the role of DH in those first few seasons.

FRANK ROBINSON: I told [the Angels] I could still play in the field. Not in 162 games, but I don't want to become an everyday DH.

OSCAR GAMBLE: With the DH, I thought I had an advantage if I made the team. There weren't many teams that had five good-hitting infielders but there were plenty of clubs that had four outfielders who could hit. One year with Cleveland we had five: George Hendrick, Charlie Spikes, John Lowenstein, Rico Carty, Rick Manning, and me. The designated hitter would give us all a chance to stay fresh but stay in the lineup.

RICO CARTY: I love the DH, because of my arm. I hurt my shoulder in 1967. I dislocated it seven times in 1969, so I was always in pain. But I have a strong mind. With all of those pains I still have—well you could look at the numbers [a career .299 average and 204 home runs]. When things happen you have to ask the mighty God to help you get over it and keep on going, and don't say, "Why? Why me?" If it's not you it's going to be someone else. That's just part of your life and those things are going to happen throughout your career and your life. It's already written down.

HARMON KILLEBREW: If you lost the skills to play the field, you probably also lost the skills that made you a good hitter. Now, when I was traded to the Kansas City Royals I had to think about it a lot, because the plan was to DH me. But my knees were still hurting and that turf in Kansas City didn't help them. Soon I was platooning with Tony Solaita, with me playing against left-handers.

TOMMY DAVIS: My favorite DH memory was the time I'm on the phone in the trainer's room talking to my first wife. The [Orioles] trainer came up and tapped me from behind. I said, "What do you want?" He said, "Tommy, you're up." "I'm *what*?" "You're due up right now and everybody's looking for you. They're waiting on you out there." I had to run all the way through the tunnel and as I get to the dugout, [manager] Earl [Weaver] is standing there, just looking at me with those eyes of his. He's burning. I don't even want to look at him. I grab my bat and run up to the plate. Man on second and I can feel Earl staring at me. Good thing I got a base hit, knocked in the run. When the inning's over, I get back to the dugout, and Earl's turning away, trying not to look at me. What could he say? I drove in the run. That was funny. Then I went back to the trainer's room. The phone's still open and I just picked it up and continued the conversation.

My other memorable game was a game I didn't play, if you could believe it. I had just DH'd in two games with the Orioles and went six-for-nine. I come into the clubhouse and look at the line-up. I'm not in it. So I walk into Earl's office and, like it's a joke, say to Earl, "Hey, baby, six-for-nine and he's not even in the lineup." Now, what you have to know about Earl is that he was a human computer before they had computers in baseball. He had stats for everything—who you hit, who you didn't hit, how you did in certain parks at night or during the day. He grinned at me and said, "Hey, Tommy baby, do you know who's pitching tonight? Luis Tiant," he grabs some of his stat sheets and says, "Oh-for-two years, baby! You got to sit your butt down today." I hadn't realized it was oh-for-that-long because Tiant would give you a nice, easy oh-for-four. So I sat down and Earl put in Tom Shopay and Tommy goes out and gets two hits. What could I say? Earl knew what he was doing out there.

THE DIFFICULTIES OF THE ROLE

When the serious talk about the DH started, there was concern about the difficulty of essentially pinch-hitting three to five times a game. After all, the stats through the late '60s showed that the batting averages of pinch

*hitters were about 30 points lower than those with regular lineup assign-
ments. Would designated hitters suffer a similar fate? What would they do
to adjust to their new roles? How would managers react? Did anyone truly
have an understanding of what this would mean to the game?*

HARMON KILLEBREW: The hard part about DH-ing is
staying in the game mentally and physically. You can cool down
and get tight sitting on the bench. Now I had to contend with
not playing most of the time, since most of the pitchers in the
league were right-handed, and DH-ing as well. I didn't have a
very good year [.242 average, five home runs, 32 RBIs in '73].

TOMMY DAVIS: The toughest thing about DH-ing was just
staying warm on cold days, staying loose. Remember to go into
the clubhouse or down the runway to swing a bat. I used to
swing a lot. In Baltimore I'd also duck into the clubhouse and
watch the game on TV, get a view of the pitcher from behind
the plate and in back of the mound, get an idea of what he was
throwing. I'd also check the umpire, see what he was giving you
that day. Is he going to call that pitch on the outside corner a
ball or give it to the pitcher? Umpires in the American League
had a more liberal strike zone than the umpires in the National
League. In the AL the umps wore a different chest protector, so
they couldn't get down low, and they called a lot of high strikes.

OSCAR GAMBLE: Staying warm and keeping your head
in the game is the hardest part of DH-ing. When you're playing
the field, you're moving a lot more, your body's staying warm
and ready, you're breaking a sweat. You're loose. But when
you're sitting for inning after inning, you can get cold and
tighten up. I would go into the clubhouse to warm my hands,
run in the runway, take practice swings, that sort of thing.
It wasn't the same as playing in the field, but it was something.

RICO CARTY: You get cold, you know, you have to be
moving around. When you first start you don't realize it. I
can recall lots of times when it was cold—that was my enemy,
the cold weather—and I would always be up in the clubhouse

drinking hot chocolate and coffee, and lots of times they had to go, "Rico, it's time for you to hit!" So, I'd be running down the runway and getting down on the field. I was lucky that lots of times I got a base hit or hit a home run.

OSCAR GAMBLE: Staying focused was the challenge. You know, when you're out there in the field, standing at your position, from the stands it might look as if you're doing nothing, but in order to play the game right, you have to be anticipating, following each pitch so you can get a good jump if the ball is hit your way. You're always focused on something. When you're sitting on the bench, waiting to hit, you have to force yourself to stay in the game. Watch that opposing pitcher carefully, see how he's setting up the guys hitting in front of you. What's his pickoff move look like in case you get on base? What pitch does he go to in certain counts? Concentrate on that while your team is up and go over it again when your team is on the field. Look out in the bull pen and think about who might come into the game if your club knocks out the starter. When you're DH-ing you have to think even more about the game.

EDGAR MARTINEZ: At the beginning it was very hard. The first thing that came to my mind was, if I don't hit, I thought my career would be over. I could be just a part-time player; it was more up in the air if I do not perform. After a while I played good and it helped me. It was the right time and the right place for me to get into that position. Mike Blowers had a lot of potential at third base, and he was swinging the bat well, and we were a better team with me at DH in 1995. We really had a good team. In 1994 I struggled to stay healthy. In 1995 I was able to come back healthy and be there all year.

OSCAR GAMBLE: You do get pigeonholed. Managers start looking at you as nothing but a DH, when I could play the field. That really hurt me more in the later part of my career.

EDGAR MARTINEZ: I had to do a series of things. I had to make sure I stretched a lot, took swings, and adjusted to the lights, so I'd get outside at the right time to make sure my eyes adjusted. I also wanted to anticipate situations, so I paid lots of attention to the game in order to know what was going on and what might happen.

FRANK ROBINSON: I didn't get a rhythm because each guy, I think, has to do what he feels is the best way to handle it himself. What I did was I never left the bench. It was just like if I was playing. I stayed in the dugout. I watched what was going on in the field. Watched the other pitcher's pitches. Tried to help my teammates. Rooting, keeping them up, try to help them win the ball game by picking up on what the other pitcher is doing. I stayed right in the dugout.

DH VS. PINCH HITTER

The roles have their similarities, but most hitters agree: it's much easier to DH than it is to pinch-hit.

RICO CARTY: Lots of us have to be grateful because the DH lengthened our careers. If the DH wasn't there, lots of us would have been out of baseball a long time ago. Or I would have just been a pinch hitter. And that role as a pinch hitter, I never liked it. I loved to play, because as a hitter you have four chances. If you pop up twice or ground out twice you have two more times to recoup.

TOMMY DAVIS: Pinch-hitting is much harder. DH-ing is a piece of cake compared to that. Pinch-hitting you have one chance to come through, usually during a critical part of the ball game where the whole game might be on the line. The pressure is enormous. You're facing a pitcher you haven't seen all day. Maybe I've been able to watch him from the dugout, but if they bring in a reliever, you have no idea what he might have that day, no matter how he's pitched you in the past. And late in the game there's a good chance that you'll

face someone from the bull pen. Pinch-hitting is all pressure.
DH, you're a regular. By that second at bat you've seen the
pitcher's velocity, his location. You have some idea about what's
working for him that day. And you know if you don't get it
done in one at bat, you'll have another chance to redeem yourself. Much easier.

I was lucky, though, because my managers, almost all of
them, used me in [pinch-hitting] situations that played to my
strengths. They didn't put me up when a home run was needed.
I could hit the long ball, but it wasn't my game. Instead, they'd
send me up with runners in scoring position in close games
where a base hit would plate one or two runs. I had to stay
warm before that at bat, if it was a cold day, but I also had to
spend a lot of time examining the pitcher, to see what he was
getting over that day. Some players would review scouting re-
ports, but I never used them.

RALPH HOUK: When I went to the Tigers, I used Rusty
[Staub] as the DH for two reasons. First, he was a tremendous
hitter, someone who drove in a lot of runs for us. Second,
Rusty was as prepared as any player on the team. He studied
pitchers all the time and he concentrated on them when he
was on the bench, looking for something that might help him
pick up a pitch. You know, I watch baseball on TV, and I've
been noticing pitchers who show a lot of white in their gloves
when they throw their curveballs. We used to remind pitchers
not to do that, but I see it happening today. Rusty would
pick up on something like that immediately. So he had the
sort of focus you wanted in a designated hitter. He trained himself to be a good DH. I used to send him to the trainer's room
to take extra swings and stay warm while our team was in
the field. Then he'd come out and watch the opposing pitcher.
He did very well for me in that spot in a position that's a
lot tougher than people realize, both for the player and the
manager.

THE DH AND MANAGERS

As for the AL managers, the DH was literally a whole new ball game. Different skippers took different approaches to implementing it, and of course many people have opinions on how the DH changes strategy, especially when it comes to managing.

RALPH HOUK: Sparky Anderson used the DH as an open spot, rotating players through the position to keep them fresh or allow them to contribute to the offense if they were too hurt to play the field. Being able to do that depends on your personnel, how many hitters you have on your bench. But I pretty much felt it was a job for one man or, as we did with Ronnie [Blomberg] and Jim Ray Hart, a two-man platoon; two hitters who knew the night before the game whether they'd be starting depending on whether we'd be facing a left-hander or a right-hander that day, and then they could prepare better. Hitters who haven't DH'd before have to get used to the spot.

RON BLOMBERG: As a DH you want to know you're going to come to the park and see your name penciled in the lineup and you're going to get your four or five at bats that day. That way you're already thinking about the pitcher long before you get to the ballpark, you can prepare better. And you want to get into a routine. Rotating your guys is like being platooned. Give one hitter the job so he can focus on it. It's hard to adapt to the position, so when you find someone who can do it, you have to give him as many at bats as you possibly can. Like David Ortiz.

BOB COSTAS: It has always diminished strategy to some extent. I don't think it eliminates strategy, but you can't argue that it doesn't diminish strategy. There are just more moves that have to be made when the pitcher is part of the batting order. Some of those moves involve double-switches and pinch-hitting. Another involves sacrificing with the pitcher. Another is more subtle than that, the way the opposing pitcher works an inning, knowing that the pitcher is coming up.

WHITEY HERZOG: It's a much better game with the pitcher hitting. It gives the fans the chance to second-guess the manager. With the DH you lose the fundamentals, the finer points of strategy. With the DH, if you have a one-run lead in the eighth inning, you can bring in your best relief pitcher with no questions.

RALPH HOUK: The one thing I had to get used to with that rule was the way it affected your pitching staff. I know that people think the DH makes it easier to manage. They think you just fill out the lineup and then go to sleep. It's not that way at all, especially if you were used to managing without it.

EDGAR MARTINEZ: In the National League there is more strategy around changing pitchers, more pinch hitters, it's more of a strategic game. The American League, with the DH, you have a lineup of nine that as a pitcher you have to go through. In the NL, the seventh and eighth hitters are at a disadvantage because they're not going to have good pitches to hit with the pitcher hitting behind them.

LUIS TIANT: When they came out with the DH they took a lot of strategy out of the game. Before the DH you could be pitching a hell of a game and they have to put in a pinch hitter for you. The good thing now is you stay longer in the game. You're going to be in the game as long as you can be.

RALPH HOUK: It was much easier to know when to take out a pitcher without the DH, right? Late innings, your pitcher due up next, you send up a pinch hitter for him. Or if your starter's getting hit and you know his spot is due up in the next inning, you might bring in a pitcher to get one or two outs, knowing you're going to pinch-hit for *him* in the next inning. But with the DH you might have to think about bringing in someone who can give you a few innings or even pitch the rest of the game. You also had to watch that you didn't drain your pitchers keeping them in too long. So you had to watch your pitchers very closely and talk to your catcher more, find out if the pitcher was losing his stuff so you could get him out of there. You do that anyway, but with the DH you had to stay on top of it more. I don't think many people realize that.

FRANK ROBINSON: The differences in managing in the two leagues are overemphasized. The basic thing is the handling of your pitchers, especially your starting pitcher. In the AL, because he doesn't get a turn to hit, you can leave him out there a little longer. You don't have to take him out as quickly. In the NL, say, in the seventh inning of a close ball game, you have to make a decision whether you're going to let that pitcher hit, and stay out there. Or are you going to pinch-hit for him? I think the next thing is that in the NL a little bit more than the AL, you have the double switches. They come up more often than they do in the AL. There's no reason why an AL manager can't handle those two things, as long as he looks at his pitchers and handles his pitchers as though the DH wasn't there. If you feel like you're losing a little bit in the seventh inning, you go get him. In the NL you pinch-hit for him. Either way you don't let him stay out there. I think that's really it. I think that's overrated, really.

JOE TORRE: It certainly makes it easier than when I was with the Mets, Cardinals, or Braves. It's one less thing you have to worry about. I can take the pitcher out when he's tired, not for any other reason. With the Yankees we're not going to play small ball very much regardless.

WHITEY HERZOG: I never minded the second-guessing that came along with managing without the DH. That's part of being a baseball manager. I always kept in mind that the second-guessers were not good enough to make a first guess. That's what I was hired to do.

THE DH'S LEGACY

No other rule change in baseball has had as divisive an impact among fans as has the designated hitter. History does not report fan outrage at the reduction in the number of balls required for a walk or the mound being moved back to 60 feet 6 inches in the 1800s. There were no bumper stickers on buckboards protesting those moves, or the creation of the foul strike, or any other movement on baseball's part. None have caused such a passionate outcry that resonates to this day.

For more than three decades, baseball has had it both ways, as the National League has never followed the American into the world of the DH. Since the reasons for the designated hitter's institution have long since ceased to be relevant (scoring and attendance are not in danger of sinking to late '60s/early '70s levels anytime soon), there isn't much chance of the rule being adopted in the senior circuit. (At least the two leagues have settled on a reasonable compromise: using the DH in American League parks for interleague games, All-Star Games, and the World Series.)

And if the DH were eliminated, who would protest? Would the American League suddenly lose its allure? Now that a whole generation has become fans without knowing any other way, there's a good chance we'll never find out. The DH has practically been around long enough to be considered an institution. But some fans might not remember that the DH rule did come up for a vote in the NL in 1977, and that baseball came a lot closer to having the DH in both leagues than people may know.

> **BILL GILES:** If Ruly Carpenter, the president of the Phillies, had not been fishing in the Atlantic Ocean in 1977, both leagues would have the DH. Ruly had asked me to represent him at the National League meeting in 1977 and to vote for the DH because he and Phillies general manager Paul Owens felt that the Phillies would be a better team with the DH. The Phillies had two very good hitters, Greg Luzinski and minor leaguer Keith Moreland, who were not very good defensively. But when I got to the meeting, I was informed that even if it passed, the DH would not become effective until the next season because the players' union had to approve it, and they never approved an owners' unilateral decision. The owners could implement this kind of decision in the next year. The National

League needed seven votes (out of 12 teams at the time) to pass the DH. There were six teams in favor and four against when the vote came around to Philadelphia and Pittsburgh. Harding Peterson, general manager of Pittsburgh, was told by owner John Galbraith to vote the same way as the Phillies because the teams were big rivals at the time. I tried to reach Ruly by phone but was told that he was out on the ocean fishing. I did not know how to vote because of the year delay in adopting the rule, so I abstained and the Pirates abstained. An abstention is the same as a "no" vote, and as a result of my inability to reach Mr. Carpenter that fateful day, there is no DH in the National League. The issue has never come up for official vote again and, if it did today, the result would more likely be the elimination of the DH in the American League.

HARMON KILLEBREW: The DH turned out to be exactly what the AL owners wanted. Attendance improved and you can see where the game is today. Pitching and defense may win pennants, but fans like to come out to the park to see offense. At least I do.

JIM KAAT: When we first had the DH, the lineups weren't as deep as they are today. There were still a lot of teams that weren't equipped to field lineups with the prototype DHs we've seen in recent years, like Chili Davis and Paul Molitor. For instance, when we played the Angels, I think Dave Collins was often the DH, and he was a singles hitter with speed but little power. From a pitching standpoint, we adjusted pretty quickly because it was the same for both teams, but I can understand what pitchers coming over from the National League today are experiencing, because the National League lineups are softer. You look at the bottom third of a typical National League team, and you have the pitcher hitting and the normal seven and eight hitters usually are not as much of a threat as you find in the American League. I think one time last year the Yankees had Jorge Posada hitting seventh, Hideki Matsui hitting eighth, and Bernie Williams batting ninth. There's not a team in the National League that can match a bottom third like that, and there's several other American League teams, such as the Red Sox, that have lineups that are similar.

TONY OLIVA: The DH gives a chance to a lot of really good players, like David Ortiz. Everybody thinks he can't play first base. But he is a player who can hit. Now it's a position that can help their team win pennants and be in the race. I think the DH has been a blessing to the American League. I wish that someday the National League would apply the DH, but they don't want to do it. They do really well without it.

BILL GILES: Today I actually like the fact that one league has the DH and one does not. It creates healthy debate and permits popular players the opportunity to stay in the game when their defensive skills have deteriorated.

BUD SELIG: Look, the American League clubs like it, the National League doesn't. The National League at one point almost did it, but they'll never do it now. And, the American League clubs—I really believe it would take a cataclysmic event for there to be a change. What does that mean? Maybe overall, geographical realignment. Otherwise, I think it was Bill Giles of the Phillies, who's very much like I am, very sensitive to baseball, who said, "You know, a little controversy between the leagues isn't bad and maybe this is all right." And so that's why everybody has left it the way it is, including me.

THOMAS BOSWELL: From the very beginning I preferred that the two leagues be different and that the two forms of baseball exist. I never had any idea why that was, except it just seemed fun to see the game played two different ways. Both seem viable and interesting and it was not clear to me which was intrinsically better. In periods where pitching might have a little bit of an advantage, the existence of the designated hitter helped the sport as a whole from becoming too pitching-dominated. In periods where there was too much hitting, I'm not sure it was as easy to justify. Baseball survived too much hitting much, much better than it survived too much pitching.

The only time you had attendance problems was when pitching was too dominant and the existence of the designated hitter keeps some of your older and better hitters in the game as long as they can still walk to the plate. It doesn't bother me to have a sport where there are 14 jobs that can be occupied by Cecil Fielder as long as he can waddle to the plate. The existence of a 270-pound slugger who can't play a defensive position doesn't insult me as much as it does some people. I wouldn't want the whole sport to have that. I wouldn't want every team to have a beer-league guy at that position. But I don't consider my position on the DH logical and I really can't explain it.

LUIS TIANT: When the National League plays their way and we play our way, it's strange. I don't know why they don't change it one way or the other. Both put in the DH, or the American League comes back to the way it used to be.

WHITEY HERZOG: It's a fundamental rule and I think it should be the same in both leagues: no DH, the pitcher should hit. It's a great handicap for AL clubs to lose the DH. If the rules are going to be different, then no interleague play. Let all the managers who have managed at least one year in each league, since 1973, get a vote. Let them decide. I don't know how the vote would go. You can't get rid of it right away. If you vote it out in 2007, then phase it out by 2010. The best place for the DH is the All-Star Game, and they don't use it there all the time.

THE DH, THE HALL OF FAME, AND THE FUTURE

Paul Molitor, who amassed 3,319 hits in 2,683 big-league games—1,173 of them as a DH—was elected to the Hall of Fame in 2004. With great hitters such as Edgar Martinez, David Ortiz, and Travis Hafner serving the bulk of their careers as designated hitters, the question will keep coming up: Does a player who spent the majority of his career as a DH deserve a spot in Cooperstown?

TONY OLIVA: [Hall of Fame voters] use all kinds of excuses. I don't think it's fair the way they've been treating [some candidates]. They treat us worse than they treat the dog. The way they do it right now, the system is very bad for players. The players who are on the [veterans'] committee, the way the system is, it looks like they don't want anybody there.

EDGAR MARTINEZ: DH is a big part of the offense now. The player can contribute offensively and can be a leader and can make the team better. There are different attitudes that other people have. But I look at relievers. They can get into the Hall of Fame, and they don't get into games as much as the DH does. The thing is, the DH is a position teams rely on, so I think there's a good case for it. It can play a huge role.

TONY OLIVA: The DH helped some other players get into the Hall of Fame. We had a young guy like Paul Molitor. The DH helped him a lot. Every time he played in the outfield he got hurt. He played the game very hard. He'd dive for the ball, he'd steal, but he'd get hurt. When they made him the DH, he was able to keep it up for another 10 years. When he finished, if he wanted, he could've played a little bit longer. Edgar Martinez in Seattle. He was a very dangerous hitter in the American League. It helped him to stay in the big leagues for a long time as the DH. He might have played first or third, otherwise, though he might have only been pinch-hitting. If it wasn't for the rule, nobody would have been able to find out what kind of ballplayer he was, what kind of hitter.

RON BLOMBERG: People ask me, "Should they put a DH in the Hall of Fame?" I look at Ortiz and say, "Absolutely." I mean, if he keeps hitting like that and winning ball games, why not? [Relief pitcher] Bruce Sutter is in the Hall of Fame, and he was a specialist, just like Ortiz. What's the difference?

BOB COSTAS: I don't think that having played DH should hurt Edgar Martinez's Hall of Fame argument, because his numbers are great enough. But if a guy is on the bubble and you were comparing him to a guy who was a non-DH? Then I think it's worth taking into account that his numbers were padded by the DH rule. Or even if a guy who played DH is a legitimate Hall of Famer but you're making historical comparisons, then you have to take that into account if you're going to have an enlightened conversation.

TONY OLIVA: The last eight years, [the Hall of Fame veterans' committee] didn't put anybody in. There are a few guys who should have been there before they went to the veterans' committee. The veterans' committee, the way it is now, it looks like, maybe I'm wrong, but that they don't want anybody inside that little club. They don't want us there and this is the way it is.

FRANK ROBINSON: Today they're developing kids at the minor-league level as DHs. I think that's wrong. You hone your skills. That's where you get better, at the minor-league level. I would prefer not to see the DH at the minor-league level. Let those kids play. If he's a bad defensive player, third baseman, let him go out there and play. Then, they come to the big leagues you can plug him in and use his bat on given days, or take him out after six, seven innings, or plug him in here and there to get his at bats at the big-league level until he gets better at that level. But still put him out there in the field. To me, if they don't have [the DH] in both leagues within the next few years, get rid of it.

BOB COSTAS: The argument that no longer holds any water is that you need the DH because you need more offense. Because over the last generation not only is offense fully restored to well past the level of before the late '60s, it went to the point of distortion, where dozens of guys were driving in 100 runs a year, where the league ERA rose two runs higher than it had been before. It's not possible to argue with a straight face that the DH is still needed for the boost in offense it provides. It's now a remedy for a problem that no longer exists.

THOMAS BOSWELL: We have to wait to find out how good our steroid testing is going to get over the next few years before we reevaluate the need for the DH. As the number of cheaters decreases—and, of course, there are pitchers who cheat, too—we need to find out what the real level of power is and we also have to find out to what degree we can catch and limit cheaters. If baseball can do a better job than football does—and I assume football isn't doing a very good job based on what I've seen walking through their clubhouses—and it turns out that offense in baseball gears down over the next few years, presumably because there's less cheating or people don't feel the peer pressure to cheat as much because they think they can get caught, then you'll need the DH. Why get rid of it if it turns out that people with less muscles hit less home runs? If, on the other hand, three or four years from now you've done everything you can to make people as honest as you can get them to be, and the league leaders are still hitting 50 home runs, then maybe you can get rid of the DH.

BOB COSTAS: Now the only argument for the DH is that there are some potent offensive players who are best used as DHs. But the counterargument to that is that it's a game of balance and counterbalance. It's not like David Ortiz wouldn't play; they'd have to play him at first base. If there were no DH, it's not like Edgar Martinez wouldn't have had a career, he just would have had to play third base or first base. Or some lumbering guy would have to play a fairly crummy left field. He'd be a four in Strat-o-Matic.

What you get for the DH isn't worth what you give up, especially now. I think it should be eliminated over a period of time, so you don't pull the rug out from under anybody currently playing.

THE FIRST AFRICAN AMERICAN MANAGER

Featuring

DAVE ANDERSON: *New York Times* columnist and coauthor, along with Frank Robinson, of *Frank: The First Year.*

RICO CARTY: Career .299 hitter who served as Robinson's primary designated hitter in 1975 and '76.

BOB COSTAS: Longtime sportscaster who was in his early twenties, working as a broadcaster at KMOX Radio in St. Louis, when Robinson managed the Cleveland Indians.

BILL DAUGHTRY: Sports commentator for the Madison Square Garden Network.

DENNIS ECKERSLEY: Hall of Fame pitcher who was a rookie on the '75 Indians.

OSCAR GAMBLE: One of the most productive platoon hitters of his era, he played in 120 games for the Indians in Robinson's first year managing the team.

DAVE GARCIA: Veteran coach whom Robinson hired for his first staff.

WHITEY HERZOG: Robinson's rival manager with the Kansas City Royals and later with the St. Louis Cardinals, when Robinson was in charge of the Giants.

MONTE IRVIN: Negro League star who became a Hall of Fame outfielder with the New York Giants.

DOC "GEORGE" MEDICH: Nineteen-game winner for the 1974 Yankees who was tabbed for the Opening Day start against Robinson's Indians in '75.

FRANK ROBINSON: Finished his Hall of Fame playing career as the game's first African American manager with the Indians in 1975. He is the only player to win Most Valuable Player in both leagues (with the Cincinnati Reds in 1961 and the Baltimore Orioles in '66). He also won the Triple Crown in '66, leading the American League in batting average (.316), home runs (49), and RBIs (122), and played on two World Series–winning teams ('66 and '70 Orioles).

BUD SELIG: Current baseball commissioner who was the owner of the rival Milwaukee Brewers in the mid-1970s.

KEN SINGLETON: All-Star outfielder for the Orioles in the mid-'70s and currently a broadcaster for the YES Network.

JEFF TORBORG: Former catcher who played 10 years in the majors with the Los Angeles Dodgers and California Angels and was a teammate of Robinson on the 1973 Angels. Robinson hired him as a coach in Cleveland in '75 and he succeeded Robinson as Indians manager two years later.

THERE WAS NEVER ANY DOUBT that, when given the chance, Jackie Robinson and any number of other Negro League greats would not only succeed but also thrive in the all-white major leagues. The history books are filled with quotes from white players extolling the virtues of African Americans they had faced in interracial exhibition games or barnstorming tours. Barring their entry into the playing ranks was a clear-cut case of denying greatness. Even their detractors at least paid lip service to their abilities. The same could not be said about African American managers, however. Because of the often-hard-to-quantify nature of a baseball manager's qualifications, those bent on keeping the ranks an all-white fraternity had ambiguity as a flimsy fallback defense as to why they were choosing to do so. Because it was difficult to know if someone was managing material until they had actually managed, and since African Americans were not being given that opportunity, a vicious cycle of denial was in place.

As more and more African Americans began to arrive on the big-league scene, however, it was only a matter of time before one of them would be the first behind a desk in the manager's office. How much time, though, would it take? The easiest solution would have been to draft an African American manager from the Negro Leagues soon after Robinson and Larry Doby broke the color lines of the respective major leagues in 1947. "The best Negro League managers," recalls legendary Negro League outfielder Monte Irvin, "were Vic Harris, with the Homestead Grays, and Ben Taylor, with the Chicago American Giants and two or three other clubs."

To have tabbed someone such as Harris or Taylor and given them, say, the reins of the Boston Braves in 1952 would have been a move of audaciousness in a sport that often moved at a glacial pace in all facets. In fact, for once, baseball was ahead of the societal curve by finally breaking its self-imposed color line. When it came to race relations, it was beating a lot of institutions to the punch. "Look at how long it took for Jackie to break the color barrier," says YES broadcaster and former big leaguer Ken Singleton. "Same reason. Baseball moves slowly and it always has."

"Jackie Robinson's coming to the big leagues—I've said it often—is the most powerful moment in baseball history," says baseball commissioner Bud Selig. "Clearly the most important, I think, in American history in the 20th century. I mean when you think about what Branch Rickey did in 1945 when he signed him. It was years before *Brown v. Board of Education,* it was at least two to three years before Harry Truman desegregated the United States Army, and it was 17 or 18 years, really, before the Civil Rights Movement."

Even though it had just fought a two-front war to help rid the world of two of the most racist governments of modern times, the United States was largely unprepared to confront its own racial inequalities. Major-league baseball was, apart from its teams in St. Louis and Washington, still a game of the industrialized north, but it was still taking its cue from those parts of the country where segregation was the norm. In this atmosphere, slipping a few African American players into the majors was pretty radical stuff. Giving one of the 16 major-league managing jobs to an African American would have been downright anarchic—especially considering that, five years after Robinson and Doby, fully half of the big-league clubs still had yet to make room for their first African American player.

Since taking a manager from the Negro Leagues and putting him in charge of a big-league team was not going to happen (and the dissolution of the Negro Leagues was removing what few managing opportunities there were for African Americans), the first African American manager was going to have to come from the big-league playing ranks, and that was going to take time for those men to cycle through. Provided, that is, that they were even offered minor-league managing jobs at the end of their careers—which didn't happen until 1961. It wasn't until then that an affiliated minor-league team was helmed by an African American. Former Cub Gene Baker was hired by the Pirates to run their Class D team in the New York–Penn League. (While a coach with the big club two years later, he would serve as an interim manager for two games in 1963 when Danny Murtaugh was thrown out of a game, much like Roy Campanella had done for Walter Alston in 1946 when both were at Class B Nashua of the New England League.) So it wasn't until 14 years after Robinson and Doby came to the majors that the meter began running on the first African American managerial career in organized baseball.

In *The Bill James Guide to Baseball Managers,* the author wondered if the quality of big-league managers didn't suffer because of baseball's disinclination to turn over their teams to minorities. James wrote, "It may be that the percentage of managers who had been outstanding players was pushed downward from 1950 to 1990 because many of the best players were blacks and Latins who were almost never going to manage."

Meanwhile, the easiest and most obvious transition for an African American man into the managerial ranks would have been for Buck O'Neil to have done so with the Cubs in 1962. He had been hired as a coach by the Cubs, the first African American to have such a position. Frank Robinson took notice.

"You know, you felt like it's time," Frank Robinson says. "That's a step in the right direction. Then, maybe a little easier. Maybe the time is getting near, that they're willing to give an Afro-American an opportunity to manage a major-league ball club. But again, too, it was a small step. But it was a step in the right direction."

How hard would it have been for the Cubs to go one step further and make O'Neil one of their infamous College of Coaches? (Instead of a manager, the Cubs in 1961 and '62 used a battery of coaches who rotated in and out of the top position.) One can argue the relative merits of appointing the first African American manager in conjunction with an experiment that is still widely derided, but it would have nominally jump-started the timetable by more than a decade.

Instead, the '60s passed without an African American at the helm of a big-league club. A time of great general upheaval saw baseball merely marking time in this regard. Recalls Selig, "Jackie Robinson said to me at the '72 World Series—he couldn't see any more [he was blind from diabetes]—he hoped someday to look over and see a black man managing. I'm sorry he didn't live to see that."

ROBINSON MOVES TO THE FORE

By that time, though, it was, at least, an ongoing topic of discussion. There were African American players and former players who were seen as managerial timber. Larry Doby and Tom McCraw were two men who were often named in such discussions. Was it going to take a big-name player to make it happen, though? Could the first African American manager be an anonymous sort of organizational lifer, or would one of the game's now-aging superstars be the answer?

DAVE ANDERSON: I wrote at the time [early '70s] that Hank Aaron should have been asked to manage the Braves by Ted Turner. Whether he wanted to or not, or whether he would have been a good manager, I don't know, but he should have been asked and that would have been a couple of years before Frank. Overall, the great players are celebrities and celebrities don't take jobs where you're hired to be fired. They're not generally geared to it or want to do it.

JEFF TORBORG: When Frank and I were teammates with the Angels in '73, we were playing in Boston and Bobby Bolin, the former Giants pitcher who was with the Red Sox at the time, knocked Frank down. Frank went after Carlton Fisk, who was the catcher at the time, and people ran out of the dugouts and the bull pen. And I remember him pointing at Bolin and saying, "You better not throw at me again." And only the good ones can do this: He steps in the batters' box and hits one over the light towers. I don't just mean over the Green Monster; he hit one over the light towers. And we all went, "Holy Christmas, how did he do that?" What he had just said, what just happened, emotions flowing on both ends—the great ones can do great things.

BILL DAUGHTRY: I remember Buck O'Neil was coaching, but no one was thinking of him as managerial material, in part, I suppose, because he made his reputation in the Black Leagues. Baseball could be shortsighted. Junior Gilliam was talked about a lot, but when a Dodgers coach did get hired as a manager by another club, it was Danny Ozark [a white coach]. I looked at Ellie Howard as a potential manager had he been healthy and lived. What interested me, though, were the guys you never heard mentioned, like Willie Mays, Hank Aaron, and, for a while, Frank Robinson.

FRANK ROBINSON: It was around 1961, '62 that I started to think about managing. At the time you don't know how long your career might go. Something might happen or an injury may end it. It's something that I focused on, because I wanted to stay in baseball. I wanted to be where the action was, so I figured that managing would be a good idea.

DAVE ANDERSON: As far as great players being great managers, there have been very few great players that have wanted to manage. Stan Musial, Willie Mays, Joe DiMaggio, none of them managed. The great players have other opportunities and generally make a lot more money playing, so there's less interest in a job that until recently has paid so little. Now that has changed dramatically. I think Joe Torre will be remembered as the best player to become a great manager.

The meltdown of the Ted Williams–led Senators/Rangers—after a promising 86 wins in 1969, Williams's record declined in each of his four seasons, bottoming out with 100 losses in '72—was certainly doing a lot to inform the attitude toward superstar-players-turned-managers at that time.

BILL DAUGHTRY: You know there's always been this thinking in baseball that great players can't be good managers because they always set the standards for everyone so high. The theory was they wouldn't be able to understand why the players they managed weren't as good as they were. If that was the theory, you could imagine how that applied to Willie Mays. He was arguably the best player ever, certainly the best of his time, and who could reach that? So there was another kind of prejudice, against the superstar, at work there, but you never heard that guys like Willie or Hank were even interested in going to the dugout after their careers ended. The names we kept hearing were all from the next step, Bill White for a while, Maury Wills, who got his chance with Seattle [in 1980].

FRANK ROBINSON: The barrier is there. You don't know when an organization would be willing to hire an Afro-American as their first minority manager in baseball. But, you prepare yourself. And the one thing I kept hearing is, you know, you need experience to manage at the major-league level. If you had experience they'd be willing to hire an Afro-American.

So instead of taking his winters off, Robinson, still an active and very successful player, approached and was hired to run the Santurce club of the Puerto Rican winter leagues.

FRANK ROBINSON: So I got the opportunity in 1968 to go down to Puerto Rico. I went down there for six years and managed. I got that experience and it certainly helped me. It wasn't [the only thing] that prepared me for it. I listened and watched other managers. I played for them and played against them. Just learned the game itself, what would work and what you felt like wouldn't work. That's the way I prepared myself, mentally and physically, for the game. I was still playing, but I was willing to go down to Latin America, Puerto Rico, during the off-season and manage down there.

DAVE GARCIA: One thing that he did, that I give him a lot of credit for, when he managed in Puerto Rico for several years. He didn't start out managing in the major leagues. He went out there and worked what was probably the equivalent of Triple-A ball, the winter leagues, and he learned a lot about handling people.

DAVE ANDERSON: Baseball, and the owners, always move slowly to do anything. I think Jackie Robinson should have been the first black manager, but his health was certainly a factor. Maybe Larry Doby. Those guys didn't do what Frank did, go to Puerto Rico, etc., to prepare to become managers.

BILL DAUGHTRY: Two things separated Frank from all of those other guys, and you have to respect him for it. First, once he made up his mind that this was what he wanted, to manage, he went after it with everything he had. He had no ego about it. I don't know how appealing it would have been for some other superstar to spend the winter in Puerto Rico managing for next to no money the way Frank did. Here he was one of the biggest stars in baseball, but, in this particular field, starting all over again like a rookie. But he knew it was the next thing he wanted to do after he finished playing. So he went [to Santurce] and worked his ass off. The second part of this was his personality. What do we think of when we think of the ideal manager? Someone who is feisty and hard-nosed, always hustling, breaking his butt to win. Guys like Billy Martin and Leo Durocher, that was their reputation as players, and that was their reputation as managers. Now think about this. Did Willie Mays play hard? Mickey Mantle? Harmon Killebrew? You know they did, but no one ever wrote about them as hard-nosed or praised them for their hustle, because they were sluggers. All those home runs overshadowed how hard they played. Frank was that rare slugger who was famous for playing hard. We all remember how he went after Al Weis [in 1967] to break up that double play, the collision that nearly ruined both of them that season. He was trying to break up the double play, he was trying to break up Weis with a good, hard-but-clean hit. And he played that way all the time. Frank wasn't one of those scrappy, little guys we always read about like David Eckstein or Freddie Patek. He was a scrappy big guy who gave everything in every game he played. Those are qualities managers want in their players, and that players want in their managers.

WHITEY HERZOG: Being a star and a minority, he proved himself, paid his dues, learning to manage. He put himself in a position to be the best candidate, not just the best black candidate. He did it on merit so the people around MLB would judge him accordingly, by his ability.

MONTE IRVIN: As a player, I knew he'd be a star when he came up in 1954. His expertise that he developed as a manager didn't surprise me. He was a very knowledgeable baseball man. He was a good choice.

DAVE ANDERSON: Frank was the perfect choice because from an early time in his career he *wanted* to manage. He paid his dues by going to Puerto Rico in the winter to gain experience and gain credibility. He put himself in a position, that when an owner [Ted Bonda of the Indians] had the guts to do it, he was ready to do it.

In addition to cutting his managing teeth in the winter leagues, Robinson was spending the rest of the year playing for one of the great managers of all time, Earl Weaver of the Orioles.

FRANK ROBINSON: You always try to take from a manager that you're playing for; even playing against, when you see things happen: their work and their good, sound, fundamental moves. Things that they do, you tuck that away in your memory. But the one thing about Earl, I really took to how Earl handled us as a roster. He involved people. On any given day, he'd use a player. He was not afraid to use a player, in certain situations. He would give a guy, a right-handed hitter, a chance to play against a right-handed pitcher. Then he'd have a left-handed hitter that he'd platoon with that guy. You knew when you came to the ballpark if you didn't start the game, you had a chance to get in it before the game was over, because Earl would use his roster. He didn't mind discussing his moves with players. They could talk with him about why he didn't do this or why he didn't do that. He was the first manager I'd ever seen that let his players argue with him. He understood. He kept you prepared. He had his teams prepared for anything the other team might do that might come up in a ball game. When he was caught by surprise, he'd make those moves. He was a great strategist. A great manager, using his players.

ROBINSON GETS HIS SHOT

Traded by Baltimore to the Los Angeles Dodgers after the 1971 season, Robinson was dealt to the California Angels a year later. The Angels then sent him to the Indians on September 12, 1974. A promising season (the Indians had been 57–50 at one point) had long since degenerated into another chapter in franchise futility. By the end of the '74 season it was clear that manager Ken Aspromonte, whose leadership skills were in question, would not be retained. Apart from other issues, Robinson discovered that the team appeared to be split along racial lines. At the center of that problem was Cleveland icon Larry Doby, a coach for the '74 Indians, who died in 2003.

FRANK ROBINSON: That ball club was divided. They were having problems when I got there. The manager had lost control of the team.

OSCAR GAMBLE: We were under .500 that year, but it was a better ball club than that, with a good lineup. When Frank first came over it was to DH and help us with the bat,

but we started hearing rumors that he might be the next manager. The club wasn't happy with Ken Aspromonte.

FRANK ROBINSON: I was a little surprised by what
I saw there with that ball club, as far as the nonblack
players—the way they conducted themselves during the
course of a game, in the dugout, and also the Afro-American
players gravitating toward Larry Doby. When I got there I
could understand it a little bit, why they did it. Because I guess
they thought about Larry maybe possibly being the manager
of the ball club. Aspromonte was let go. I guess they started
to align themselves with Larry, hoping that maybe they'd get
some favors, if he became the manager. But, it wasn't a good
situation there with that ball club.

OSCAR GAMBLE: Yes and I'm sure Larry wanted [the
manager's job]. Cleveland was his town. He became the first
black player in the American League with the Indians and
I think he would have been a fine manager for us. He was
a terrific coach. A lot of people thought he would get it, and
I know Larry was disappointed when they passed him over for
Frank. But he didn't show it. He had that game face, so you
couldn't tell.

*Robinson likes to tell the story that he was paid only $20,000 to manage
the Indians in 1975—a pretty low sum for a manager in those days. He
was, after all, being paid $180,000 to play.*

BILL DAUGHTRY: You might find this funny, but I had
mixed feelings. We all knew what he had done in winter ball
and that he knew how to manage. But I thought, Why Cleveland? It was the Siberia of baseball. These weren't the Indians
of Lou Boudreau, a team that was expected, year after year, to
contend with the Yankees and had the players to do it. It was
such a bad club, I didn't see what he could do to change it.
So in that sense I thought this was partially window dressing.
I was glad to see, it was historic and about time, but I wondered

if he had gotten the job because no one expected the team to do anything. It wasn't like Willie Randolph coming to the Mets [in 2005] as they started their revival. There were no expectations in Cleveland; .500 was the goal there. So I thought, "It's great that they gave the brother the gun, but they didn't put any bullets in it." Obviously there weren't many teams looking to hire a black manager, and had Cleveland been a contender, a team with something to risk, I don't know if the Indians would have hired him. I don't think anyone thought this consciously, but it's as if they said, "Hey, stick him here, what difference does it make? That team's going nowhere." Also, Frank was placed in a situation where he could easily fail, or create the perception that he had failed through no fault of his own. I was concerned that if he did fail, that would be used as an excuse not to hire another black manager.

OSCAR GAMBLE: When he was hired I felt proud. Definitely proud. It was about time.

JEFF TORBORG: I knew of Frank and we had played against one another in the NL and then he went over to the AL and I played against him there. But in 1973, my last active year with the Angels, we acquired Frank. He came over in that big deal from the Dodgers; there were five guys in that deal coming our way: Bill Singer, Bobby Valentine, Billy Grabarkewitz, Frank, and Mike Strahler, a pitcher, came to us from the Dodgers for Andy Messersmith and Ken McMullen. That year being with Frank I really got to know him; we spent quite a bit of time talking, and he really liked to talk baseball. During the year it just so happened that we spent a lot of time talking about philosophy and what we believed in. After the '73 season I was traded by the Angels to the Cardinals for John Andrews, and then I got released that spring. So during the latter part of that year I took a job as an athletic director at a high school in New Jersey. And one morning [my wife] Suzie and I and the boys were having breakfast and we heard that Frank Robinson had been traded to Cleveland and that he was in line to be the manager. And my wife said, "Why don't you call Frank?" And I said, "He knows I'm available." She said, "I don't know—outta sight outta mind, you haven't played with him in a year." So I did call him, and strangely enough I got a wire asking if I'd be interested in being on the coaching staff. So obviously I called back quickly and said, "Boy, would I ever." And we had more fun, because we only had a four-man coaching staff: We had Dave Garcia, Harvey Haddix, and Tommy McCraw. Tommy, Frank, and I had all played together with the Angels, and Tommy was a player-coach with us in '75. So here you have a first-time manager, the first black manager, who is a player-manager. Frank is unbelievable; people who know him [know] this guy is really bright. So that first spring, I was a first-time major-league coach, Tommy McCraw's a first-time major-league coach, and Harvey and Dave, of course, had been coaches before with a lot of experience, and we really had fun. And Frank handled all the publicity and also getting himself in shape.

OPENING DAY

As was often the case with the Indians of that era, the largest crowd (better than 5 percent of the season total) showed up for Opening Day. On this occasion the fans got to witness history in the making. For one of the few times in the 1970s the eyes of the baseball world were on Cleveland, where 39-year-old Frank Robinson was making his debut as player-manager for the Indians, against the New York Yankees. Rachel Robinson, Jackie's widow, threw out the first pitch and commissioner Bowie Kuhn flew in for the occasion and made a speech before the game.

FRANK ROBINSON: I wasn't going to play the first day. But [Indians general manager] Phil Seghi talked me into it, when I went by the office that day. We talked about different things. He said, "You're in the lineup, right?" I said, "No." I hadn't thought about putting myself in the lineup. He said, "Why?" I said, "Because I told you, I'm going to manage the

ball club." He said, "Oh, I think you ought to put yourself in
the lineup. You know you rise to the occasion, and do some
special things in special situations. I think you should put yourself in the lineup." So, I went downstairs and thought about it.
I said, "Well, maybe I'll put myself in there." I had to find a
spot. I said, "You know, I think I'll put myself second, because
if we get a man on first base, I can try to teach these guys the
right thing to do." Man on first base, I'm going to try and get
him over. Man on second base, I can either bunt him over or hit
the ball to the other side to get him over. That type of thing. So
I put myself in the second slot.

DOC MEDICH: It was cold, it was about 38 degrees and
the mound was frozen. There were 55,000 people there and the
place looked empty. You know Municipal Stadium in Cleveland
over by Lake Erie. It was exciting and a lot of noise, but the
playing conditions were kind of tough, coming out of Florida
where temps were in the high 70s and low 80s; to walk into
that, it was hard to feel the ball, control lacking because you
really can't feel it.

FRANK ROBINSON: I wasn't really focused when I went
up to hit. Doc Medich got two quick strikes on me and I got
back in the batter's box 0 and 2 and he dropped down to the
side and threw another strike. I just kind of flicked the bat out
there and fouled it off. Then, I got out of the batter's box, I
said, "Holy smokes" and a light went off. I got in focus and
I said, "You know what, this guy is trying to embarrass me on
my day, in front of my fans here on Opening Day by striking
me out on three pitches. He's not even respectful enough to
try to waste a pitch on me." So I got back in and I focused. He
threw a pretty good pitch, low and away. I got most of it and
pulled it to left field. It wasn't hit high, it was a line drive.

DOC MEDICH: He hit a low and outside fastball, it was a
really good pitch, I asked [catcher] Thurman [Munson] about it
afterward and he said it was a really good pitch, he just got it.
He said he was sky high and you weren't going to get him out

anyway . . . that's about all I remember, that and Frank seemed pretty happy with himself.

FRANK ROBINSON: I didn't know if it was going to clear the fence or not. It did. I kind of floated around the bases. I really didn't come down to earth and really wasn't in focus until I turned toward home plate, and saw a group of players jumping up and down at home plate. Then, it dawned on me. I said, "Wow, this is kind of special."

DENNIS ECKERSLEY: Lou Piniella was playing left field and he hit it over Piniella's head, over the fence. And, the next time up he did the same thing and Piniella jumped and caught it. It would have been two home runs. I had a bird's-eye view. I was maybe 40 feet from the home run. And that's all I can remember. I didn't even want to pitch in that game. It was too much for me.

JEFF TORBORG: I don't think I've ever heard an outdoor stadium as loud as that one was that day. I don't know if it was just being a part of it for the first time, knowing history was being made, but when he hit that home run, they didn't stop hollering. It was cold, it was bad conditions. In fact we took batting practice with ski hats on. The field was wet, which in Cleveland it usually was in that old ballpark. For him to step up and do that, that was incredible. I don't remember how many people were there; close to 60,000. That was an unbelievable day. That goes down as one of the most exciting days I've ever had a uniform on.

FRANK ROBINSON: That was a tremendous lift for me. I was very proud that [Rachel Robinson] would make the trip over there. The thing about it, I hoped and wished that Jackie could've been there. The next best thing was having her there. And I really appreciated her being there. It really helped me, on my first day, because it kept me focused. I wasn't thinking too much about the circumstances. [Having her in the ballpark] had kind of a settling effect on me on my first day managing the ball club.

DAVE ANDERSON: You look at his career, World Series, Triple Crown, MVP . . . I really think that home run was the biggest moment of his life in baseball.

ROBINSON THE MANAGER

After the hoopla of Opening Day there remained the task of running a team for another 161 games. Robinson the groundbreaker would now have to settle into the role of Robinson the manager. In his recounting of the season in journal form in the book Frank: The First Year, *it becomes quickly apparent that there are enough pressures on a big-league manager without him having to worry about matters of race. Having to worry about a player's skin color is about the last distraction a man in charge of 25 talented and diverse personalities wants. That was never more apparent than when the one player who had come to him and reported that he was thrilled to be playing for an African American manager—John "Blue Moon" Odom— turned out to be one of Robinson's most problematic charges.*

A better title for the book would have been simply Frank, *for it is decidedly that. Robinson pulled no punches. He and coauthor Dave Anderson did an excellent job of putting the reader into the day-to-day grind of the long baseball season. It is not the kind of book that would have been written before* Ball Four *came along, in that it names names. If Robinson was not happy with someone, he said as much in the book. Problems with the Perry brothers, pitchers Gaylord and Jim, and catcher Johnny Ellis, as well as run-ins with any number of umpires, are recounted in detail.*

Robinson's goal in Cleveland was, to some extent, to re-create the atmosphere that existed when he was with the Orioles.

FRANK ROBINSON: We had tremendous chemistry on that ball club in the six years that I was there. It started right from day one. As a matter of fact, yesterday I was with Luis Aparicio. We were talking about the first day that I appeared in spring training after the trade [to Baltimore]. I got into the cage. I couldn't hit a ball hard. All of a sudden I hear this voice outside the cage, "Is this who we got for Milt Pappas?" "This is what we got in the trade?" "Let's take Milt back." You know, everybody laughed about it. I laughed about it. But, it made me feel comfortable, it made me feel more relaxed. You know, going out there, not knowing a lot of the guys, personally. And it was just that way, all year long. People tried to come between Brooks [Robinson] and me. Creating problems that weren't there. Saying that, you know, he was the leader of the ball club. I couldn't lead the ball club. That kind of stuff. We, to this day, have never had a cross word. We got along great together. No competition. We were there to win ball games. We were there to do whatever we had to do to help the ball club. There were no superstars in our minds. We treated everybody the same. We looked at everybody the same. And we embraced everybody the same way. It was not, "I'm better then you. I'm the big guy here." None of that on those ball clubs I played for in Baltimore. And that's what creates winning on the field. Because you'll go to any lengths to help your ball club win games, or try to set up situations so the next guy coming to home plate, say, has a chance to drive in a run or whatever. Defensively, you're going to go out there and bust your tail to try and make that play to help that pitcher on the mound; because you want to help win a ball game. It was a great atmosphere on that ball club.

DENNIS ECKERSLEY: Frank knew what he was talking about. Frank knew the whole game. I think he understood the psychological side of things through players. He knew about pitching. He understood. Not that he's a contradiction, but I think he understood a lot of facets of managing. Now, was he a little too firm? Maybe. He didn't put up with shit.

JEFF TORBORG: I was amazed that he was so good and had a handle on everything. I remember going to spring training and one of the things he said to the coaching staff was, "We are here as a coaching team and just because you have expertise in a certain area doesn't mean that person has a territory that can't be stepped on." And what he did was bring the four of us together and there was such a camaraderie. That's a small coaching staff, only four guys. Harvey Haddix was the pitching coach, I was the bull pen coach, Tommy McCraw was the first base and hitting coach, and Dave Garcia was the third base coach. There was no bench coach. Frank had planned for this for a long time, going to Puerto Rico in the off-season to manage winter ball. I was impressed that he had a grasp on the entire game. Frank must have had tremendous vision to start with to be a great hitter, but he could tell what was going on in the bull pen. If someone was screwing around, I'd get a call saying, "What's going on down there?" He didn't miss a trick, and I was unbelievably impressed. There were a lot of managers I was familiar with that wouldn't even be aware that there was something going on in the bull pen. And that spring there was so much flying—the media was in town constantly because of his being the first black manager.

OSCAR GAMBLE: He was very straightforward. Frank wasn't afraid to tell anybody what was on his mind. That first spring training he had us running a lot, made sure everybody went into second hard, broke up the double play, hustled all the time. He taught us to play the way he played the game. He had an open-door policy with the players. His door was always open, but you couldn't say anything once you walked in. I'm just kidding. Frank would talk. Actually, I went in there and told him I wanted to play more. I remember he took the time to explain that we had a lot of players competing for playing time. We had all those outfielders, plus Rico Carty and Boog Powell. That was a lot of bats to get into the lineup. And you have to remember Frank was a player-manager that first year with the club and he could still hit the long ball.

FRANK ROBINSON: They talk about Earl Weaver and Jim Palmer, and this and that. Earl allowed that. There was no ill feeling there. That's the whole thing about it. Earl didn't have a doghouse. As soon as you finished what you had to say, or he said—or screamed at you—what he had to say, when you walked out of that door with him, it was over. It was forgotten. You know it's the old saying, that kind of sums up those Oriole teams, "Get the ship into port and you worry about who the heroes were later."

DAVE GARCIA: I liked [Robinson] because he was fair. One time [as third base coach] I had Rico Carty thrown out by about 20 feet at home plate. The fans jumped on me about how stupid I was and when I came into the dugout I told Robbie I didn't think he was going to pinch-hit for [Ed] Crosby [the on-deck hitter] and I was going to gamble that the cutoff man was going to make a bad throw and I was wrong. He threw a perfect throw and Rico was out. The pitcher who was going against us that day was pretty good and Crosby was a pretty good little shortstop, and I didn't think that Robbie would pinch-hit for him, and I gambled and I was wrong, but he understood. He said, "Okay, Dave." He was fair with me.

RICO CARTY: He is a great man and he knows about baseball, but when it comes to playing, Frank wants the players to play exactly like he used to play.

KEN SINGLETON: Frank coached me in Baltimore in 1979. He had tremendous knowledge of the game, but he was a tough guy to get to know because he was very tough and old school.

DENNIS ECKERSLEY: He liked people to play hard. Was it a talent thing? I don't know. How could it not be? When you're so good like that, it's got to be tough for such a great player. When you're a Hall of Fame–type player watching guys in mediocrity it's got to be difficult. I think it's difficult for anyone that's great to turn into a manager.

OSCAR GAMBLE: He was straight with me and everyone on the club. He did have to learn how to deal with umpires. Frank could be pretty vocal when he got on them. Except some of those umpires could hold grudges and they could take it out on our team. Frank realized that, though.

DAVE GARCIA: He did some very unusual things. Like signs. He would give me a hit-and-run with nobody on base. We had signs that were different. If my right hand touched my left wrist and my left hand touched my right wrist, the right hand on the left wrist was for a ball one [count]. My left hand on my right wrist was for a ball two [count]. He could give me a squeeze with 1-and-1 on the hitter but only if there was one out with a man on third base but we didn't have anybody on base. The reason that he would give me signs ahead of time was because years ago managers would have a player stand between them and the other dugout so they couldn't see the manager giving the signs.

JEFF TORBORG: We spent hours talking—the coaching staff and Frank were so close . . . Frank as much being a boss as he was a friend and, in a way for me, a mentor, and yet I felt really good that I could help him from the standpoint of pitcher-catcher relationships and communication, signs and all that. He was not familiar with that. But that was the only part of the game he was not familiar with. To give you a bit of an idea, he was the best I've ever seen at picking up a pitcher's pitches just by some mannerism—he might have the glove open, or he would bite on his lip, or he would go back further over his head on his windup on his breaking ball. Frank once took his hat off and looked through one of the little holes, and I said, "What are you doing?" He said, "I can focus on the pitcher this way." In one particular game we beat Frank Tanana 2–1 when Tanana was throwing really hard. Frank hit two home runs to beat him. He knew what was coming.

DENNIS ECKERSLEY: We went down to play a Triple-A team in Toledo. I think this is '76, you know, during like April or May—might have been April, because we always had a day off and you got to go down and play a Triple-A team. So we go down there to play, and what had happened in spring training, and don't hold me to what the date is, a guy named "Bullet" Bob Reynolds [right-handed pitcher], he had gotten sent down, and Frank Robinson didn't tell him.

OSCAR GAMBLE: He had been Frank's teammate with the Orioles and now he was with Cleveland. He wasn't getting people out so Frank sent him out to Triple-A to rehab.

DENNIS ECKERSLEY: [Reynolds] was holding a grudge in Triple-A. Frank was DH-ing in the exhibition game in Toledo and people were chatting among themselves, "Bullet is going to be pitching and he might throw one at Frank." So the situation that came up, there were guys on first and third and Frank was up—something like that, first and second—and [Reynolds] threw one way high over [Robinson's] head. Not even close. Next pitch, wherever it was, he flies out, sacrifice fly. So, the guy on third tags up and scores. Frank ends up jogging to the third-base dugout and "Bullet" Bob Reynolds is in the middle of his path on the way back. He says something to Frank and Frank drops him. He drops him in the middle of an exhibition game. I'm talking *dropped him!* Boom! Bang! Gone! The crowd went—it was crazy. It's not like the benches emptied. This was the manager. Reynolds had no business doing that. He asked for it. I'm telling you I was in awe.

OSCAR GAMBLE: Frank charged the mound and we ended up having a fight with our own Triple-A team. So in his own way, Frank could be as fiery as Billy Martin.

Like Earl Weaver, Robinson had some very heated confrontations with umpires. Unlike Weaver, though, Robinson was convinced there was a racial component to his treatment by the men in blue.

FRANK ROBINSON: I still feel that way to a certain extent. I brought a lot of it on myself because I wanted to really protect my players. I went overboard sometimes. Stayed out on the field, arguing too long. Arguing about some of the things I shouldn't have even been out of the dugout on.

DENNIS ECKERSLEY: Part of it was brought on by him. He didn't let anything go. I think we're talking about a chip on his shoulder. I thought that they stuck it to him after he didn't let it go. If he had turned the cheek a couple times— to me looking back, easier said than done because I'm just like he is. If you let it go, maybe be a little more lenient: "Whatever. The next time." But, if you're too hard from Jump Street, it's a battle. It just got really bad. It's almost like, "We're getting screwed here, just let go." I thought I was getting screwed because I was a rookie. I threw balls right down the middle they were calling balls. And I never changed. I was always pissed off. All I can say about Frank is he backed me every time I got pissed. So it wasn't like he was dissing me. He never dissed me. If anything I felt the same way he did. He was easygoing to begin with. My picture of Frank is this intense, competitive guy who was a relentless battler. That really rubbed off on me. That's what I took away from being with Frank for three years. I was yelling at umpires. I thought, "That's the way it goes." It was almost like he had a chip on his shoulder. And that's what rubbed off on me. I carried that my whole career. When I talk about that chip, I think it's taking everything personally. It helped me, too. It gets to you after a while, because it's hard to do all the time. Sometimes, it's not personal.

TWO JOBS IN ONE

While Robinson is famous for being the first manager of one kind, he is also one of the very last of another. Playing managers appeared to be a thing of the past by the time he took the reins of the Indians. The list of men who had taken on the dual role since the end of World War II was under 20. The last playing manager who had maintained anything like a starting role with a club was Lou Boudreau with the Indians of the late '40s. The last traditional player-manager at all had been Robinson's old skipper from the Orioles, Hank Bauer, who had done both jobs in 1961 while with the Kansas City A's. Robinson's hiring signified a resurrection of a seemingly defunct practice in this regard. Once he stopped playing in 1976, only three player-managers followed: Joe Torre with the 1977 Mets, Don Kessinger with the '79 White Sox, and Pete Rose of the '84–86 Reds.

JEFF TORBORG: Frank handling that "first African American manager" position, and playing at the same time, is incredible to me. I don't know how he did it. And he was successful doing it. And people don't realize this, but that year he had a bad shoulder. And that year there was a game when he pinch-hit himself against Terry Forster, throwing probably 100 mph. And by God he wins the game with a home run, only because he knew how to do it, and it amazed me. I honestly can't remember having the feeling that Frank was feeling the pressure.

OSCAR GAMBLE: That was one thing, though. I don't think it was a good idea for anyone to play and manage. It's too distracting, plus you have the pressure of having to sit someone to play yourself. That's tough. But Frank would always say, "Don't worry. I'm going to get you in there." And he would.

DAVE GARCIA: Robbie would DH once in a while and he would pinch-hit, and one time the count was three balls and one strike and he was batting. And he looked at me as though I was supposed to give him a take sign or go ahead and hit. All I did was shrug my shoulders. I said, "You're on your own." He would give me signs to give to the players. When he was batting and he looked at me with 3–1 as though he were saying, "Dave, do you want me to take this pitch or you want me to go ahead and swing?" And I'm not stupid. He's the manager. I just shrugged my shoulders, which meant "do whatever you want." Robbie smiled.

What his players probably didn't know was that he was being pressured to put himself in the lineup more often. After all, the bulk of his Indians salary was being paid to him as a hitter. General manager Phil Seghi [who died in 1987] often suggested to him that he play more. It created an unusual dynamic that rubbed one of his players the wrong way.

JEFF TORBORG: With every manager there's going to be one or two guys that they don't see eye to eye with. Frank had problems with Rico Carty. Rico was an interesting guy that I had known since he was a rookie; we played against each other in the Texas League when he was with Austin in the Rangers organization. Frank, I think, even suspended Rico at one point.

But I do know one thing, that most of the players loved Frank. First of all, they respected him, but Frank was good. You knew where you stood with him, and if you realize that the sarcastic needle he had was his way of making his points and having fun with you and you didn't take it with a thin skin, you were okay. The players I remember commenting about it really liked Frank and appreciated him. Frank was a guy who was so intense, so emotional, so fiery, yet one of the things he would do if he had a run-in with a player, if he could, he would sleep on it. Now I had a tough time doing that. You don't want anything to fester. You want to address it now. But if there was something that really hit him up, he would wait, and his comments to you would be made with a clearer mind when you sat down to discuss the thing. I mean he would address it if there was a problem during the game right away, but he wouldn't keep it going, if you know what I mean. Watching how he handled a game was interesting: He was very respectful of his pitchers. You know a lot of times great hitters don't like pitchers and don't respect them and won't give them enough time to warm up, don't understand that there's a psychological side to pitching as much as physical. Frank understood that. Frank was really patient with his players. I had seen patience personified in [Dodgers manager] Walter Alston, but to see it from someone who was on another level in terms of competitive nature was really something.

RICO CARTY: When I had trouble with Frank Robinson was when I used to tell him, "Frank, if I hit, leave me in the lineup. Don't take me out." But he always took me out if I went 3 for 4 or 4 for 4. The next day I'm out of the lineup because he wants to play.

FRANK ROBINSON: Rico got to the point I guess he thought I was taking playing time away from him, because I would DH once in a while. I guess he thought that. But that would never enter my mind because I was a manager first, player second. I only inserted myself in the lineup when I thought it was the right thing to do. Just like any other manager would use me.

DENNIS ECKERSLEY: He and Rico didn't get along. It was kind of threatening a few times. Frightening! These were big guys.

RICO CARTY: I got hurt one time in Detroit. I was coming around third base and I hurt a hamstring. And Frank says that he didn't see it, and I asked him, "How didn't you see that?" He called a [team] meeting, I think, the following day and I didn't go because I was taking therapy. And he says, "Well I told you we had a meeting." I said, "I was taking therapy." And he told me, "You know some day I'm going to fine you a thousand dollars." "For what? I said I was hurt." He said, "I didn't see you get hurt." That's the type of fellow that Frank Robinson was. Then [he did fine me and] I said it on the radio and TV and the fans paid my fine. They sent in $3,500 and it was only a thousand. But he didn't want the fans' money, he wanted my money. And that was me and Frank: we had a problem.

DENNIS ECKERSLEY: His being a player-manager didn't really affect me. He DH-ed a lot, so it wasn't like he was playing first base and he came out to the mound to talk to you. It was normal.

JEFF TORBORG: I saw Frank break the handle off the bat in a spring training game. Billy North threw his bat—he didn't intentionally throw it at Frank—but it ended up rolling under Frank's folding metal chair in Rendezvous Park in Mesa. Frank just grabbed the bat, turned around, and hit it on the back of the chair. He broke the handle of that bat about three inches above the knob just as clean as if you used a saw. And we all went, "Whoa!" I would have been pounding on that chair and it wouldn't have broken. He just broke that handle off. He was a tough competitor and yet he defended his players, and I think they appreciated that.

One of Robinson's triumphs as a rookie manager was plucking Eckersley, a 20-year-old fireballer, out of spring training and making room for him on the big-league roster. Robinson used the future Hall of Famer in relief first, sometimes long and sometimes just to get a batter or two, before putting him in the rotation for good in the middle of May.

JEFF TORBORG: I remember putting the club together and we wanted Dennis Eckersley to break camp with us that first year, and Phil Seghi saying, "He's only just finished Double-A, I really think he's not ready." We said, "He's ready. This kid can pitch, we were going to use him in the bull pen." I remember Phil Seghi saying, "If he doesn't get enough work we're going to take him back to get enough work." And ironically he moved from the bull pen into the starting rotation, and was as good as we had. He had a different angle delivery. He threw from the side, and he had that cocky way about him. He'd strike someone out and he'd almost shoot him with a gun from his fingers. He was really sure of himself. But he had nasty stuff. And as a young kid, besides being sure of himself, he had good command. In fact he pitched a no-hitter later on [May 30, 1977, against the Angels].

DENNIS ECKERSLEY: Frank was pretty good at handling pitchers. First of all, you have to have patience. He wouldn't take the ball from you. He gave you an opportunity. For me as a young pitcher, I think he had a plan for me. He brought me along real slow. Then again, the first time I ever pitched in Cleveland he brought me in with the bases loaded and the hitter was Hank Aaron.

Robinson was also very high on another 20-year-old, Rick Manning. For two years Manning looked like he would justify Robinson's intuition about him. Both his rookie and sophomore seasons under Robinson were filled with great promise. Instead he was felled by injury in 1977 and never again played as well. He became one of those rare players who are better at 21 than they are in the prime years of 25 to 29. He was out of the majors by the age of 32 and currently works as a broadcaster for the Indians.

ROBINSON'S LEGACY

As a manager it was Robinson's fate to inherit a series of troubled teams (here are each club's record in the season before he took over):

1974 Indians: 77–85
1980 Giants: 75–86
1987 Orioles: 67–95 (0–6 in 1988)
2001 Expos: 68–94

In each case Robinson got the team over .500 within a season or two of his hiring. In Cleveland, Robinson's teams finished 79–80 in 1975 and 81–78 the next year. But on June 19, 1977, the Indians, 26–31, fired Robinson and replaced him with Torborg. (By the way, here's a bit of trivia that's anything but trivial: Robinson is not only the first African American manager in the American League; he's also the first African American manager in the National League—with the '81 Giants.)

JEFF TORBORG: '77, when I was hired to replace Frank, was one of the most difficult times that I've ever had. It was on a Saturday morning that I was asked to come in to see the owner [Ted Bonda] and the general manager before a game we had that evening. And they told me that they were going to replace Frank and they wanted me to manage. And I told them they were making a mistake. Five times I turned the job down. I said, "Ted, I've said this to you so many times; you're really making a mistake. You can't do this. This man is really good." So finally, on this morning—and ironically we had won two in a row—they were replacing him. We had a doubleheader on Sunday against Detroit, and before the game I gave in to them. But before I even went to the press conference I went to see Frank, and I said, "Frank, I don't want your job." And he said, "Jeff," and we're sitting there facing each other, and I can see the tears well up in his eyes, and I know they're in my eyes, and he says, "It's not my job anymore. They're taking the job away from me. If you think you can do it and want to continue what we've tried to do here, take it." I looked at him, and . . . it was the most difficult thing. Just thinking about how he had spent all those off-seasons preparing for this job, and here I am, never having made a lineup out on any level, taking over from this man who meant so much to me and the change in my career. So now listen to what he did: I take over, and that day in the doubleheader we beat Detroit two games. I didn't do a thing: Just sat there and watched two complete games. I think it was [starters] Wayne Garland and Jim Bibby; I didn't even have a change of pitcher. We go from there to Toronto—we may have won eight in a row. And Frank called me every day, during the day, before those games to help me. "What are you gonna do? What are you thinking?" This is a guy who could have very easily thought that I had worked behind his back for that job, who could have felt so hurt that a guy he brought in took over for him in the job that he really wanted so badly and prepared so diligently for. He called me at least 10 days in a row to help me. We didn't play anywhere near as well in the years I managed the Indians as they did for Frank. And in fact, years later, Ted Bonda came down to me, I was either coaching with the Yankees or managing the White Sox, and Ted Bonda came down to the railing in West Palm Beach and said, "You were right, I should have never fired Frank Robinson." And I looked at him and said, "Thanks a lot. Now you tell me."

BILL DAUGHTRY: Once Frank left Cleveland, he kept getting jobs where the expectations were low. Think about it. In San Francisco he took a team that everybody said was too old and didn't have enough pitching and he made them contenders. Frank did that, but at the start of the season no one gave them a prayer. When he went back to Baltimore, the Orioles were one of the worst franchises in the majors. In 1988 they finished last and lost almost 110 games [107]. And over the winter they did next to nothing to improve the club. Everybody expected them to flop again, but Frank brought them in second and almost won the division. That was one of the greatest managing jobs ever. Just look at that roster. It was Cal Ripken and Phil Bradley, past his prime at the end of his career, Mickey Tettleton hit more than 25 home runs and that was pretty much their offense—that was about all the offense he contributed. They had maybe a four- or five-man lineup in a DH league. And their pitching staff was pretty much guys you had never heard of before and haven't heard much of since. But Frank almost went to the World Series with that club. And then they gave him the Montreal Expos–Washington Nationals job. Same thing again: a club with zero expectations. I don't think that's a coincidence.

DAVE GARCIA: Next to Jackie Robinson, Frank Robinson has done the most for the black ballplayer. One of the reasons I say that is because he stayed in the game. He stayed in the game as a manager, he managed in the big leagues, he was my coach when I was managing with the Angels for the 1977 season, and I remember I was talking to him and I said, "Do you want to manage in the big leagues again?" And he said, "Sure." Then I said, "Well you've got to be in uniform, then." So he came to be my batting coach.

DAVE ANDERSON: Frank is one of the great *baseball* men of all time . . . maybe the last. He's done it all, contributed to the game in so many ways. I mean he was the commissioner's office "dean of discipline." Who better than Frank to handle situations with knockdown pitches!

BOB COSTAS: Frank has had a tremendous and varied career in baseball. He's a citizen of the game. Frank had some success as a manager, but I don't think the point of his baseball career is to compare him to Earl Weaver or Tony La Russa or Whitey Herzog. He's a clear first-ballot Hall of Famer as a player who also had an estimable career as a manager and a front-office guy. It's a very full baseball life.

FRANK ROBINSON: I had a lot of people saying, "Oh you're going through the same thing that Jackie went through." I say no. I mean it sincerely. I mean it to this day. It wasn't even anything close to what Jackie went through. Because times had changed. Different atmosphere, different situation. Afro-American players were playing in the big leagues. They were playing on teams. They were stars. A lot of them were some of the highest-paid players in baseball at the time. Times had changed. But it was still a focus to compare a black manager, unfairly, I thought. On account that every move you made was being scrutinized, anything that went wrong was magnified. Even when things went right, it was second-guessed. It was tough in that respect. Other than that, it wasn't even anything remotely close to what Jackie did.

BOB COSTAS: After Frank, it wasn't exactly a torrent [of African American managers] as it was after Jackie Robinson broke the playing color line. With managers it was a trickle and it went in stops and starts. The graph didn't move smoothly upward.

BILL DAUGHTRY: There have been great strides since Frank broke in. Cito Gaston and Dusty Baker winning helped that along. But in the case of Cito, you still had to ask some questions. Here's a guy who wins back-to-back World Series with the [Toronto] Blue Jays—only Joe Torre has done that in the last 25 years—and after he is dismissed by Toronto, his phone suddenly stops ringing. Davey Johnson won one World Series and parlayed that into how many jobs? Jim Leyland won a World Series in Florida, one World Series, and he was always in demand, you heard him mentioned for jobs every year, until he took the manager's job in Detroit. And if Joe Torre were fired at the end of this season, there'd be a line outside his door of general managers with job offers. Cito didn't receive a call and that gets me.

Of the managers who have won World Series titles since 1970, a number have retired or passed away without managing again for another team. This group would include Sparky Anderson (1984 Tigers version), Tom Kelly, Tommy Lasorda, Danny Murtaugh, Whitey Herzog, and Dick Howser. Ten of the Series-winning managers have gotten other opportunities after losing their job with the team they took all the way. This group includes Dick Williams (four other clubs), Davey Johnson (three), Lou Piniella (three), Billy Martin (five, depending on how you count his various Yankee incarnations), Jim Leyland (two), Dallas Green, Tony La Russa, Chuck Tanner,

Alvin Dark, and Sparky Anderson ('75 and '76 Reds version). The managers who have won world championships and have never gotten a shot with another team is a much smaller group: Joe Altobelli, 1983 Orioles; Bob Brenly, 2001 Diamondbacks; and Cito Gaston, the first African American manager to win a World Series.

BILL DAUGHTRY: Frank laid the groundwork for all of that. But I'm still waiting to see more. I'm disappointed that Chris Chambliss, who played with [Willie] Randolph, has never gotten the shot he deserves after winning two minor-league manager-of-the-year awards with two different organizations, Detroit and Atlanta. The best major-league offer he can get is batting coach. And when you ask why, you hear nothing but excuses. Here's where I get insulted. Don't tell me you didn't hire Chambliss or Willie or whomever because they didn't interview well. We all know that Buck Martinez is a charming guy and you can see how polished he is on TV, right? I bet he gave a great interview when they hired him to manage the Blue Jays. How long did he last in that job? Baseball has to drop its tunnel vision and look past the interview process to what a man has done. Until then, it still has some work to do.

In 1975, the year that Frank Robinson became manager of the Indians, 25 percent of major leaguers were African American. As of this writing, African Americans made up 8 percent of big-league rosters. Naturally, Robinson is looked to for his opinions about the causes of and solutions to this issue.

FRANK ROBINSON: Well, there's no one answer to this problem. It didn't happen overnight. It's been slowly going in this direction for a number of years. It hasn't gotten anyone's attention to the extent that, "We've got to do something about it." Everyone has a solution to it, and an opinion on why. But I think baseball is doing some good things. Setting up youth academies across the country. Getting youth involved in baseball again. That's one step in the right direction. There are other things that have to be done. They say that the Afro-Americans are going into football and basketball. Well, I say to myself, Is that all the athletes we have in this country now? Playing football and basketball? When I was coming along, baseball was the ugly sport. The glamour sports were football and basketball. Nobody watched us play baseball in high school. People say, "A lot of scouts don't go into the inner city. Baseball is played more in the suburbs now. A lot of schools have dropped baseball programs, so the kids don't have a chance to play anymore." There are a number of reasons. People who would like to see more Afro-Americans in baseball are going to have to listen to the people that are not playing the game. The young people of this country. You've got to get into the inner cities and find out their reasons why they are not playing. And try to correct that, and then get them interested in the game itself. People say the game is too slow. Baseball is not played by a clock. It's not a boring game. I don't have one answer. I think it's time for the people who can make a difference, to try and find out what the problem is, and try to correct it. It's going to take a while. It's going to take years.

CAL RIPKEN'S STREAK

Featuring

RICHIE BANCELLS: Baltimore Orioles trainer responsible for keeping Ripken fit during the streak.

THOMAS BOSWELL: Award-winning *Washington Post* writer and author who covered the Orioles and Ripken for almost the entire length of the Iron Man's career.

JOHN EISENBERG: Baltimore *Sun* columnist who was also present for much of the Ripken canon.

MIKE FLANAGAN: Cy Young Award winner and All-Star. Won 141 games as an Oriole and later became the team's executive vice president of baseball operations.

LOU GORMAN: Longtime baseball executive who was assistant farm director for the Orioles in 1964 and '65 and farm director in '66 and '67.

DEREK JETER: Perennial All-Star and a member of the new wave of bigger, slugging shortstops that followed in Ripken's wake.

JAMIE MOYER: Winner of more than 200 games in his long major-league career and a Ripken teammate from 1993 to '95.

BILLY RIPKEN: Cal's younger brother had a 12-year big-league career, mostly with Baltimore but also with the Cleveland Indians, Detroit Tigers, and Texas Rangers.

CAL RIPKEN JR.: Orioles Hall of Fame shortstop who broke Lou Gehrig's record of 2,130 consecutive games played, extending the mark to 2,632.

ALEX RODRIGUEZ: Another member of the new shortstop wave and the youngest man to enter the 500-home-run club.

BUD SELIG: Purchased the Milwaukee Brewers in 1970 and became baseball's de facto commissioner in 1992, a title he formally assumed in '98.

KEN SINGLETON: Orioles standout from the mid-'70s through the beginning of Ripken's big-league career.

MIGUEL TEJADA: The Orioles' current All-Star shortstop, Tejada played in 1,152 consecutive games, the fifth-longest streak in major-league history, before a broken wrist sidelined him on June 22, 2007.

EARL WEAVER: Ripken's first major-league manager. Weaver had already won six divisional titles, three pennants, and a World Series when Ripken's career began in 1981.

HAD CAL RIPKEN JR. spent a week in Tahiti each summer instead of showing up at the ballpark every day, he would have still had enough credentials to be enshrined in the Hall of Fame. Yet it is because he *did* show up at the ballpark ready to play every single day that he will be remembered. The night Ripken tied Lou Gehrig's consecutive games-played streak was voted as the number-one Most Memorable Moment in a 2002 poll sponsored by Major League Baseball. Ripken's record-breaker beat out countless other events that had many qualities it lacked, namely the spontaneity, unpredictability, and drama inherent to the pursuit of a pennant or world championship. Ripken's passing Gehrig was, after all, a moment that was all but inevitable for weeks, if not months or years, in advance, yet it was more memorable to fans than any other. Why?

One possible explanation is that at the time Ripken's streak began, Americans were being told that, when it came to hard work and productivity, other portions of the industrialized world had passed them by. It was something of a national joke that one never wanted to buy an American car made on Monday or Friday for fear that lazy American workers, their minds wrapped around their weekends, had done a slipshod job assembling it. The United States, once alone at the top of the industrialized heap in the wake of World War II, was being constantly reminded that this was no longer the case.

It also seemed as if baseball players were an embodiment of this situation writ small. Their salaries were increasing exponentially and they had just cut short the 1981 season with a strike. In spite of the fact that statistics show that players moved around just as much in the old days as they did in the wake of free agency, the perception existed that the new breed of ballplayer was an itinerant mercenary who would pledge his sword to the highest bidder. Where, it was asked, were the Gehrigs of old, the men who played for the same team every day of every year until only an act of God could take them away from the game?

CAL SR.

Into this stew of self-doubt and retribution came Cal Ripken Jr., a player whose team was also a link to his family. Ripken's father, Cal Sr., who died in 1999, was a baseball and Oriole lifer. He had joined the Baltimore organization in 1957—three years after it escaped St. Louis. He was an outfielder who also caught and played third base with Phoenix in the Class C Arizona-Mexico League. Except for a five-day period in 1959 when he was released by the organization, he had been with it ever since. His managerial career began with Leesburg of the Florida State League in 1961. Cal Sr. was 26 at the time.

JOHN EISENBERG: When he was manager, he wasn't necessarily in his element. He wasn't a man of many words. He did what he could to give the press what they needed. His strength was in instruction. I would say he was better suited for that. Out of all the roles he had with the Orioles from manager on down to minor-league farmhand—the bottom to the top— everything: coach, instructor, third-base coach, minor-league manager—he was at his best as an instructor. He could teach the fundamentals of baseball better than anybody who came

through that system. That's how the Orioles used him most effectively—as an instructor of young players to teach them to
play the game right. I think Cal Jr. came to embody that. The
guy he had the most influence on was Cal Jr.

BILLY RIPKEN: We were taught from an early age to
respect the game. The clubhouse was where Dad worked. If
we were at the game, Dad moved fast after the game to get us
home. We'd just hang by his locker.

JOHN EISENBERG: His teaching style was no-nonsense,
too. He wasn't a screamer or a yeller. He wasn't one of these
guys who would yell, "Dammit, what the hell were you thinking?" It was like, "Let's just get it right." It wasn't personal,
like, "You moron," it was very much the art itself. It offended
him to see things done poorly. In spring training there was a
little half-diamond next to the cramped stadium in Miami.
That was church for Cal Sr. more than anywhere else. They
would spend hours on infield plays like the pitcher covering
first on a ground ball to the right side. There's a reason why the
Orioles were so fundamentally sound for all those years. It's
because they would just do that over and over and over again.
It bugged him when it wasn't done right. When a veteran player
would do it wrong, he wouldn't yell at the player, he would just
say, "Come on, let's get this right." He had a very patient way
of detailing what the fundamental was and what the footwork
should be and where the glove should be. He just knew the
game and the little details that make the difference in many
baseball plays. He would do it over and over every year. The
Orioles were a veteran team throughout much of his tenure but
that didn't stop him from starting from scratch every year with
some pretty basic stuff.

LOU GORMAN: Cal Sr. worked with me for the better part
of six years. He was one of my minor-league managers in Aberdeen, South Dakota. They were called the Aberdeen Pheasants.
And he ran the club and was kind of a legend in that town. Everybody there loved him. And Cal Jr. used to go with him to the

ballpark all the time. Cal Jr. was a little guy then, and he'd play catch and field with his dad. He'd come to the ball games all of the time with him. Cal Sr. was a devoted, hardworking, marvelous baseball guy. Loved the game, knew the game, great teacher, great instructor, great working with kids, just one of those kind of employees that you wish you had a hundred like him.

RICHIE BANCELLS: Cal Sr. was a coach when I first came to the big leagues, so he meant an awful lot to me. As a young athletic trainer for a major-league team, he kind of took a liking to me, took me under his wing, showed me a lot. The one thing he taught me is about the game on this level. What he taught me baseball-wise made me not just a better athletic trainer, but a better baseball athletic trainer. I kind of valued that. Any time I had a question, he spent the time to explain it to me. He would teach me from a skill standpoint, he would show me that if the guy possessed skills and did things the right way, it also kept a guy from injury. The prime examples that I can use were his sons, Cal and Billy. They both were so proficient turning the double play around second. They did it right the baseball way, but they also did it in a way that kept them away from injury.

EARL WEAVER: On my way up [through the system] he followed me up the ladder. In 1968, when I took over in Baltimore, I inherited coaches George Bamberger, Billy Hunter, Vern Hoscheit, and Charley Lau. I lost Charley Lau and I brought Cal Sr. up to the Orioles as a bull pen coach. When Billy Hunter went to Texas, I sent Sr. to coach third base.

BILLY RIPKEN: Earl always had that aura about him. He was all business. He could be an intimidating presence. He'd go right to his office and get to work. If Cal and me were around, he'd see us and say, "Just what we need, another Ripken in here." The Orioles club was truly a tight-knit family.

LOU GORMAN: Cal Sr. was one of those guys that everybody in the organization loved. They knew he was a great instructor, hard worker. He managed Aberdeen all those years with me. Weaver loved him. And when Weaver became the big-league manager he ended up putting Cal on his coaching staff. Cal spent his entire career of 30, 35 years or more as a Baltimore Oriole. Just a marvelous man, a great example for Cal Jr.—for both boys—because he loved the game. He knew the game. You couldn't find a more solid, qualified baseball guy. And he was a very good teacher and great with young players.

JOHN EISENBERG: Cal Sr. was the definition of old school. He was tough, he was like an old piece of leather. He didn't tolerate any sort of nonsense on the field. Baseball was church for him. He was physically different than Cal Jr. He was a wiry, strong little guy. He was not big. He was very fit even though he smoked and he drank.

THOMAS BOSWELL: He was as color-blind as anybody of his baseball generation could be. Everybody from Eddie Murray on down felt that Cal Sr. was the stern but caring surrogate father. In some sense Cal thought he shared his father with an awful lot of other baseball "children." I think that was one reason he was so pleased when he got to spend time around his father when he got to the major-league level.

BILLY RIPKEN: The best time, as a kid, was hanging out at the minor-league park. When Dad was coaching with the Orioles, it was different. There were a lot of things that kids couldn't do at the big-league level. We participated in a summer [baseball] program, in [Baltimore], as we got older. But we spent less time hanging out on the field at the Orioles games.

THOMAS BOSWELL: My favorite story about Cal Sr. comes from Jim Palmer, who played for him at Aberdeen, where there were long bus trips. One day the bus broke down on a hot afternoon. They were waiting around with time to kill and Cal Sr. had his golf clubs in the back of the team bus. He sent the players out 500 feet into an open field and they shagged golf balls. He was driving them out there and they were having a ball. They had a great time.

KEN SINGLETON: Cal Sr. was the best coach, the hardest-working coach I have ever seen. You could say to him, "Rip, I want to take batting practice at 3 o'clock in the morning," and he would be there ready to throw to you. That's the kind of guy he was. Great person and a great coach.

JOHN EISENBERG: He grew tomatoes in his backyard. In 1995 I went to his house to talk to Cal Sr. and [his wife] Vi Ripken about Cal Jr. and he spent most of the time showing me the tomatoes he'd grown. These were plum tomatoes, and he was every bit into the details of growing tomatoes as he was into the details of baseball. These were huge vines of tomatoes in long rows. He talked lovingly and in great detail about his tomatoes. I don't think I got what I needed for my story but I sure learned a lot about growing tomatoes.

THOMAS BOSWELL: The kids' nickname for Vi Ripken was "Brave Mom," because she was the one who would take care of their cuts or deal with snakes on the property because Cal Sr. was away every summer. She's where Billy Ripken gets his humor. It was a classic marriage from that period: stoic, tough-guy dad and feisty, funny, brave mom. You couldn't have a more classic, clichéd Aberdeen, Maryland, marriage from that period and you couldn't have a much better marriage.

BUD SELIG: Cal Ripken Sr. was a great teacher. He taught Cal not only how to play, but how to act.

LOU GORMAN: I think Cal Jr.'s dad impacted him greatly. When he realized what kind of a guy his dad was, what kind of a baseball man he was, how committed he was, how dedicated he was, how he went about his job, how he worked with young players—that had to impress Cal, there's no question. I think the great things about Cal—length of seniority in the game and the records he obtained: number of games—I think he got that from his dad. His dad's whole life was baseball and I think that rubbed off on Cal Jr.

YOUNG CAL

Born August 24, 1960, in Havre de Grace, Maryland, Cal Jr. was raised in nearby Aberdeen as part of a baseball family. He has two brothers (Fred and Billy) and one sister (Elly), but at an early age Cal Jr. proved to be a breed apart.

BILLY RIPKEN: He always had a different motor than everyone else. We'd play basketball in the driveway, and everyone had enough . . . tired, hungry, ready to go home. Not Cal. He just loved to play. He didn't need anybody to push him. He wanted to go to the park every day.

MIKE FLANAGAN: He was about 14 years old, but you could tell this kid has got a chance. He hadn't hit his growth spurt yet. He was a late bloomer. It was a question about how big he was going to get, how he was going to develop physically.

EARL WEAVER: I remember him at the park. Maybe 12, 13 years old. Sr. hitting him ground balls at shortstop. When he got a little bit older, maybe 15, 16, Sr. began throwing him batting practice before the games. He was hitting 'em in the stands at Memorial Stadium at that age.

BILLY RIPKEN: My first memories go back to '72, '73, and '74, between seven and nine years old. Dad managed in Asheville, North Carolina [Double A], for those three summers. I remember playing catch and hanging around at the ballpark. We had our family dinner at 2 p.m. [on days of home games at night] with Dad. Then we would ask to go to the ballpark. Jr. was 11–13 years old. He would take infield before the game with the club.

MIKE FLANAGAN: First time I saw him, I think it was 1974, in Asheville, North Carolina. He came down when school got out. He was always hanging around the ballpark. You could tell how much he loved to play.

BILLY RIPKEN: I can remember Cal taking batting practice as a 15-, 16-year-old and hitting balls into the stands.

KEN SINGLETON: I remember Cal Sr. bringing Cal Jr. to Memorial Stadium when he was 16. He took batting practice and was hitting balls in the bleachers. I remember thinking that whoever got him was going to be pretty lucky. What people forget was that at that time, there was a question whether he was going to be a shortstop or a pitcher. He was a heck of a pitcher. But when I saw that power . . .

RICHIE BANCELLS: As I recall in Bluefield, he wasn't a big kid by any means. He came out of high school and showed up at Bluefield and he was thin and wiry, just not that big. He was just like all the other kids. You really didn't know at that time. He was just out of high school, still kind of working on his skills. He would throw balls away. But it was kind of between his Double-A years and his Triple-A years, especially for me because I had gone from Bluefield to Rochester and he caught up with me in Triple-A. It was during that time where he was growing and maturing, both physically and skill-wise as a baseball player. It was kind of in that era in Rochester in the high minor leagues where you could see that this guy might be something.

JAMIE MOYER: His upbringing made him go and motivated him. I never had the good fortune of knowing his dad, but I heard a lot about what his dad stood for, how he respected the game and believed it should be approached and played. Cal took that and moved on with it. Billy, too. Cal respected the game, his teammates, and his opponents.

EARL WEAVER: As a rookie, he was a field general. Once again it has to do with his background, the baseball family. He just took charge right in the center of the field—directing cutoffs, rundowns.

A ONE-OF-A-KIND SHORTSTOP

While Ripken was not necessarily an original—there had been a few tall shortstops before him and a few who could be relied on as power mainstays in a lineup—he was certainly out of the norm. While games such as basketball and football are driven by assigning the correct position to the correct body type, baseball is not immune from it either. The instinct is always to have the player's position conform to the physical parameters previously defined by his predecessors. Thus the instinct was to get Ripken away from shortstop.

EARL WEAVER: The Orioles originally wanted to sign him as a pitcher out of high school. His parents didn't want him to be a pitcher in professional baseball. The best athletes [in high school] are always playing pitcher and shortstop. Hey, Mantle was a shortstop. But that would have been a terrible waste of speed not having him in the outfield.

ALEX RODRIGUEZ: The thing that stood out for me was how big he was, that he played shortstop, that he played every day, and that he hit in the middle of the order. Those were all things I aspired to do as a young player. He had a huge impact on me personally.

THOMAS BOSWELL: Everyone on Earth saw that he was a prototypical third baseman except for one person: Earl Weaver. Only Weaver had the imagination to see that Bobby Bonner needed to go and that Ripken would work as a shortstop. I was covering the team then as the daily beat writer and there is no question that this was 100 percent Earl Weaver against universal indifference or mild hostility to the idea from everybody else in baseball. Nobody else thought Cal Ripken could play shortstop. Period. Anybody who says differently wasn't there and is wrong.

BILLY RIPKEN: Earl had the authority. He wasn't a first-time manager. He knew how to handle the front office, the media. He said, "He's my guy," and moved Cal to shortstop. He believed in him as a shortstop.

EARL WEAVER: Your typical shortstop, I think of the great ones . . . Pee Wee Reese, Phil Rizzuto, Ozzie Smith. That's pretty much the average size. The two guys I think about (in relation to Cal) are Joe Cronin—he had home run power—and Marty Marion, who was 6'2". Cal was graceful playing the position like him.

DEREK JETER: Just the fact that he was so tall . . . I wasn't accustomed to seeing that. Usually shortstops were smaller guys. Cal really paved the way for the taller shortstops.

ALEX RODRIGUEZ: I don't think he was a new kind because he's one-of-a-kind. I don't think it was a trend by any means. But it definitely gave me a lot of hope as a young player that I could play that position.

EARL WEAVER: It would take a Marion or Cal one or two steps to get to a ball that others would take four steps to get to.

DEREK JETER: There were some guys who changed the position and turned it into an offensive position. You had guys like Alan Trammell and Barry Larkin. But Cal was the biggest one. He had the most influence on changing how people viewed the position.

EARL WEAVER: He was very smooth playing the position. He just seemed to glide around, like Marty Marion. He could really make it look easy. I think being from a baseball family had a lot to do with it.

THOMAS BOSWELL: Earl grew up watching Marty Marion. His nickname was Slats, so it gives you the idea he was tall. Mark Belanger was tall for a shortstop. Most shortstops seem to be that scrambling, point-guard kind of athlete. Jim Kelly, the Buffalo Bills' Super Bowl quarterback, was a big guy. Listed at six-foot-four-inches, 220. One day he was in the tunnel at Camden Yards and standing behind Ripken, and Ripken was much bigger. Kelly turned to a friend, pointed to Ripken's back, and just rolled his eyes as if to say, "This guy is huge!" He had NFL size. I saw him play against a Washington Wizards team in a celebrity game. He was matched up with a 6'7" forward. The rest of the game had a real charity feel to it but these two were trying to dunk on each other and beat each other off the boards. Ripken clearly felt he was as good as this NBA guy and was going to show him. I'm surprised they didn't end up in a fistfight. He played like a wild man.

MIKE FLANAGAN: There was never any question among the players. Maybe the public or the media. We all thought that he could handle the position. He was such a great competitor, terrific athlete, tremendous instincts.

EARL WEAVER: I mean, to be a shortstop that could give you 20 to 25 homers—what a bonus.

DEREK JETER: There were whispers about moving me away from shortstop when I struggled in my first year, but nobody ever approached me about it. Did Cal's success help with that? Yeah, probably. When I was younger, people used to say I was too tall to play shortstop. But I would always say, "Look at Cal Ripken." That was my first line of defense.

ALEX RODRIGUEZ: There was no talk of moving me. I came up as a defensive shortstop. That was my strength as a player at that time. The question was whether I was going to hit enough. Watching Cal gave me a lot of confidence and everything starts from there. I could always say, "If he did it, why don't you give me the chance?"

EARL WEAVER: He had the advantage of signing as a 17-year-old and coming up through the system. He was a good base runner; no Mickey Mantle speed but he knew how to run the bases. He made a lot of errors in the minor leagues but a lot of that has to do with the [poor quality] of the fields.

THOMAS BOSWELL: When he moved from third base to shortstop, Earl Weaver told him, "Just make the routine plays. Field the ball, throw it to first. If the guy's out, he's out. If he's safe, no problem. I don't care—just do it at your normal speed, don't be rushed." What Ripken discovered over the years, it almost never happened that people beat him.

JOHN EISENBERG: He was raised in a baseball tradition and the tradition was that shortstop was a fielder's position. He very much saw himself as a fielder first.

THOMAS BOSWELL: My feeling was that he was always a better defensive than offensive player. He was certainly aware of it. With the exception of Ozzie Smith and a very small handful of acrobatic shortstops that played in the last 50 years, Ripken was at the very top of that second group of shortstops. What made him unique was that from the time the ball hit his hands until the play was completed, I'm convinced he was the best shortstop of the last 40 years. He had the softest hands on ground balls. He charged the ball like a third baseman, because that's how he began. He was wonderful going out for pop-ups and catching the ball over his head. The ball barely seemed to touch his glove when he turned the double play at second base. He was wonderful at turning the double play because he was so big. He would throw sidearm and underarm and make the runners who were sliding into him dive out of the way, and if any of them dared to try to take him out, he simply landed right on top of them and, at 225 pounds, they didn't tend to come into him spikes-high anymore.

CAL RIPKEN JR.: As a shortstop I was big and didn't have the same physical range as someone like Ozzie Smith, but I was able to figure out through positioning and anticipation in counts and situations how to cover certain parts of the field as effectively.

MIKE FLANAGAN: He had the ability, like Mark Belanger, of not playing the same hitter the same way within the same game, making the adjustments along the way. I remember him making a play in the hole on a hitter and then on the hitter's next at bat he sent one back through my legs. I figured it was in center field, and there he is . . . right up the middle, making the play. As pitchers, me and Scott McGregor were pretty good fielders. We got in the habit of letting balls go so we wouldn't tip a ball. We'd pull off and let the sure hands have it. You didn't know how good he was 'til he wasn't there. There was a spring training game where I pulled off a ball and forgot he wasn't there. Base hit.

THOMAS BOSWELL: You could literally watch him for years and never see a ball clank off his glove. His intuition for where hitters were going to hit the ball, his study of where they would hit, his understanding of how pitchers pitched to their defenses so that he could play according to the pitcher and the pitch. He was constantly cheating, by the time the ball was off the bat he was already in full motion, which meant that he had anticipated and was not just on the balls of his feet but was often leaning and breaking in one direction or another because he would see as the pitch was being thrown, he could just sense that any ball hit was either going to be to his right or to his left. That's a remarkable gift you almost never see. He has one of the strongest shortstop arms of contemporary times. He didn't show it off. Early in his career you saw it a lot. As his career went along it was almost like he was saving his arm the way John Havlicek saved his legs. He said he never dunked on breakaway layups because he wanted to save his legs and play a very long time. When Ripken unleashed a throw from the hole, it was like a grown man playing on a Little League field. It seemed like he could practically reach out and hand the ball to the first baseman—especially if you were sitting down the third-base line behind his throw.

JOHN EISENBERG: He was not the superquick, agile little shortstop, but he approached it very scientifically. You could listen to Cal Ripken talk about each pitch and where to position himself and how many factors he brought into it, and it was just unbelievable. He wouldn't actually say, "Well, the wind is blowing S/SW at five miles per hour, this batter tends to hit the ball to left-center, but the last time up he hit to right-center against the left-handed pitcher who was throwing 80 miles an hour as opposed to 87. . ." He just instinctively factored in 10 different things and would position himself on the field four steps to the left or three steps to the right or whatever it may be. For a shortstop that's critical.

THOMAS BOSWELL: Look at the five directions you can go for a ball on defense: because he was tall, nobody got up higher on a line drive; because he'd been a third baseman, nobody charged slow hops better than he did or had softer hands to finish that charging play; because his arm was so strong, he could go deep in the hole as well as anybody; because he was confident on balls over his head he was as good on pop-ups as anybody I've seen and was courageous going into the box seat railing along the third base line; on plays to his left there were people who were better, but Cal was very good at getting the ball, whirling, and getting a lot of steam on the ball. He compensated by not having to throw across his body.

JOHN EISENBERG: It was a scientific approach and he was right a lot more than he was wrong. He would be in position. He maybe didn't have the speed that many shortstops had, but he was always in the right place and he had great hands. If he could get to the ball, it was in the glove. And he had a very strong arm. He wasn't a guy with a gun, but it was very strong and very accurate and he rarely threw it away. Brooks Robinson, who is considered the ultimate fielder in Baltimore, did not have the greatest arm, but he knew how hard he had to throw and he always beat the runners by half a step. Cal was, in many ways, the same. He was not a hot dog as a defensive player. He was no-nonsense: get to the ball and beat the runner—that's all you have to do.

THOMAS BOSWELL: He studied footwork at shortstop far more than any shortstop that I'm aware of. Because of his size, he felt that he couldn't be freelancing and improvising with his feet. He felt that a bigger man would move more slowly, so he really had to choreograph every move.

CAL RIPKEN JR.: I often wondered, the type of player I was, if I wasn't so switched-on by the other parts of the game, would I have been able to focus on myself a little bit better, and would that mean I would have better at bats and be 100 percent engaged in my bat as opposed to thinking about what happened the inning before. I can't remember who told me that sometimes they thought that knowing too much could be a burden. You knew the patterns around you and you were constantly thinking. I guess if you didn't have that you wouldn't be burdened and you'd be able to focus on your areas [of excellence]. But I always thought it was a gift and one that you have to manage. By understanding the game and by being in the middle of the infield, you can see the different pitches and the thought processes and where things are going. You could add any situational aspects of the hitter and the counts and that part of the game, and that gave me a better understanding of what to do. I only knew how to play the game that way. I was able to have better success and maximize my talent just by knowing the game.

DEREK JETER: I tend to learn a lot from watching, and from Cal I learned a lot about positioning yourself for certain hitters. I think that helped him out and I paid attention to him. I'm more a learner by watching.

BUD SELIG: I have a lot of memories of Cal, because we played Baltimore a lot. We had a young shortstop by the name of Robin Yount. They were very much alike. Robin's in the Hall of Fame and Cal is about to go in. I knew his father through a lot of Baltimore/Milwaukee connections. I remember in '82 we battled right to the end of the season.

ALEX RODRIGUEZ: I first met Cal in 1992, spring training in Bradenton. Johnny Oates was aware of me from a story he had read, and called me over to say hello and he called Cal over. He came right over and spent three or four minutes with me. It was terrific. I was just a kid. He was better than I even hoped he would be. He was great to me.

JAMIE MOYER: It was amazing how much he was into a game. He could be in the dugout having fun, flicking sunflower seeds into a cup, then all of a sudden say, "What do you think this guy will start me with first pitch next at bat?" That told me he was into the game. He was a cerebral guy who loved the game.

JOHN EISENBERG: He definitely changed the expectations of what a shortstop could be. I think Robin Yount changed it too. The prototypical shortstop was Mark Belanger. It was a position where you put your best fielder and you didn't worry much about what he contributed with the bat. It's hard to believe that that's how people viewed the position. Cal came along and had some power. He changed the expectation: A shortstop could be a big, powerful guy. A shortstop could hit home runs. A shortstop could bat third or fourth in the lineup. These things were unheard-of. Earl Weaver thought it was like stealing. He said, "This is the opportunity to get production out of a position that no one has gotten before, and it's just a bonus. You've already got a good-fielding shortstop and he can hit, too."

JAMIE MOYER: He taught me a lot about pitching. He was a student of the game. I remember sitting with him on the airplane or in the dugout and he'd say, "Why did you throw that pitch in that situation? You had him set up for this and you did that. I think you could have done this and been successful." I always listened. He knew what he was talking about.

MIKE FLANAGAN: Cal always talked about the advantage of coming up with veteran pitchers [on the Orioles staff]. It allowed him to cheat up the middle, or toward the hole. Depending on the pitch selection and with the veterans, they could execute more consistently. He also talked about how much more difficult it was later on, with a younger staff.

THOMAS BOSWELL: Earl was ahead of the game on a lot of numbers issues. He understood that certain hitters hit certain pitchers better than others, so he was constantly going to his statistical book to see if anybody had better stats against a pitcher. He would bat Mark Belanger leadoff against Nolan Ryan because he hit Ryan very well despite the fact that he couldn't hit anybody else. He was always looking to steal something in that sense. He was always looking for a statistical advantage. He realized much earlier than other people in baseball that offense was slotted by position, that everybody looked to the corner positions for power. He appreciated that you could steal extra offense. One was by platoon, which Casey Stengel had already innovated. John Lowenstein and Gary Roenicke were a wonderful tandem for Earl and in another one of his pennant-winning years Jim Dwyer and Disco Dan Ford. The other way was to have people who were better-than-average hitters up the middle. Cal was the most extreme example, but he also did it with Elrod Hendricks and Andy Etchebarren at catcher. Some years they'd hit 20 home runs combined. He also had Davey Johnson and Bobby Grich at second base. He was 10 years ahead on shortstop.

THE STREAK BEGINS

Very few players—even the most famous—get to be remembered for more than one thing—and that's if they're lucky. A large majority of ballplayers do not have a signature accomplishment or moment to which they can lay claim. Even many of the Hall of Fame's luminaries exist in this light. Because of this, the memory of their careers among the masses is often not as strong as their skills should have warranted. That Ripken does have a signature achievement should not detract from his overall credentials, just

*as it did not detract from the man whose consecutive-games-played record
he broke, Lou Gehrig. While neither was a one-trick pony, each of their
careers is defined by one of the more innocuous columns in a stat profile:
the G for games played.*

*On April 29, 1982, the Baltimore Orioles and Toronto Blue Jays played
a doubleheader. Ripken played in the first game and, as he had done in a
previous doubleheader on April 17, he sat out the second game. The Orioles
played five more doubleheaders that year, but there were no more nightcaps
off for him. In fact, there was no more anything off for a long time. Ripken
was not only starting every game, he was finishing them, too. He played
every inning of every game until his father, who had by then become the
Orioles' manager, decided to give him an inning off at the tail end of a
blowout loss to the Blue Jays on September 14, 1987.*

*The Streak, of course, had its critics. In 1993 Bobby Bonds said that by
never taking a day off, Ripken was hurting his team and putting personal
goals first. It was a comment that Ripken would learn to deal with.*

CAL RIPKEN JR.: Dad took the responsibility as the
manager of the team; he thought it was right to take me out.
In actuality when I came off the field after the Blue Jays had
hit 10 home runs—a record 10 home runs in a game—we were
getting beat very bad in Toronto and I think Dad in the weeks
coming up to that thought it was a little bit of a burden that
I constantly had to respond . . . because people started thinking
about [my] playing every inning, every game, and there was a
certain burden of managing that kind of thing when you came
to a new city.

When I came to the bench he asked me, "What do you think of
taking an inning off?" and I immediately posed the question,
"What do you think?" He said, "I think it would be a good
thing." And I said, "Fine." And I sat on the bench. Having
played in the field so long, naturally, I felt out of place. I didn't
know what to do. I didn't know if I should go in and take a
shower or should I sit on the bench. It was a weird sort of feeling and I guess I'm the kind of person that analyzes everything,
so when I was sitting in the hotel room later, I started to think

back on it, reflect a little bit, try to understand it so I could deal with it. There was a certain kind of numbing feeling and I thought as an exercise to put it behind me I would sit down and start to put my thoughts on paper and see where it would go. Then it was done and you start over.

The irony is that I don't think I missed another inning the rest of the season. I think it was just a point to break it and see if that would help. I trusted my Dad's judgment as a father and I trusted my Dad's judgment as a baseball person. I think if any manager would have come to me and done the same, whether it was Joe Altobelli, Earl Weaver, or Frank Robinson, I think the same response would have happened. Looking back on it, I think people were making a bigger deal out of it than I was; I was just playing.

MIKE FLANAGAN: He was very into the game—all the time. He had an acute curiosity about the game. He always asked a lot of questions. He wanted to know everything. The veterans in the dugout would tell Earl Weaver, "Please put the kid in the game! He's driving us crazy on his off-days." Then the Streak got started.

CAL RIPKEN JR.: My approach to the game was not to break Lou Gehrig's record of consecutive games; it really was a culmination of many one-game streaks. I always felt that you came to the ballpark and my responsibility to the team was to be available to the manager to play. That was something that Dad gave me, and it's one of those things that principally I felt was right. I felt that every player in the big leagues should come to the ballpark and if the manager wants you to play and puts you in the lineup, you try to perform as well as you can and try to do the job. That was the approach I had. When I think back I'm tickled to death that people recognize you and remember you and think that you made a positive contribution to the sport in any way. It could be the simplest way; it could be the biggest way. So if someone wants to remember me for the sake of the Streak, or if someone wants to remember me as the shortstop that was big and had a little success and maybe contributed to the change of the mind-set of the middle infield, that's great. If they want to remember me as a gamer or someone that had a joy for the game, I think that the important thing is that people remember you at all. I know I said that in some way, shape, or form in a speech and maybe the speech at the end of my career I might have said that, but I truly believe that I went out and tried to do the best I can, and I'm comforted to know that I had a very fulfilling, long career and I played the game the way my dad taught me and I thought was the right way.

JAMIE MOYER: Obviously the Streak stands out, but he never discussed it. I don't think that's what made him go.

CAL RIPKEN JR.: I was blessed to have the managers I had, starting out with Earl Weaver, who saw the bigger potential in me and kept me in there even when I struggled.

RICHIE BANCELLS: People always bring up injuries, but the most amazing thing to me about the Streak—and it has to be pure genetics—is just the illness part. He never really got sick. There were times he maybe didn't feel great and he may have had a fever, but he never got the plague or anything.

JOHN EISENBERG: First there was the innings streak. That in itself was remarkable. Very early on it was established that here was a guy with some amazing instincts in terms of longevity and amazing ability in terms of being strong and fit and able to battle his way through the rigors of a long season. He got thrown out of a game in the late '80s at Memorial Stadium for arguing balls and strikes. The umpire said, "It was like throwing God out of church." Once he got over a thousand and he kept going people were saying, "He's not coming out," because this was getting into historic proportions.

CAL RIPKEN JR.: Once I got my feet on the ground with the managers who wrote the name on the lineup, no one ever discussed with me, "Do you want to play today, do you want to have an off-day, do you want to stay in the game?" So as the games played out, almost without realizing it, I was playing every inning of every game. I think Joe Altobelli had some small comments with me in the middle of the '83 season. But I was so early in my career, I was learning all the time, I was having a great deal of success and we were winning. I think that was the first year that I played every inning of every game. Joe would say, "How about an inning off?" I really thought I would lose my feeling at the plate if I was hot and I really wanted to fix something if something wasn't quite right, and it wasn't a big deal. I didn't think missing an inning would give me this renewed rest and I would feel better the next day, so I think Joe mentioned it once very briefly and that's the way it was and from that point on the managers just kept writing my name in the lineup. The Streak was formed, looking back, not because I went in there and said, "I have this goal: I want to play every single day," the Streak was formed because the managers kept writing my name in the lineup and I responded and played well enough to be considered for the lineup every day.

MIGUEL TEJADA: For me it wasn't hard to play so many straight games because, like Cal, I love the game. And when you have a good year, that's when they want you to be on the field all the time. I wanted to show people how much I love the game, and that's why I kept playing every day. I never really thought about it. Every time I woke up, I just thought about the game I had to play. That's why I played so many games, because I just thought about that one game that day. I didn't think about playing 162 games.

MIKE FLANAGAN: There was so much on his shoulders. He handled everything with such grace and class. He was really a role model for the ages. Such an amazing talent, a great combination of intelligence and athletic ability.

THOMAS BOSWELL: The most interesting thing about the Streak to me was his complete indifference to physical injury. He wrestled and horsed around in the clubhouse more than any player on any team that I saw. When Albert Belle came to the team he was considered the big huge bully. Now Cal had gotten into wrestling matches with every other big guy that was ever on the team and they would throw each other around and flip over sofas. He just locked up with Albert Belle and he was so strong he just threw him around the room. He had natural strength. Not weight-lifting strength. I think of it as farm strength where you don't just lift things in repetition that develop the muscle in one precise way but where the act of being a farmer or logger forces your body to move in every conceivable position. I think one of the reasons Ripken was such a wonderfully reactive player at shortstop and never got hurt was that he had natural, old-fashioned 19th-century farm strength—frontiersman strength, logger strength—that was not developed through weight lifting, which may overdevelop some muscles but not develop every muscle around it that compensates for the strength of that muscle. I think that's the difference between the player that concentrates on weight lifting as opposed to Babe Ruth and Lou Gehrig, who you always saw chopping wood in the off-season.

CAL RIPKEN JR.: Certain comments were made during the course of the Streak by different people who didn't understand the full context of me playing every day. When [Bobby Bonds] made that comment I remember thinking that everyone is entitled to their opinion. To me it was never about personal goals or selfishness. That was the easy way out for everyone to talk about. It was about the ultimate feeling that you had a responsibility to the team. I think selfish would be taking yourself out when your team needs you the most. I've seen over the years many times, when you're facing a tough pitcher and things weren't going well, you would dodge Roger Clemens or Randy Johnson or somebody else in that particular game, and I always looked at that as being selfish. You protected yourself and let the rest of the team battle against the hard challenge.

JAMIE MOYER: There were always skeptics who, whenever he wasn't hitting, said he should take a day off. But you see guys who are not in streaks have the same results. That's just the game. I thought it was great.

BUD SELIG: The one thing you want from your players is the ability to play every day. They've got to play through injury. They've got to play through pain. Because, after all, when all is said and done—and a lot of division and pennant races are very close—you need your best players in there. And I don't think there was anything selfish about it. I know people have been critical and I think it's not only unfair, I think it's just plain wrong. And, who would they rather have had playing shortstop? That's the question I would ask those people. I think it shows an unselfish attitude that you wish all of your players had.

MIGUEL TEJADA: Oh my God. I can't believe it because for me, I've been through a lot of stuff: pain, losing streaks, injuries. I can't imagine how Cal Ripken did it. That's unbelievable.

CAL RIPKEN JR.: In some cases people looked at it and said I was selfish for wanting to play every day, but I always thought that the approach of every baseball player should be to go out there and play. To put yourself out there to be able to play. That's all the Streak was, just a collection of times coming to the ballpark and saying to the manager, "Okay, I'm here if you need me." The manager wrote my name in the lineup and I responded the best I could. In a lot of ways, if you look at how the Streak was born, the Streak wasn't born from personal goals or personal power over the managers. The managers wrote my name in the lineup consistently and all I did was play. It wasn't until later on . . . of course when you're struggling offensively or maybe your team wasn't looking good and people were looking for reasons why, that seemed to be a subject that would come up. To me it was always the same. You came to the ballpark and there was a game to be played and in your role as a baseball player, you came ready to play. The role of the manager was to say, "Which team can I put out there that gives the best chance to win today?" If the manager wrote my name in the lineup, I played. I always tried to focus on what my approach was and I knew that my approach was honest and true. I knew there was no other agenda that I had, and other people interpreted that in any way that they wanted, but that was their opinion. They didn't have the benefit of knowing what I knew.

KEN SINGLETON: That was a big question in Baltimore, and I personally don't think so. He was always the best choice to be out there, even if he wasn't feeling well. I don't think he ever hurt the team.

CAL RIPKEN JR.: I was only criticized when either I wasn't hitting real well or the team wasn't doing real well. Sometimes I couldn't understand why people would offer up opinions at certain times, but I always respected the fact that people had their opinions and the way I dealt with it was to understand that their opinion doesn't make it true.

JOHN EISENBERG: I don't think that sitting out a game or two would have helped his batting average. I don't think a day off or two days off would have made a difference. Toward the end, the Streak became larger than life at a time when the Orioles were sort of off course as a franchise. Maybe there was too much attention on that as opposed to the condition of the team. It became such a monster—it was larger than the team. I don't think taking a day off along the way would have changed anything about Cal's career, but if you're looking for a negative, it did become bigger than the team. They needed to be more worried about what was going wrong and they weren't. They were relieved as an organization that they still had Cal out there. He was popular and they knew he kept people happy when the team was falling apart.

CAL RIPKEN JR.: For me, I didn't feel that I was imprisoned or I was obligated to continue. I always thought it was my job and the job of everyone else to come to the ballpark to play.

I felt an obligation toward the end, people had made all these plans, there was an expectation and I felt there was a little pressure for me to actually get to the finish line. But I never thought there was a finish line.

CLOSE CALLS

On his way to playing 2,130 consecutive games, Lou Gehrig was no stranger to pain. During a game in 1933 he was knocked out by a pitch but recovered and kept playing. He had no official pinch-hit at bats after 1925. He did, however, nearly miss a game the next year with a bout of what used to commonly be called lumbago—a lower-back problem. Since the team was playing in Detroit, the Yankees cleverly listed him at shortstop and had him bat leadoff, keeping the streak alive with that one at bat. But Ripken was starting and, with a few scattered exceptions, finishing every game. For him there would be no such single-at-bat cleverness. But that doesn't mean everything always went smoothly.

Ripken avoided injury for the most part, but there were several times that he thought the jig might be up. He says that a herniated disk in 1997 was the worst injury he ever played through, although he had long since passed Gehrig by then. The Streak also nearly came to an end very early in its fourth year, when Ripken sprained his ankle on a pickoff play in the second game of the season.

CAL RIPKEN JR.: It was so alien to me because I never set out to have a consecutive-game streak. That wasn't my focus and it's not how you're supposed to play the game. So if you were thinking about those things then you'd be acknowledging that, "Yeah, I'm playing for selfish reasons, I'm playing for the Streak." But that wasn't the case. If you come back to the simple approach of what can I do to help us win today, and I'm here for that purpose, then you have to put yourself in the hands of a manager and that day's game. I can't imagine how one at bat at the start of the game would help your team win or pinch-hitting or something to extend it . . . you're compromising how the game should be played at some point during that game.

In 1985 we had a Wednesday-afternoon game, when I suffered a bad ankle sprain, and a Thursday off-day when we played an exhibition game against the Naval Academy, I believe, and then a Friday-night game against the Toronto Blue Jays. The ankle was a really hard thing to play with. But because it was a Wednesday-afternoon game I had the rest of Wednesday, all of Thursday, and almost all of Friday to get some of the swelling out. I had almost two full days to get the swelling down and to get used to it. It was still very difficult, I taped my ankle really tight and I went out and played. I don't think I could have played the next day. I don't think the swelling would have been down far enough. There was a moment where I came up with a guy on third base and two outs and hit a line drive off [pitcher] Jimmy Key's glove. It rolled behind the mound, in-between second base and the mound, and I had to beat it out to get the run in. I jumped to first base and I landed on my ankle in a hard way and it was pretty painful, but I was called safe, just barely.

RICHIE BANCELLS: Whether they play or not, it's ultimately their decision. That's the way it was with Cal. He just had this unbelievable ability that when he had a problem, he'd treat it and take care of it. But when he got between those lines and the bell rang, that seemed to be put aside and he'd play. The decision of should he play or not was left solely up to him.

JOHN EISENBERG: Richie Bancells was the perfect guy; very no-nonsense and as low-key as they come. He and Cal understood each other. There's no doubt that a lot of things contributed to the Streak and one of them was this relationship with the head trainer. I think Richie knew he had a special player on his hands who was capable of special things. I'm sure there were many cases where Cal showed up and said, "This is hurting," and Richie said, "Well, let's go to work on it." There was also an obligation. If Cal ever showed up Richie couldn't just say, "You're done." He never had to do that, and I'm sure he's probably relieved that was the case. It would have taken an unbelievable act for that to be the case. The guy played through a lot.

CAL RIPKEN JR.: A herniated disk in '97 was the worst injury I've ever played through. I couldn't sit down between innings. I had to kneel and stretch my back out to give it any sort of relief. It was a constant source of pain for about six weeks.

I remember being diagnosed with it and the doctor saying, "That's it [in terms of playing]." I asked him, "If I could play and bear the pain, would I do any further damage?" And he said "No." So I said, "I'm going to give it a try"—almost to the medical people's disbelief because that hadn't happened before. I remember playing and the nerve pain moved down my left leg and affected the electrical impulses to my leg and had my muscles firing in a certain way like I was always losing strength out of the leg, where I didn't have total control over it. At times it felt like I was gimpy and I couldn't move and I just felt like I wasn't stable. I remember I couldn't really stride out on it, so I shortened my swing a little bit, which probably had less power but I was able to hit the ball and I think I hit pretty well for average during that period of time. I was able to contribute pretty well offensively.

I remember being out at Oakland during a day game and I remember how much pain I was in; it seemed to get worse when I traveled from coast to coast. There was a slow-hit ball—full-swing bunt—and I came running over and I tried to reach down bare-handed and I felt very awkward; I felt like I couldn't stand up or I felt like I was going to fall on my face. So there was a brief moment where I thought while I was standing out there that this was ridiculous. I think I should just walk off the field right now, and walk into the clubhouse and that will be it. So I thought for a minute and said, "Get through the inning and see what happens." I led off the next inning, almost looking for some sort of indication offensively that I couldn't do it. I hit a line drive to left field on the first pitch—I got a single and I'm standing on first base and I said, "I guess it will be okay." There were certain moments where I had to push myself through, and I remember that being one because I had a moment of truth standing out on the field after the full-swing bunt single, and I felt like I couldn't attack that play. I asked myself what was I doing trying to go through this, and I had a moment where I could almost visualize myself walking straight off the field. In Oakland there was this little door behind the backstop that accessed the tunnel to the clubhouse, and I pictured myself opening that door and people asking, Where's he going? What's he doing? Disappearing without a word. It's funny that when you reach that moment and you're looking for some sort of confirming part, that maybe if I had struck out off balance on three pitches, maybe I would have walked into the clubhouse, I don't know. But the fact that I went there looking for some sign and hit a sharp single to left field, I guess that was the sign I was looking for.

Perhaps the closest call came as the result of a brawl with the Seattle Mariners on June 6, 1993.

CAL RIPKEN JR.: Chris Bosio had started the game for the Seattle Mariners and we had a couple of guys—Harold Reynolds and Mark McLemore—that tried to bunt on him, and I think that Chris responded by hitting McLemore in the leg and threw behind Reynolds. There was some sense in the dugout that we needed to retaliate. I wasn't involved in those sorts of decisions, I know Johnny Oates was the manager and I think Rick Sutcliffe was on the bench and Mike Mussina was our pitcher. I don't know what transpired or what was said, but I think Bill Haselman had hit a home run from the time before and he came back up. Mussina was trying to push him back off the plate and ended up drilling him. He immediately charged the mound, and I remember reacting and coming to the mound trying to help Mussina and protect him, and I think Paul Carey was the first baseman and he was down there already at the mound wrestling around and helping. I turned my attention to the Seattle dugout to try to stop them from jumping on top of the pile. I hadn't been involved in a whole bunch of those things, but once in the minor leagues I found myself on the bottom of the pile, and it's not the right place to be. So when I turned my attention toward the whole Seattle dugout—in a sense to put up a barrier—my cleats slipped in the grass a little bit and I was twisting at the same time and I felt a little pop in my knee and then I got hit with about 2,000 pounds worth of people and ended up on my back on the bottom of the pile, which is not where I really wanted to be.

JOHN EISENBERG: It was a huge brawl—all over the field. People swinging in a huge pileup. It took 20 minutes to clear it and he was in the middle of it, that's for sure.

CAL RIPKEN JR.: You had to fight to try to get back to a point where you felt protected. There were a lot of words and a lot of punches thrown in different areas that came across there. My adrenaline was pumping pretty good and I didn't feel much pain in my knee but I remember that sensation in slow motion like something had popped, and after it was all over, I came back to bat and I started to feel a little weird sensation. After the game was over I put a little ice on it and I thought it was just a strain of some sort. The next morning I woke up and I went to put my feet on the floor and start to walk and I couldn't put any weight on it. It really scared me because I thought something was really seriously wrong. I thought it was something so seriously wrong that I called my parents up and tried to give them a heads-up, I gave them a warning and said, "Looks like today might be a day that I won't be able to play. I don't think I can do it, I think it's that serious."

My parents live 45 minutes from my house and in exactly 45 minutes my parents showed up at my house. My mom sat with me, my Dad was there. A couple of times I was icing it and treating it. A couple of times during the in-between periods, I would walk down the driveway to try to test it to see how it would feel and slowly but surely I got a little more feeling in my knee and I went to the ballpark and tested it out. It's kind of funny how these things work out; I decided I would give it a go.

RICHIE BANCELLS: I was concerned because at the time he was playing shortstop and he had sprained the medial collateral ligament in his knee. That ligament is going to be involved moving laterally. That was my biggest concern, whether he was going to be able to move laterally at shortstop as well as when he rotated when he hit and ran the bases. I was concerned that he could injure it further being out there. He called me quite often, but never at 8:30 in the morning during the season. I remember it distinctly. He called and my wife answered the phone and said, "Cal is on the phone for you." I thought, This is odd. I was just waking up. That is the first that he had mentioned the knee. He didn't mention it the day of the fight. But he said, "I think I hurt my knee in that fight last night." He said it was sore. We started turning the wheels. I called our orthopedist at the time and we had him see him and then come to the ballpark early to start treatment. We went from there. I actually thought there was no way that he'd play.

JOHN EISENBERG: They shielded [the press] from this, but Cal woke up with his knee all blown up. Somehow, by hook or by crook he played. He had an amazing ability to play through little nicks and cuts and bruises and twists and strains where you couldn't believe he was out there.

THOMAS BOSWELL: I'm the guy who broke the story about how the Streak almost ended. I went over to him and said, "I can't believe that son of a bitch Bosio didn't break your leg yesterday when he tried to clip you." Bosio was just a headhunter as a pitcher and it was a vicious thing to do. I had the binoculars on him when it happened and he just appeared to clip Ripken and maybe even deliberately tried to injure him. You can't prove it, but it sure looked that way to me. Cal gave me this funny look and I said, "Did he hurt your knee?"

RICHIE BANCELLS: After treating it, treating it, and treating it, I took him into the hitting cages and I was rolling balls to him side by side to see what he could do in lateral movement that would represent what he had to do at shortstop. There were times we were doing that where I thought, God, I don't know if this is a good idea. I don't know if I feel comfortable with this. I explained all the risks to him, but someway or another, the closer it got to game time, the more it looked like it was going to be all right and he was more comfortable with it. He actually did say, "Well, I'll play the game. Let's treat it after the game."

CAL RIPKEN JR.: I remember thinking maybe I'll play one or two innings before I'm tested, but sure enough it was the first hitter and he went right to the play that's going to cause you the most problems. Very few times in my career have I thought, don't hit me a ball, or I really don't want to get a play, but in the very first inning and on the very first hitter there was a two-hopper through the hole with a topspin. What that represents to the shortstop is he's got to go to his right, catch the ball, and plant really hard with his right leg to throw back across the diamond to first base. I remember doing it instinctively and naturally and made the play fine.

THOMAS BOSWELL: He told me he had told his wife earlier in the day that he couldn't play, and she said, "Can't you just pinch-hit?" to which he replied, "You too?" Meaning, "You also think I'm about the Streak? You don't understand that I just play because I can play. That's my job. I come, I play—I'm not doing it for the Streak." It was a real *"Et tu, Brute?"* moment.

CAL RIPKEN JR.: If there was ever a point where I had to test it immediately, it was in that moment, and I planted my knee and put all my weight on it, threw accurately to first base. Then I thought if I can do that, I can continue to play. There was pretty good pain associated with it and it took a while, by playing through it, to heal. Maybe it would have taken less time if I didn't do anything on it, but I was able to compete, I was able to play, I was able to perform, and I got through that.

JAMIE MOYER: You'd hear something in the clubhouse, "Is he going to play?" Then, all of a sudden, he's healed! He was amazing. I think he was able to stay so healthy because he worked so hard. He worked hard after games and he still would sign autographs until 12:30 or 1:00 in the morning. I remember I'd shower and eat and be on my way home and there would be lines of people near the players' parking lot waiting for his autograph. He'd sign until they all had one.

Within three days of the brawl with the Mariners and the near-end of the Streak, however, Ripken was mixing it up again.

THOMAS BOSWELL: There was a game where Terry Steinbach was catching for the A's and a pitch hit Cal in two different spots. It hit him on the arm and then on the helmet as it went by and Ripken didn't say anything. He just went to first base. Later in the inning there was a hit to the outfield on which he had to decide whether or not to score. He came around third base and he just obliterated Steinbach with a forearm to the catcher's mask. He knocked him out of the game. He never looked back and ran straight into the dugout. It was absolutely deliberate and it was absolutely revenge. After the game he still had the marks from Steinbach's mask on his forearm.

CAL RIPKEN JR.: Well, I didn't [compromise to protect myself] in all those years; I didn't really give it much thought. I know I played every game and I thought that if you didn't play hard you were increasing your chances of getting hurt. So you needed to play as hard as you can and play the right way and that would insulate your injuries because you would always be ready for the unexpected. I guess the collision at home plate came after I was hit. I was hit on a 0–2 pitch, I think, and probably was a little perturbed when I was hit and so I was more determined. I didn't equate the two, the knee with the collision.

RICHIE BANCELLS: During the knee thing and during the back thing, there were times I thought in the back of my mind, Gosh, it really would be better if he didn't do this. With the knee, I was always afraid of risking further injury. But along with that, the aspect and terminology of *Should he not play?*, at this level, that's up to the ballplayer. I can have concerns about the risks and I always express those risks to the ballplayer—what I think could happen if they go out and play with a given injury.

THE RECORD FALLS

One of the most amusing things to appear as Ripken neared Gehrig's record was a list of the many offbeat reasons why various players had missed games during the course of Ripken's streak—everything from Tony Gwynn missing a couple games after he smashed his thumb in the door of his luxury car (while going to the bank, of course) to Wade Boggs being sidelined after straining his back while pulling on his cowboy boots. It illustrated how every player is just one mistimed door slam (or in the case of pitcher Mark Portugal, felled by food poisoning, one bad serving of mahimahi) away from being out of the lineup. Ripken played in his 2,130th consecutive game on September 5, 1995, tying Gehrig. He was set to break the record the next night. For an event that was utterly foreseeable, it managed to generate an atmosphere of incredible drama.

CAL RIPKEN JR.: It was very spontaneous, a celebration in the middle of the game, which is rather odd. And I know there was a building-up about a week before and I thought that the numbers on the warehouse [at Baltimore's Camden Yards] were an extraordinary idea because it really provoked a buildup and a feeling. I remember the first time they turned the numbers down on the warehouse [counting the games of the Streak], nobody was really sure what that meant, and the song that came on and the emotions that poured out because it made you go back and think about your whole career and how you got to that point. I think it's probably very similar to what you witness at the Hall of Fame. I saw Eddie Murray and Gary Carter go there and their whole career flashes before them and they start to think who was instrumental in their success and getting them to that point and it seems like an emotional journey. A lot of people cry and they break down acknowledging all the people that were important to them. In that brief moment when the numbers started turning down, it made me take a snapshot all the way back. The actual September 6th day, there was no way anyone could have said this is how it's going to play out, where people are going to clap continuously for 22 minutes . . . in and out of the dugout trying to say thank-you in the best way you could and then have that move to a lap around the ballpark, it was all so spontaneous. Really once you went around the whole stadium, I was really concerned about having the game interrupted and we really owed it to have the game continue. It wasn't fair to the pitchers, it wasn't fair to the players, but once I got around past the California Angels and into my family, I could care less whether the game started or if it was completed at that point. It was that special of a moment. I don't think there was any one thing that I can say was a total surprise, but there's no way you could have planned it out or thought it was going to turn out a certain way; it unfolded in a very nice way.

MIKE FLANAGAN: I was in the dugout, as pitching coach. It was incredible watching him go through it. He never pandered to it. He was the same guy, playful in the dugout, wrestling with the clubhouse kids. I think I would have worn a suit of armor. Instead, he was always open, never guarded, stayed animated; seemed to enjoy it.

JAMIE MOYER: It was a very exciting day. [President] Clinton showed up. The Secret Service and the dogs came through the stadium. That was cool. I thought the Orioles did a very tasteful job of celebrating it.

CAL RIPKEN JR.: As a personal human moment, the September 5th and September 6th celebrations were one of the best you could ever have. To really fully understand that, when I think back on September 5th and September 6th, there were a lot of these interactions personally. My favorite was looking up and communicating with my dad through my eyes. There was a lot of meaning when he was there. He was in some cases pushed away from the Orioles and in Dad's way he would say, "Okay, if you don't want me anymore, that's fine," and he really didn't come back. There was some sentiment coming up to the celebration whether Dad would even show up at the ball game or not, and I guess down deep inside I was pretty certain that he would. So when I looked back up to him after I ran around the ballpark, he waved, and there were a few seconds where you're actually communicating through the eyes. No words were spoken, but it's a pretty powerful memory and one that is very special to me.

JOHN EISENBERG: Cal Sr. was in tears. The shame is he wasn't on the field. He'd been on the field for 50 years. But this was when he wasn't working for the team. He was up in a box in a suit. The moment where Cal Jr. looked up to him and pointed was an incredible moment because it was a real moment. That was as genuine a moment as there was that night.

EARL WEAVER: It was quite a thrill, it was unreal. The night he tied the record, I had the opportunity to throw out the first pitch. I got Cal to sign the ball and I have that with the Baltimore *Sun* photo in my house.

CAL RIPKEN JR.: Again, if you're looking at human moments in one's life or a compassionate moment or interaction with another human being, those particular days have to be the highest memory you can come up with. And even coming all the way around, I saw a lot of the people; I stopped to talk to them. I even remember talking to [Ripken's agent] Ron Shapiro down at his seats on the third base line and then coming upon the California Angels team. Again there are very, very few moments in one's career where the people that you're competing with are the peers within the game and you have an opportunity to have some sort of personal exchange. I always thought All-Star Games were probably the best for having a chance to meet the other great players and being a teammate with them for very brief moments. But in this particular case the California team was right there and I got a chance to talk to and embrace every one of them and they said certain things to me that were very good. I wish I could remember some of the words that Rod Carew said, but I was very touched.

BILLY RIPKEN: You could tell there was something really big going on. Such electricity. The game that night meant nothing. When those numbers flipped on the warehouse: 2 . . . 1 . . . 3 . . . 1 . . . You couldn't have written a better script. If you tried, it would have gotten fouled up.

MIGUEL TEJADA: I didn't see it, but they show it here [on the scoreboard] all the time. It's amazing. It really is unbelievable to see. I always talk to him when he comes here, but I don't talk to him about that. He just comes here for a little bit of time and I don't want to talk about baseball with him. I just want to say hi and talk about something else.

CAL RIPKEN JR.: I came along all the way down through the California Angels guys and then I came to my own family at the end by the screen and Billy was there and I shook hands through the fence with Billy with two fingers because you couldn't get your whole hand through. Said hi to the whole family who were there. And my two kids, who were very young at the time, I remember Rachel leaning down and kissing me on the forehead and I was soaking wet with sweat and she said, "Oooh Daddy" and pushed me away. Ryan was there and I showed Ryan the back of my shirt that they gave me that morning. When [I'm] looking back at that moment or over my career, I do categorize it very much into a professional accomplishment, which was more the World Series and knowing what that feels like, and then the personal, human moments where you might have had success and you're able to share that with the people around you. There's nothing greater than September 5th and September 6th in that regard.

THOMAS BOSWELL: It was one of the unique, authentic, and powerful moments of this whole baseball generation, and the thing that made it so special was that it was the same guy that signed all those autographs after the [1994 players'] strike.

This is a guy I saw signing autographs 90 minutes after a game in Kansas City at midnight in the fading light for the very last person in the ballpark. We used to joke that Cal had devalued his autograph to the point where someday it might not be worth anything on the autograph market because everyone in America would have one. We used to also joke that if the Streak were ever broken it would be by carpal tunnel syndrome.

CAL RIPKEN JR.: With the autographs it was a kind of a sharing of what was going on on the field and trying to bring that sharing of information back to the stands; the autograph was just a vehicle with which to do it. It kind of bridged the actual action and playing on the field and brought it to the fans who create the excitement and watch and care. The autograph has always been a part of baseball and I was always honored when someone asked me. I always enjoyed the interaction and I think I learned early on that when you see a kid's face light up, that was meaningful and there was a certain power to bring happiness at that moment. It really wasn't much of a price to pay by signing your name.

JAMIE MOYER: It was great to have been there, to have been a teammate, to have been a minute part of that, to watch him go through it. To see him break it was cool. My wife had the video camera out. Every once in a while we break out the video.

CAL RIPKEN JR.: When I first started running the laps after Rafael Palmeiro and Bobby Bonilla pushed me down the line, I first wanted to go out with the mission to get it over with, but then you start looking into other people's eyes and start seeing it as a one-to-one celebration as opposed to 50,000 people collectively clapping. I recognized faces; I recognized some people's names and the joy and feeling that came out of each individual person.

JAMIE MOYER: He didn't want to do the lap. It was very unscripted, but it was a pretty cool thing to do.

JOHN EISENBERG: Bobby Bonilla and Rafael Palmeiro pushed him out of the dugout because people kept cheering. I think Bonilla has it on camera somewhere.

BUD SELIG: I cried when he took that victory lap around the ballpark. We were coming off the strike and it was unbelievable. He just conducted himself so well. Breaking Lou Gehrig's record that night of September 6th, 1995, was legendary.

THOMAS BOSWELL: The trip around the perimeter was an extension of that same person who signed autographs until midnight in Kansas City. When Cal signed an autograph, he looked everybody in the eye and had a mini-conversation with everyone who came through. It was a very slow line. He told my son when my son was little, whenever you ask someone for an autograph, ask them a question so that you have something more than just a signature. Cal would ask the kids who came through: "Do you have anything you wish to ask me?" The only other athlete I saw who had a similar level of intensity and concentration while interacting with fans was Jack Nicklaus. So, when he went around that stadium, he just couldn't go around because when he looked into the crowd he really did know, if not everybody, at least hundreds of people. He knew their faces. He knew where they lived. He may not have known their names, but they were people he couldn't jog past. He had to go over and shake their hands because he knew them well enough that it would almost insult them not to. Cal wasn't pretending to pick out people to go over and shake hands with—which would be such a typical thing for some asshole in sports these days to do.

BILLY RIPKEN: When he took that victory lap, I had former players tell me that they just stared at the television, in disbelief, at the accomplishment, overwhelmed. That type of tribute, to me, that's what matters.

CAL RIPKEN JR.: It is very true that when you're in the moment, it's hard for you to understand what's going on around you because your focus is very much in the present, and it's counterproductive to think too far back or even think too far ahead, so you just keep plugging away. Now that I've been away from the game a little bit, I look back on all my experiences in two distinct categories. When someone asks me what is my favorite and best moment, without question it's being part of a World Series team and all the team accomplishments jump out right away at you. And that's not BS or anything else, it's a much different meaning when I caught the last out of the World Series and the feeling that comes over you . . . the sense of accomplishment, the sense of fulfillment, the goals . . . it's almost like a fulfillment of a dream. But when you go back to some of the individual things, I think the Streak, because it was celebrated as an individual accomplishment, I was always torn about that.

BUD SELIG: Baseball has survived everything. I believe that September 6th was really the beginning of the bonding of our fans to the sport again after all of the drama of '94. There were a lot of good things going on already, and the sport now is more popular than it has ever been. [In 2007, it] set another attendance record for the fourth straight year. It was a seminal moment in baseball history and certainly brought the fans and this sport closer together. There's no question of that. I was the acting commissioner at that time, so believe me, I understand that.

THE LEGACY OF THE STREAK

Coming as it did on the heels of a strike that wiped out the World Series for the first time in 90 years, there are some who posited the theory that Ripken's passing Gehrig, in effect, saved baseball. It certainly provided a story line that brought out all that was good about the game.

Forty-eight thousand people came to see the Yankees play the Orioles at Camden Yards on September 20, 1998, in Baltimore's home finale. What they didn't see that day was the real story, though. For the first time in more

than a decade and a half, Cal Ripken Jr. was not in the lineup. About 30
minutes before game time that night Ripken had walked into manager Ray
Miller's office and simply said, "I think the time is right." And with that
the Streak was over at 2,632 games. "I look at this as a happy moment,"
Ripken would say afterward. "But now that I know what it feels like, I
don't want to sit and watch a game anymore."

Gehrig's record was long hailed as one of the game's unbreakable marks,
but a player with the right genetics, disposition, attitude, fortune, and tal-
ent—because it has to be done by someone whom a team wants on the
field for the better part of two decades—came along and broke it. Ripken
then set the bar even higher by tacking on another 500 games to the record.
Can anyone really say for certain, though, that there isn't some kid play-
ing Little League right now who won't someday play in 2,633 consecutive
major-league games?

THOMAS BOSWELL: There are never too many moments
in sports that feel entirely authentic, and Ripken's finishing of
the Streak was. Not necessarily all the aggravation in earlier
years when people asked, "Should the Streak go on?"

DEREK JETER: We were there when his streak ended,
we were playing in Baltimore. I was hitting second and that
was around when everyone in the stadium realized he wasn't
playing, and they gave him a standing ovation. That was a
special moment.

THOMAS BOSWELL: No one person or record can save
a sport. That's silly hyperbole. Baseball would have gone on
and found its way back without Ripken. However, he had been
generous with his time before the strike, but nothing like on the
scale it was after the strike. You saw someone who understood
the game down to his bones and said, I am the man for this
moment. I am going to give every drop of myself to the sport.
I am going to pay back in the most genuine way possible. And
he didn't do that thinking that's going to make him a megastar
beyond the level he already had. He did it because it was the
right thing to do. However, he put the game back in touch with
its roots. He shamed countless players into acting better in their

roles with the public and even their media relations. I can't tell you how many players in 1995 and 1996 said Cal's example shows me how we should all be acting, how we should all respect the game. People on both sides of the labor issue said, We should all be acting more like Cal, we should be putting the game first.

BUD SELIG: I actually had a lot of contact with Cal. The finest compliment I could pay him is that, like Robin Yount or George Brett, he's a great player who worked hard every day and conducted himself the way you would hope not only an athlete but a human being would conduct himself. It was a privilege to watch Cal Ripken and to know him. I have enormous respect for Cal Ripken as a player and a human being. I think that he has represented this sport so beautifully, so gracefully, so graciously that I'm profoundly impressed with Cal off the field, and he was truly a Hall of Fame player on the field.

MIGUEL TEJADA: I appreciate everything that he did. He's a role model for every baseball player, especially for myself, to keep playing every day, because to play so many games like that and never get hurt, it's unbelievable. He's got to be proud. I am proud to see what he did and it makes me keep pushing myself every day. Every time [the media] mentioned Cal Ripken, I really put myself in a situation where I had to go out and play every day. But I was never trying to catch Cal Ripken. I am just really happy to see what he did.

RICHIE BANCELLS: I know you never say never, but the way this game is, the travel that's involved, the chance of injury, especially in that position—the middle infield—it's hard for me to imagine that it could be done again.

MIGUEL TEJADA: I don't want to say never. In baseball, anything could happen. But it is going to be hard. It is going to be very hard.

CAL RIPKEN JR.: From where I sit, if I could do it, some-body else could do it. I wasn't Superman. I had a great passion for the game and certain things have to come together. You have to be deserving to start and play every single day. You have to have a little luck and you have to be durable. But I think the biggest thing is you have to have a sense of purpose and a passion for what you do.

ICHIRO COMES TO AMERICA

Featuring

PAT GILLICK: General manager of the Seattle Mariners at the time Ichiro Suzuki came to the United States.

DEREK JETER: Perennial All-Star shortstop and a teammate of Hideki Matsui since Matsui joined the New York Yankees in 2003.

EDGAR MARTINEZ: One of the stars of Ichiro's first U.S. team, the 2001 Mariners.

HIDEKI MATSUI: Yomiuri Giants center fielder who hit 332 home runs in his Japanese career—including 50 in his final season—and then became an All-Star left fielder with the Yankees.

JOHN McLAREN: Mariners bench coach who helped Ichiro transition to the American game. Succeeded Mike Hargrove as Seattle manager on July 2, 2007.

JAMIE MOYER: Ichiro's teammate and a 20-game winner with the 2001 Mariners.

DON NOMURA: Agent who was instrumental in bringing star Japanese pitcher Hideo Nomo to the Dodgers in 1995. Nomura's other clients have included Japanese stars Hideki Irabu and Masato Yoshii and Dominican import Alfonso Soriano, who cut his teeth in Japan before moving to the Yankees.

HIDEKI OKUDA: A freelance writer who covered Ichiro's Mariners for *Sports Nippon*.

ALEX RODRIGUEZ: The youngest man to enter the 500-home-run club, he joined the Yankees in 2004 and has been Matsui's teammate for the past four seasons.

KEN SINGLETON: Three-time All-Star outfielder in the 1970s and early '80s, mostly with the Baltimore Orioles, and currently a Yankees broadcaster.

ICHIRO SUZUKI: Batting champion from the Orix Blue Wave who smoothly transitioned to the Mariners in 2001.

BOBBY VALENTINE: Former Mets and Rangers manager who led the Chiba Lotte Marines to the Japanese championship in 2005, the first foreign manager to do so.

ROBERT WHITING: Author of *You Gotta Have Wa*, *The Meaning of Ichiro*, and *The Chrysanthemum and the Bat* and a foremost authority on Japanese baseball.

FOR MOST AMERICAN FANS, Japanese baseball was, until the 1990s, a distant and vague presence. There were tours by American teams and All-Star concordances that called some attention to the Japanese game. Reciprocal spring-training visits by Japanese teams would also generate a modicum of interest. Everyone had heard of all-time home-run leader Sadaharu Oh, of course, especially after he and Hank Aaron squared off in a home-run derby on national television in 1974. Hard-core American fans might sport a cap featuring the logo of the Yomi-uri Giants—the New York Yankees of Japan—just to prove how hard-core they really were. Former big leaguers would call attention to the Japanese game by their presence there, but they were rarely players of note.

It was always understood that second-line Americans and Latinos could excel in Japan if they could bridge the cultural differences and adjust to the different approach that Japanese teams took to training and discipline. The question that no one could answer, because it had been tried only once—and very briefly—was this: What would happen if the very best baseball players from Japan came to the United States to ply their trade? In late 1964 and '65 a 20-year-old pitcher named Masanori Murakami pitched in 54 games for the San Francisco Giants, relieving in all but one appearance. He was fairly successful, striking out 10 batters per nine innings but posting an ERA higher than the league average.

The pressure on Murakami to return to Japan was great and he eventually did so, commencing a long professional career there. His appearance in the big leagues actually had the opposite effect of opening a door. He had joined the Giants through an exchange program, and it was never intended that he would play anywhere but in the minor leagues. When he was promoted to the big club and succeeded to the point where both he and the Giants wanted him to stay, it caused a diplomatic meltdown between the professional leagues in the two countries and led to a codification of the restrictions against further movement by Japanese players.

"There was a misunderstanding of the option clause," explains author Robert Whiting. "The Giants took [Murakami] for a couple of years and ignited this international dispute in which baseball relations were severed. A scheduled trip by the Pittsburgh Pirates to play after the season was canceled. The majors and the Japanese signed a working agreement in which they agreed to obey the rules of each other's standard player contracts. They would keep their hands off of each other's players unless both sides okayed it."

The NPB (Nippon Professional Baseball) no more wanted to give up its best players than it wanted its rosters diluted with too many foreign players. Unlike the world's best soccer leagues or the NHL or even Major League Baseball, Japanese baseball welcomed a kind of professional isolationism, limiting the number of foreign players on its rosters and making it practically impossible for its own players to move outside of the major Central and Pacific Leagues or the minor Eastern and Western Leagues. Because of this, Japan's best players—not to mention fans on both sides of the Pacific—wondered how they would fare on the larger stage.

HIDEO NOMO PAVES THE WAY

So, for three decades, nary a Japanese player went against the flow of talent from the West. Although a number of major-league teams coveted Japanese stars and several tried to set the wheels in motion to bring them to the United States, the strictures imposed by the NPB—not to mention the societal pressures to stay at home—kept them in Japan. In many ways, to paraphrase Winston Churchill, these were two people divided by a common sport.

One player changed all that: Hideo Nomo. Unlike the groundbreakers from Latin America or the African American community, however, Nomo's greatest challenge was not how he would be accepted by American fans who were, by the '90s, used to polyglot sports rosters, but by the people of his own nation. That was his great risk: becoming alienated from his own homeland.

DON NOMURA: Everybody misunderstood the agreement between the United States and Japan. It was like, you're not supposed to go to the United States, you can't do anything illegal to cross over. With that mentality in mind, [Japanese] players never thought of going [to the United States], or even competing over there. It was like a party for them every two years when U.S. teams came to Japan. To get to play against each other, getting major-league players' signatures, meeting famous players like Roger Clemens, it was a fantasy for them. I think there was so much talent in Japan, that even though they wanted to go [to the United States], they didn't know how to go over there, and also they were informed that they were not supposed to go over there.

HIDEKI OKUDA: Back then, I remember in the late '80s, Joe Montana became popular after the NFL sent the 49ers and Rams to Japan for a game. Some company used Montana for their commercials, and the NFL became quite popular. Michael Jordan, before his first retirement, won three championships in a row, and he became very popular, and the NBA became a very popular sport in Japan. Back then only limited people saw and enjoyed major-league baseball. Maybe on some satellite channels you could see a couple major-league baseball games. I have to say, back then, in the late '80s, the NFL was more popular than MLB, and in the early '90s, the NBA was more popular than MLB.

HIDEKI MATSUI: There were always [U.S. baseball] games on television and you could see highlights. I remember watching the [MLB] All-Star Game with my father when I was young,

I don't know what year. I was impressed with the players.
But I also was impressed with the Japanese players, I watched
them more.

ICHIRO SUZUKI: [The U.S. major leaguers were] big in
[Japan]. I never saw a game in person, but I was watching it on
TV. I don't know if *fan* would be the right word, but I was defi-
nitely interested.

HIDEKI OKUDA: Baseball is our national pastime. Sumo is
our traditional sport, but baseball is number one. We enjoyed
the Japanese professional league, and a lot of people play in
high school, but talking about major-league baseball, there
weren't many fans back then. The majority of Japanese people
enjoyed watching Japanese players play. Every other year,
American All-Star teams would come to Japan after the season,
and we enjoyed that, we were excited, but there were no players that Japanese people really paid attention to on the level of
Joe Montana and Michael Jordan. Maybe Pete Rose became
famous when he broke the [career hit] record, and maybe Hank
Aaron when he broke Babe Ruth's [home run] record. But nothing like Michael Jordan. Now, there are a lot of Yankee fans,
and now Red Sox fans. Hideo Nomo changed everything.

DON NOMURA: It was Nomo's dream to play in the big
leagues. When he was selected to the All-Japan team, he went
to the Olympics, and he played against the U.S. team, and
some of the players he was playing against were playing in the
big leagues. He met Roger Clemens at the U.S.–Japan All-Star
game, and those were the triggers—he always wanted to play in
the United States, but he didn't know how to get over there. His
priority was to play in the United States. Money was never the
issue. It wasn't the money that motivated him. It was the desire
to play in the United States. To be with the best.

ROBERT WHITING: The agreement pretty much stayed
in place until the end of 1994. By that time it was obvious there
were [Japanese] players who were good enough to play in the

major leagues. Nomo had played in the Olympics and against visiting All-Star teams, and Americans had told him he was good enough to play in the major leagues.

DON NOMURA: I met Hideo back in 1993. He was not only concerned about his play but also how the players were treated in Japan, and was more interested in the difference between the United States and Japan. And so we got to talking in that sense, and slowly he expressed interest in going to the United States. And then in my mind it was like, Well he's not supposed to go there, that's what the rule is, as I was told. But I'd never read the rules. I told him I'd investigate and see what the actual rules were. I studied, went back to 1966 or something, and we found a loophole.

HIDEKI OKUDA: Nomo was sensational in the 1990 and 1991 seasons. He became an instant star. The big reason was that he was a real power pitcher. In Japan the majority of people are finesse pitchers, using a breaking ball most of the time. With Nomo it was fastball, fastball, fastball—then splitter. A power pitcher. People in Japan were very excited. In '94 he got hurt. He had trouble with his manager and he had trouble with management. He hired Don Nomura and he tried to find a way to go to the United States and be a member of major-league baseball.

DON NOMURA: I was searching for certain types of players. The language said that the voluntarily retired player, the suspended player, or the player on the military reserve list in the United States cannot play in Japan. So the American team was very clear that any player that they reserved, or who was voluntarily retired, or they had some kind of rights on the player, unless a team gave them or gave the club permission, were not able to go to another team overseas or play for anybody. But the Japanese side did not have that language. It did not specify a voluntarily retired player or suspended player. Now I don't think anyone wants to take a suspended player, because I'm sure he's got a problem, but the thing was it didn't say voluntarily retired player, it only said reserved active player. And then I found out more as I dug in about some players that came over to the United States on an exchange program. They were all voluntarily retired players. They came to the minor leagues and played. There was actually a major-league player that voluntarily retired in Japan and came to the States and played. As I studied more, I came to the conclusion that a U.S. voluntarily retired player cannot play in Japan but maybe a Japanese voluntarily retired player can come to the United States. And then I challenged it; I took a videotape with me to the commissioner's office in Japan, with whom I had a pretty good relationship then, and I asked him all sorts of questions and basically this general secretary of the commissioner's office said, "Yes, you're right, a Japanese voluntarily retired player can contract with the American club." I got that on tape and then asked the American commissioner if a voluntarily retired player can play in the United States. We got a positive feedback in writing. I also asked a friend of mine, an agent, to do the same, and he basically got the same answer: Yes, a voluntarily retired player in Japan can come to the United States. So I had three proofs in my hand in case they were going to argue you can't play in the United States.

The officials of the NPB were not going to give up easily. Ever since Murakami had been wrested away from the Giants—with whom he had a contract for the 1966 season—they had successfully kept American suitors at bay. For Japanese players, there had always been a way out, though. It took Nomo and Nomura to try it.

DON NOMURA: I went back to Nomo and said, "I think we have a way to get you out of here. And that is, only to be voluntarily retired. And the question would be: How do we get you voluntarily retired?"

ROBERT WHITING: America had their rule that stipulated that any player who retired had his rights still owned by the team that he last played for. These were worldwide rights. The reason the Japanese didn't have worldwide rights in their contract was that their standard player contract was copied from a 1930s American minor-league contract.

DON NOMURA: In those days Japan did not have or accept agents. Even today they don't, unless you're a certified lawyer in Japan. We figured simply if the club gets pissed off, their tactics could always threaten a player. They usually threaten their players every year to induce them to sign a contract. Their muscle was to tell the player, "If you don't sign this, you can't play anywhere. We're going to voluntarily retire you, and that means you can't play anywhere." Normally a player gets scared and they come to a conclusion of signing a contract. Those were the techniques and strategy that ownership in Japan used. We figured if the president of the club gets pissed off, he will probably come out and use that strategy. So we basically pissed him off by asking for a multiyear contract. If they accepted the first multiyear contract in Japanese history, we would have accepted it because, I told Hideo, money is very important. If you're going to get a large amount of money in Japan, you might as well take it. He had six years until he was going to be a free agent, so we basically asked the club to guarantee those six years and give us $20 million. At that point Hideo was making, at today's rate, roughly a million.

That Nomura even got to meet with management was something of an upset. The concept of player agents at that time was still a foreign one in Japanese baseball. Like American owners of 25 years before, Japanese management negotiated directly with players.

DON NOMURA: My first meeting, when I presented that figure, the president kicked me out of the room. Hideo was going to leave with me, but I insisted that Hideo stay and listen to what they had to say as a courtesy, because it was the first contract negotiation of the year. And I told Hideo, "Tell him six years, $20 million." I was waiting in the lobby, and 10 minutes later Hideo came out of the hotel room and said the president was pissed off. But I said, "You did a fantastic job. We'll wait until next meeting," which took place about 10 days after that.

That time I was also waiting in the lobby, and Hideo had gone up to the hotel room, and he came running out about five minutes later and said, "We did it." The president just said, "If you don't sign this, I'm going to voluntarily retire you." And Hideo says, "Fine, then I'll retire." We thought it was going to be more complex and tough, but at the end of the day it was very simple.

ROBERT WHITING: The players' union in Japan is very weak. The players essentially do what they're told. They take the salaries that the front office wants to give them. You can see the Japanese national character in the way they approach baseball. For years they would never strike because they thought it wouldn't be fair to the fans or the owners. They had a strike in 2004 over the merger of two teams, and they only did it after polls showed the fans didn't want the merger either. They only did it for two days and they apologized.

Getting free was just the first step, however. The next one was running the gauntlet of media and popular reaction.

BOBBY VALENTINE: [Nomo] was the protruding nail at the time and many Japanese wanted him to be hammered down. They didn't think he could succeed at that higher level— that his best years were behind him and that he was leaving for selfish reasons. There was a lot of intrigue but it wasn't necessarily intrigue with support.

ROBERT WHITING: In the beginning he was treated as a pariah, a traitor, a deserter, a troublemaker.

DON NOMURA: We didn't expect it to be such a big thing. The media made it into a big thing, and basically pounded him, pounded us. We wanted to keep it quiet. We told the club that when we signed the voluntary retirement papers we wanted to talk again at the end of the year to talk about how to deal with the media and so forth. Unfortunately the very next day the president ran to the league office and spilled the beans. And all of a sudden it was the biggest story out there. It hit the front pages everywhere and they just pounded Hideo, saying that he was a traitor. It was an everyday thing. We were stalked. Cameramen were hiding in bushes. Our cars were chased. It was just unbelievable. There was no positive thing [in terms of media response] whatsoever—it was all negative. He was going to fail. Why would he go to the States? He was washed up. Playing against the best he won't last an inning. There was absolutely nothing good written about him.

HIDEKI OKUDA: Most of the media were against him and Don Nomura. They were criticized. But at the same time baseball fans were very excited and wanted to see what would happen. Very, very curious to see what he could do. Some baseball people criticized him, saying he could not make a major-league baseball roster, he'll be back soon after a miserable time there.

HIDEKI MATSUI: I was younger at the time [but] it wasn't something I thought a lot about. I was curious about how he would play in the majors. I wanted him to do well because it would be good for Japan.

DON NOMURA: It seemed like the public, though, was rooting for him. That was the feedback I got. But the media—for instance you look at the Tokyo Giants, owned by the Yomiuri newspaper. They're also related to Nippon TV. All the baseball teams control the media in Japan. The newspapers would never write bad things about ownership. And it's still the same today.

Nomo made his debut on May 2, 1995, in the Dodgers' seventh game of the strike-delayed and shortened season, pitching five shutout innings. He was wild at first, averaging a walk an inning in his first three starts. In fact, he was pulled after four innings of his third start without allowing a hit. (He walked seven Cardinals.) He calmed down immediately thereafter, striking out 14 Pirates in his next start. He reached double figures in strikeouts 10 more times that season and finished 13–6 with a 2.54 ERA and a league-best 236 K's, earning National League Rookie of the Year honors.

DON NOMURA: So they were just beating and pounding Hideo. Until June. When June came, he won his first game, and he had six straight wins, and then all of a sudden the media couldn't help themselves and they changed. It seemed in Tokyo and Osaka, when Nomo was pitching, the majority of the population was rooting for him, except for the media and the commentators—former ballplayers, coaches—they were all pounding him.

HIDEKI OKUDA: But in 1995 he did a very, very good job. Nomo fever came. So many interesting things happened. Some baseball fans flew from Japan to Los Angeles and enjoyed the game, then after the game went back to the airport and flew back to Japan. Some fans bought a lot of souvenirs; one guy spent $10,000 in the souvenir shop at Dodger Stadium. So a lot of interesting stories were heard back then.

ROBERT WHITING: His first game against the Giants was televised live back to Japan. All of a sudden people were saying, "Here's our boy!" He was a boost to the Japanese national esteem. He won Rookie of the Year. All his games were telecast nationwide. They had set up these Jumbotrons all over Japan and you would see people standing outside watching him pitch. It was really quite a phenomenon.

BOBBY VALENTINE: The same year that he was headed across the pond to break a barrier and do something creative, I was headed in the opposite direction to break a barrier and do something creative—manage the [Chiba Lotte] Marines. Along with the rest of Japan I had the TV on at six in the morning to watch him pitch for the Dodgers.

HIDEKI MATSUI: I supported him, maybe because it was my dream, too. There were people who were critical because they were worried about Japanese baseball. But there are always new players coming up. I didn't mind that he left.

HIDEKI OKUDA: Some people said that without Hideo Nomo, maybe someone else would come to the United States and compete at the major-league level, and I agree with that.

We cannot expect that kind of dynamic performance that
Nomo gave us, we cannot expect that from just any player.
Nomo's first year: Rookie of the Year and strikeout title. He
had double-digit strikeouts many, many times. He pitched
against Barry Bonds and Tony Gwynn, those great hitters, and
he struck them out. He put on a very entertaining show. In his
second year he no-hit the Colorado Rockies.

*It can be argued that this no-hitter of Nomo's against the Rockies on Sep-
tember 17, 1996, is one of the single greatest pitching achievements in baseball history, in that it came in an environment where the Rockies and their
opponents averaged 15 runs per game. The Rockies won two-thirds of their
Coors Field games that year, averaging eight runs per game. To throw a
shutout in these circumstances would have been impressive enough—no
other pitcher did so in 1996—but to no-hit them was downright amazing.*

DON NOMURA: It took 30 years for the first guy to come
over. It had to take a guy with balls. You needed a guy of
Hideo's caliber to break the ice. He certainly had the makeup
to do it, and in breaking the ice, he was successful. Without
success, you can't pave any ways. With Hideo being successful,
that gave confidence for other ballplayers to stand up for themselves and say, "I want to go." Japanese are a little bit more
shy. They do it as a group but individually they don't want to
be outspoken. There's the saying the nail that sticks out gets
hammered down. It's that kind of society—if you're a nail, you
better be successful. Because you're going to get nailed down
pretty hard. Hideo didn't get hammered down.

ROBERT WHITING: When Nomo went to the States in
1995, all of a sudden you had major-league baseball on television when you didn't have it before. These guys grew up reading
about major-league ball but it always failed on TV because fans
couldn't identify with the players. I remember back in the '80s
they would show a game of the week and nobody watched it.
When Nomo went, all of a sudden there was a Japanese right
in the middle of the action and he was a big star, so everybody
watched. It's on live in the morning at nine o'clock. Then Hideki

Irabu went and then Masato Yoshii and soon you had major-league baseball on every day. Ichiro was sitting there and watching these guys and saying to himself, "Yeah, I can play there."

A POSITION PLAYER, TOO?

Nomo was followed to the States by a number of pitchers throughout the '90s. Hideki Irabu, Shigetoshi Hasegawa, Masato Yoshii, Tomo Ohka, and Kaz Sasaki all landed on American shores with varying degrees of success. What remained to be seen, though, was if a Japanese position player could make it in the major leagues. When assumptions were made about Japanese professionals, the general feeling was that the finesse pitchers wouldn't have a hard time adjusting to the North American game but that the hitters, used to shorter schedules, smaller ballparks, and a steady diet of those very same finesse pitchers, would struggle against the American power game.

ROBERT WHITING: [Japanese] hitters are four inches shorter and 20 pounds lighter on average. They had some big guys like Hideki Matsui, but you don't have anybody that looks like Albert Pujols or Alex Rodriguez. For a long time, lifting weights was taboo in Japan—they thought it would screw up your timing and flexibility. It's only in the past decade that they've gotten into it. So you had a lot of good slap hitters there, but they didn't have that much appeal to Americans. They're very skilled batsmen. They very seldom strike out. They teach them to hit with the lower half of the body. Ichiro spent a lot of time in the gym building up his thighs and calves. You look at him closely and you see that the bottom half of his body is solid. Americans use upper-body strength to propel the ball. They can drive an outside pitch down the line. The Japanese can't do that, but they have a nice, even swing. There's a lot of emphasis on form—that comes from the martial arts, too, that there's a right way and a wrong way to swing a bat. You'll see guys go out in camp and swing a bat a thousand times a day. One guy did it 1,500 times. Batters will take 100 swings before a game or take 100 ground balls. They try to develop hitters that have perfect swings and perfect timing, who can hit a ball to any location. In order to do that, you sacrifice power. That's why Japanese hitters have not been valuable commodities to Americans. Americans think it's easy to get a .300 hitter who slaps the ball to all fields like Rod Carew. They are not as prized as somebody like Pujols or Ryan Howard or, before that, Sammy Sosa or Mark McGwire.

BOBBY VALENTINE: There have been many pitchers who have succeeded who were of Japanese stature—not the biggest guy on the field who didn't throw it hard who were able to win 300 games. But [Japanese] hitters just weren't thought to be big enough, strong enough, fast enough.

DON NOMURA: It's only a myth that's come out of the fact that Japanese players are not big and strong. A lot of people say, "Well, pitchers, if you have good control you can get away with it. Hitters, if you don't hit, you don't survive. You have to be big and strong."

ICHIRO SUZUKI: I first got the idea I wanted to play in the United States in 1996. I had a lot of stress. I was carrying a lot of stress relating to baseball at the time and I wanted to change environments to change myself. That was the number-one reason I had, the first feeling I had. For many reasons, I was suffering. It is possible where I was in that part of my life affected the reason for that.

JOHN McLAREN: When Ichiro first came over [in the spring of 1999 for 10 days with the Orix Blue Wave], he was around [Ken Griffey Jr.] and Jay [Buhner] and I could tell from the gleam in his eyes that this was where he wanted to be. If he could have been in the outfield with Griffey and Buhner, and with A-Rod in the lineup, that would have been something.

ROBERT WHITING: Every other year since the end of the war, a major-league team or All-Star team would visit Japan in November to play their Japanese counterparts, and Ichiro would always play in those games and he always did well. In 1996 an All-Star team came, managed by Mike Hargrove, and Hargrove said he thought Ichiro could make it as a reserve outfielder in the States. That was a big insult—pissed everybody off. So the next time the Americans came Ichiro hit .400 or something like that. He wanted to show everyone that he could play. He was the best player in Japan. He won seven batting titles in a row. He is the only player with over 200 hits in a season in Japan [in 1994, when he had a record 210 hits in 130 games], where the season is shorter and it's harder to do.

ICHIRO LOOKS TO THE WEST

By the time Ichiro began seriously contemplating a jump to the States, the voluntary retirement loophole had been closed. After the Hiroshima Carp lost Alfonso Soriano by the same method that had enabled Nomo to skip town, the NPB sealed the escape route and created a posting system.

ROBERT WHITING: Free agency was implemented in 1992 by the owners, who were trying to change the dynamic and add some life to the game. It wasn't the same way Americans got free agency. As a way to solve the problem with the voluntarily retired gambit—the thing that had cost them Nomo and Soriano—they came up with the posting system. The way it works is that a player who wants to go to the States before his nine years of obligation is up and he became a free agent, the club would post his name in quotes as a player whose rights of negotiation were available to the highest bidder.

DON NOMURA: The posting system came about when Hideki Irabu came over [to the Yankees in 1997]. The straw that broke the camel's back was when I brought Soriano over [also to the Yankees, two years later]. It was a combination of both. When the Japanese finally said, "We've got to put a stop to this and find a system," this posting system was presented by the U.S. commissioner's office, putting a player's negotiating rights up for bidding. They implemented this in 1999. There's no trigger for the posting system. If a player wants to be posted, a club says either no or yes. A team is not going to say yes unless there's some kind of leverage, like in the case of Daisuke Matsuzaka, who would have become a free agent a year [after his posting request]. The Seibu Lions wouldn't have received anything in return [if Matsuzaka were to leave the team at the end of that season], so they used the posting system as a way to get a return on their investment. A player doesn't have any right or say in going to which club or negotiating with which club. For instance, if you're drafted by a Japanese club at 18 then you have to fulfill that nine-year term. On average you're looking at 30 years old. At 29 the Japanese club will post you and then you'll go to a club again where you don't have any freedom negotiating. So it goes against the liberal thought—you're always chained to something. And a ballplayer should be free to negotiate his contract and go to a company where he wants to work. Eventually the free-agency terms—now it's nine years—have to come down. I don't know when, but it'll come down, maybe to be compatible with American baseball. It's getting there.

HIDEKI OKUDA: Ichiro already had mentioned something like, "I want to come to the United States and play at the major-league level eventually." It was a very, very sensitive statement for him back then. Right now Japanese baseball players can talk freely about their desire. "Maybe next year I want to play at the major-league level"—they can say that. But back then Ichiro had to be very, very careful.

PAT GILLICK: The two guys that were responsible were Jim Colborn, who is the pitching coach at Pittsburgh now, and a fellow by the name of Ted Heid, who lives in Phoenix and who still scouts for the Mariners. It's kind of interesting: Ted is a Mormon, and he went on a mission when he was younger to Japan, so he's trilingual, not only Japanese but also Spanish and English. He learned Japanese, and so Jim Colborn had actually been the pitching coach with the Orix Blue Wave when Ichiro was a player there. He got to know him in Japan and he came back to the States and he started scouting the Far East with Ted Heid, so he and Ted together were really the ones who brought [Ichiro] over. The first time that Ichiro came to spring training in the spring of 1999, the Mariners got a look at him because there was a chance that sometime in the future he would be posted. So they got a chance to see him before I got there.

ROBERT WHITING: Ichiro felt very loyal to his manager but he stayed until the seventh year. They knew they'd lose him a year later anyway, so why not get something for him? He had just hit .387 and the team didn't have any money. They were never on national TV and the stands were always half full. The irony of Ichiro is that he's a big star in Japan but nobody ever saw him play.

BOBBY VALENTINE: There wasn't even a lot of quality video available. We [the Mets] had some video where people could see him hitting, but it was video taken from the stands or behind home plate. So there wasn't real good perspective.

PAT GILLICK: I'd seen him on tape prior to the time that he was posted. I liked what I saw on tape, and naturally I got a very positive report from Jim Colborn and Ted Heid on him, and consequently our owner in Japan wanted to bring the right player to the United States and wanted to make sure he was the right representative to the club. I think he was very supportive of us pursuing him.

BOBBY VALENTINE: He was a skinny kid who ran fast and hit a lot of balls to the opposite field, so people who hadn't seen him up close and personal might have thought that he was only going to hit singles. Turns out he was a singles hitter but he hit over 200 every year!

ROBERT WHITING: A lot of people were skeptical about how well he would do. Bobby Valentine, who had seen him in 1995, flat-out predicted he would hit .350—which is what he did. I think it's one of the all-time great predictions. He called him one of the top 10 batters in the world.

BOBBY VALENTINE: I predicted he would hit .350 because I tried to get him out. I did all these things. I had good pitchers hitting spots. I had good defense against him. I saw him in action and I was amazed. I thought he was what he is: a world-class talent. When I tried to get him to come to the Mets I told them he was one of the top five players in the world, but it turned out I was wrong—he was one of the top three players in the world.

HIDEKI MATSUI: I thought he would do well because he was a very good hitter and a very good player in general. He was an All-Star in Japan. You don't know for sure how every person will react in a new league, but I thought he would do well.

EDGAR MARTINEZ: When he first came over, the expectations were huge everywhere, given his accomplishments in Japan. But we players didn't know what to expect. We all felt it would be an adjustment period before he got going. I personally thought he would perform at a very high level, but I wasn't sure how long the adjustment period would be. It was amazing when it happened. From day one he was on for the whole year.

PAT GILLICK: We wanted him very badly. We thought at that time—of course that money is dwarfed by what's happened since that time with the guy in Boston [Daisuke Matsuzaka, for whom the Red Sox won negotiating rights with a bid of $52 million]—we just kind of, there was no scientific way, it's just like a free agent, there's just no scientific way to know exactly what amount of money you have to bid. We kept thinking or hearing that it was somewhere in the range of $10 million, so we thought we had to be somewhere above the $10 million mark. We were thinking somewhere in the area between $11 to $12 million, and we decided that if we really wanted to get him, I remember telling Chuck Armstrong, our president, and Howard Lincoln, our chairman, "Well, I would think that for sure 13 would get it done," because we were thinking 11 to 12. So we decided to go a little over 13 just in case someone else bid 13. So we went with 13.125. We thought the West Coast clubs were in it for sure. We figured San Francisco, Los Angeles, and probably Boston and New York were probably in. We didn't think, because they're a smaller market, that San Diego or Oakland were in it, but we were pretty certain that San Francisco, L.A., the Yankees, and Boston, and probably the Mets, were five other clubs that we thought were in the thing pretty deep. I have no idea what the other bids were or who was the closest. It might have been $1 million or $2 million—I don't know. We just thought, we want to get him. We were pretty determined. We thought that probably 13 was an overpay, but we weren't sure. [The bids were never made public, but the Mets were rumored to be the runner-up at $10 million.]

ICHIRO ARRIVES

While Ichiro would have made a splash anywhere he landed in the States, it didn't hurt that his debut came with the winningest team of the Expansion Era (i.e., since the 1962 season, when the schedule was expanded to 162 games). The 2001 Mariners would have won a lot of games had Ichiro never showed up, perhaps as many as 110 had right field been handled by an average player, but Ichiro's style of play was so different to modern eyes that he became the center of attention on a team that featured Bret Boone and Mike Cameron having career years as well as the always-productive Edgar Martinez and John Olerud. Trepidation about Ichiro's ability to make the transition ended early.

PAT GILLICK: We were in spring training in Arizona and Lou Piniella was running the club and Lou came to me and was kind of—I wouldn't use the word upset—but he was kind of doubtful if Ichiro was going to hit. And he said, "Everything he's been hitting has been up the middle and the other way. I'd like to see him pull the ball a little bit." And I said, "Well, Lou, why don't you just ask him if he can pull the ball. Just ask him to do it today in the game." So Lou went up to him and told him, "I want you to pull the ball." And the first time Ich went up there, he took the first pitch and pulled it to right field. I went up to Lou afterward and said, "Well I suppose he can pull it, too, Lou." That kind of made us think that if this guy puts his mind to it, he's going to accomplish pretty much whatever he wants to accomplish.

EDGAR MARTINEZ: For that 116-win season he was the last link we needed. We had a good team before that. We had most of what we needed in pitching and guys hitting in the middle of the lineup. We lacked a guy to set up the lineup for years. We had good hitters at the middle of the lineup, but we had always struggled to get the right player to lead off for us. When he came he was the right player, we had a great team and he was just a big part that we were missing.

ROBERT WHITING: He was a throwback to the turn-of-the-century players like Wee Willie Keeler—"hit 'em where they ain't." Scratch out a single, steal second and third, and come home on a sacrifice fly. He was a guy who, unlike these players who seem to come to the ballpark just to take their cuts and see how many they can hit out of the park, excelled at all aspects of the game. He is an outstanding fielder. He has one of the best arms in the major leagues. He is a great base runner. He can hit any pitch in any location. He has great reflexes.

PAT GILLICK: I was immediately struck also about his way at the plate. I kind of compare him a little bit—though it's a different sport—to Wayne Gretzky. Why I say that is Gretzky to me guided the puck into the net; he didn't shoot the puck into the net, he guided it. It's sort of the same thing with Ich. He swings, but he almost takes the ball where he wants it to go. It's very unusual. With a lot of guys you say hit the ball hard, and if you hit the ball hard enough sooner or later it'll fall in. But he gave me the impression that he guided the ball to the open places, through the infield.

JOHN McLAREN: That spring he wasn't trying to do anything but learn the pitchers. He just wanted to see pitches. He didn't care about anything else, because it was so important and he was so new. I thought he would hit .300 that first year, but with the culture being new to him and with the league being new to him, I thought it might be a little tough. Obviously it wasn't that tough. As you can see now, there isn't a pitch anyone can throw that he can't hit. You could tell right from the first how special he was. He wasn't a prototypical leadoff hitter, who hits and walks. He was from the first the kind of player who could beat on people with the way he hits. Every series that first year teams tried to put a new defense out there against him, and he'd look at it and he'd hit it where they weren't. His bat control was always incredible.

HIDEKI MATSUI: Maybe it was easier for him [than it was for me]. If he had a single, he was a success. People expected that I would hit a lot of home runs because I had a lot of home runs in Japan. I had a tough few months if you remember. We are different players. It's difficult for me to compare. I'm not fast like he is.

One play in particular put Ichiro on the map. It came in Oakland in his eighth game with the Mariners, and the first time that he didn't start. Entering the game in the eighth as a pinch hitter, he led off with a single that started a three-run rally, breaking a scoreless tie. He went out to right in the home half of the inning. Terrence Long opened with a single. With one out, Ramon Hernandez singled to right and Long tried to go to third.

HIDEKI OKUDA: Obviously the game in April against the Oakland A's, an away game, people talked about his laser-beam throw that threw out Terrence Long at third base. He showed his strong arm and everyone was excited.

JOHN McLAREN: That was his ESPN coming-out party on defense. It was one hop, right on the button. If there was ever a textbook throw from the outfield, that one was it. And it was a big out in the game. He charged it perfectly, then he had that great quick release that we now know is typical for him.

HIDEKI OKUDA: That was a defensive play, and that night ESPN *SportsCenter* showed that play over and over again.

PAT GILLICK: It was one of those special moments where most of the people today, in every sport, they're thinking offense, they're not thinking defense. That was one of the times where it's like a guy hitting a triple; it's a great thing to watch a guy, at least in my estimation. It's a pretty good demonstration of a guy's defensive ability, gunning someone down at third. Going way back, Rocky Colavito and a few other guys in history can make that throw. When Ich gunned that guy down at third, a lot of people's eyes popped out.

ICHIRO'S MAKEUP

No one knew quite what to expect from Ichiro in the United States—on or off the field. He was something of an enigma even in Japan. But he occasionally showed his sense of humor with the Mariners, and between the lines he quickly proved that he belonged: leading the league in batting average (.350), hits (242), and stolen bases (56) in 2001 en route to winning the American League Rookie of the Year and Most Valuable Player awards.

ICHIRO SUZUKI: Up to that point, No. 51 for the Seattle Mariners was Randy Johnson. But after my first year, I think No. 51 for the Seattle Mariners became me. I don't know if you could say that's the fondest memory, but I think it was something that had the most meaning.

DON NOMURA: I don't think he pioneered anything. He told the club he wants to get posted because if he didn't he would walk away. He got posted. He wanted to go to Seattle.

He came to Seattle. The deal was done in 24 hours. He didn't go against anything. Everything was already railroaded to where he wanted to be, and how he wanted it to be. He had no struggle coming in here. It was all red carpet for him.

ICHIRO SUZUKI: I don't feel I'm a trailblazer. I think there were rules and regulations that prevented it from happening. But also I think up to that point there wasn't really anybody who had that thought process to want to come over here and play. Basically for fielders, people couldn't picture themselves playing over here. Due to that, I think a distance was created. Speaking of probability, it's more likely for a person who never played in Japanese professional baseball to come over here and play. It's possible that those people existed, but I think then the problem arises that they don't have enough skill.

JOHN McLAREN: Ichiro is really a funny guy. He likes to have a laugh, and he will surprise you with some of his slang English terms.

ALEX RODRIGUEZ: He doesn't speak a lot of English in public but he does in the clubhouse and on the field. He's funny. He fits in with everybody else.

ICHIRO SUZUKI: I definitely accept [U.S. culture]. There are some things we don't want to accept, but you have to accept them. John McLaren [helped me adjust more than anyone]. More than what he did, it's that he was always concerned about what state I was in. I really felt that coming across. It wasn't a temporary thing, either. It seems like some people will do some things very temporarily. But with him I felt that he was always, always concerned.

JOHN McLAREN: I remember when he first came over, right at the end, he asked permission to ask a question. We said yes. He asked, "Spring training is a total clusterfuck, isn't it?" There was Jamie Moyer standing behind him, laughing. I asked if Moyer had been teaching him English. He said yes, and started laughing. Then he was with Ted Heid at LAX going back to Japan a little later [in 1999] and there was a huge line. He turned to Ted and said so everyone could hear, "This is like spring training, a total clusterfuck, isn't it?"

ROBERT WHITING: The first time he participated in a big-league camp he told reporters that Americans have the kind of spring training that makes you wonder if they really know how to play the game or not. In Japanese camps a lot of work is done on team play: how to defend against the push bunt and relay throws and cutoffs. He said that during his first season he stood in the outfield many times and saw the Mariners make plays like missing the cutoff man and throwing to the wrong base, and he'd think to himself, If we only worked on these things in camp, we'd be a better team. This was a team that won 116 games, mind you. He said it was a pity because spring training is the only time you have to practice these things as a team. Americans are becoming more and more aware of how superior the Japanese game is in that aspect. They got a view of it in the [World Baseball Classic] in 2006. Americans don't even take infield anymore on some teams.

HIDEKI OKUDA: Ichiro was different. He tried to deal with the media like he plays against an opposing pitcher. He has been very serious. If some reporters ask him stupid questions, he never hesitates to say, "Next question," or "That's not worth answering." That kind of response he would do. If he likes the question, he answers with a very long and quotable comment. And I think he prepares himself well for these press conferences. He takes time to think about what he should say, how he should react to different types of questions. I believe he takes time to answer as perfectly as possible. That's how he was that first year. He wanted to be perfect in every way possible.

JOHN McLAREN: There might be times when he needed a translator, but he picked up [baseball] language really quickly. And he picked up Spanish, too. It's funny to hear him talk in Spanish.

BOBBY VALENTINE: He practiced religiously and he trained to be the best. But he's a genius. He's like Mozart was with the piano. He's special.

JAMIE MOYER: He's very quiet. Driven. Always on a mission. Always doing something. Always working on something. Stretching. Working out. Very regimented and disciplined in his approach. I was always very respectful of that.

JOHN McLAREN: He's really a creature of habit and routine. It was a shock to him when he found out that we didn't practice eight hours a day. That's what he was used to. His body told him what he had to do to be ready.

ICHIRO SUZUKI: I wasn't really surprised by the way Americans prepared, because I already knew. I had an image in my head what it would be like. One thing I can say is that it's very different. I'm not saying that one way is better than the other, but it's very different. [For instance] in Japan you have to be in your uniform in your hotel lobby, all the players, then you go to the stadium together. I really hated that, so I like the American style better. In Japan, though, the dugout is very clean. Even to this day it's really tough for me to get used to the dirty dugouts over here, because I don't like dirty things. But there are good and bad in both. So the best way, I think, is to mix.

EDGAR MARTINEZ: I always thought he was unique about the way he got himself ready. But that was what it took for him to perform at a high level. He has a plan and a routine and to be good, he feels he has to stick with it. He won't allow people to break his routine, and I can understand that. He needs to do that to be the best he can be. He's very unique. Most players are more flexible. At the same time, I admire his discipline. It's not common in most athletes to see that level of discipline in his game. From when he wakes up to the way he is when he gets to the stadium, it's almost like he follows the same pattern and goes about his business the same all the time. His routine isn't just what he does at the plate. It's in everything he does.

ICHIRO SUZUKI: As far as on the field, it was tough for me to get used to the rules over here. As far as off the field, shopping [was a tough adjustment]. I can't find a lot of items I like over here. As far as eating, I don't have much problems. It's mostly about clothes.

BOBBY VALENTINE: Japanese players succeed because they train better. Their balance is better. They have better discipline of controlling their bodies through their motion, and during the game they actually know what to do when the ball is hit. Not to say that MLB guys don't, but there aren't as many. The guy who doesn't know what to do in Japan is the exception. That's not the case in major-league baseball.

JOHN McLAREN: I remember when Ichiro was first posted and we were in the hunt for him, and it was pretty exciting stuff. We got him, and he came to Arizona to work out in January 2001. Well, I live in Arizona, so I would come to the park every day and I'd throw him batting practice and I'd hit him fly balls. I'd throw him 90 pitches one day and 124 pitches the next and 148 the next, whatever he wanted. And the Japanese media was all over the place. And every day they'd ask the same question. They wanted to know why he had 90 pitches one day and 124 the next and so on. And I said, "That's just as much as he wanted for the day." And they thought there was something deeper than that in there, and he had to deal with that every day.

DEREK JETER: He has an amazing ability to control the bat and put the ball where he wants to put it. He sort of slaps it to certain holes and he's so fast that he gets a hit before you can make a play. I really haven't seen too many people who can do that so well.

JOHN McLAREN: During that first spring, he was hitting lots of line drives, but mostly the other way and not driving the ball at home. [Manager] Lou [Piniella] became concerned that he never really saw him turn on the ball. I'd seen him so much in batting practice, having thrown to him, that I'd tell Lou, "Hey, he can turn on the ball. Don't worry." But Lou was concerned and he mentioned it to Ichiro one day. The next day we were playing San Diego in a [Cactus League] game. The first time up, he turns on a pitch and hits it 450 feet to right field. After he came off the field, he went over to Lou and said, "Is that turning on the ball?"

HIDEKI OKUDA: That year the majority of media got frustrated. There were regularly between 20 to 30 covering him. Usually 30 regularly. Opening day there were over 100. But through the year we were frustrated. At the same time we were excited because of his performance. And besides his performance, the Seattle Mariners had a great season. They won 116 games with Lou Piniella, an energetic manager. They had a great team, and [Kaz] Sasaki was the closer. It was a very, very entertaining and exciting season for us. We felt frustrated but at the same time we felt Ichiro was great, and he played, offensively, defensively, better than we expected. We were frustrated and excited. We were excited because American people were praising the way Ichiro played. We never expected that—before the season, we were kind of worried. Ichiro can be a good player, but we really had no idea how good he could be. But after the season started we quickly realized that Ichiro could be an impact player on the major-league level and in that first year he was voted number one for the All-Star Game, so that year, everyone was talking about Ichiro, and we were completely amazed.

DEREK JETER: Not too much surprises me, but I was surprised that he became the MVP so quickly. You don't expect somebody to be the MVP in their first season. But he wasn't really in his first season because he had been so good in Japan.

THE ICHIRO LEGACY

One can wonder what might have been the outcome if someone other than Ichiro had been the first Japanese position player to come to the United States, someone such as Kaz Matsui, a terrific infielder in Japan who had a much rougher transition after moving Stateside in 2004 to join the Mets. Matsui washed out as a shortstop in New York and in June 2006 was traded to the Colorado Rockies, for whom he has become a serviceable second baseman.

ROBERT WHITING: If Kaz Matsui had been the first Japanese player instead of Ichiro, it would have been the end for a while. It's good for the baseball population that Ichiro was as good as he was—and that Hideki Matsui was as good as he was.

HIDEKI MATSUI: I don't think [it matters who was first]. If you are a good player, you should have faith in what you can do. I don't think any Japanese players would have stopped wanting to come here. A lot of players in Japan want to play against the best competition.

BOBBY VALENTINE: Ichiro really was the chosen one. He was the hitting prodigy who was supposed to represent the country in the other league. [Hideki] Matsui was the home-run hitter, the leader from the great Yomiuri Giants team, who was supposed to go over and represent the league. If they didn't succeed it would have been very devastating to the psyche of the baseball community.

ROBERT WHITING: It became a matter of pride. So when Ichiro went and succeeded, it forced Hideki Matsui to give it a try. Matsui played for the Tokyo Giants, which is like a combination of the Yankees, Dodgers, and Mets—the be-all and end-all. It was considered unthinkable for a member of the Tokyo Giants to leave his team and play for any other team anywhere. But most of the fans wanted him to go. A lot thought that after Ichiro went and succeeded, Matsui would have to go, too, otherwise he'd be a wimp—that he'd be scared at trying his hand. In the course of time, since Nomo went, it became a test of virility—to see how big your balls were. If Ichiro had stayed, then Matsui would not have gone, I don't think. It took a lot of guts for Matsui to do that. [The Giants] offered him, I think, a $64 million, 10-year contract and he turned them down to play for less money for the Yankees.

HIDEKI MATSUI: I was a free agent and I was able to make my own decision at the time. The Yankees were interested in me and I was interested in the Yankees because I wanted to play in New York. It was a unique situation because of the respect I had for the Giants, which I still do. But I had the choice. Ichiro was posted, it was a little different for him. We are two different kinds of players. I made my decision because it was the best decision for me, not because of anything Ichiro did.

ROBERT WHITING: Ichiro is the first full-fledged Japanese cultural icon in the United States. If you went into a bar in the United States and asked the patrons to name a Japanese [celebrity], most couldn't name the emperor, the prime minister, or a movie star, but they could name Ichiro. This gave a tremendous sense of self-worth to the Japanese.

What's more, the way in which Ichiro was accepted in the United States has had an impact on Japanese baseball. On two occasions the sacred Japanese single-season home run record of Sadaharu Oh was protected by a barrage of intentional walks issued to Randy Bass and Tuffy Rhodes, both American imports. Ichiro's approach of a long-held U.S. record—albeit not one considered sacred—was treated entirely differently by American fans and media.

ROBERT WHITING: There was a sea change in attitude after Ichiro broke George Sisler's [single-season hits] record [with 262 in 2004]. There are four Americans managing in Japan now, which was unthinkable 10 or 15 years ago. Two of them have won Japan Series. Bobby Valentine is quite popular. Valentine was the centerpiece of a marketing campaign that was all over the subways. There's a warmer feeling toward America.

THE FUTURE OF JAPANESE BASEBALL

The advent of the Japanese professional ballplayer in the United States—which culminated in the successful 2007 transition of Daisuke Matsuzaka from Japan's Pacific League to the Boston Red Sox, for a total of $104 million—has had a positive impact on the players themselves as well as the Japanese community at large. What, however, will this free-flowing talent stream do to Japan's storied Central and Pacific Leagues? And is a bona fide World Series between the champions from the two countries a realistic possibility?

HIDEKI OKUDA: Before Nomo, nobody expected a Japanese pitcher to be that good. After Ichiro succeeded, we thought only Japanese superstars could make it at this level. But after Tadahito Iguchi—good player, but not a superstar—showed he could play well as an everyday player, we saw that you didn't have to be a superstar to play in the major leagues.

BOBBY VALENTINE: I do worry that the continuing defection of Japanese stars to MLB will diminish Japanese baseball. It happened to another great professional league back in the '40s and '50s: the Negro Leagues. They had infrastructure, parks, fans, and players. And before you knew it, they didn't have great players and they didn't have fans and they didn't have the revenue to pay the rent on the parks and the league was no longer a great league—it was not a league at all. That could happen in Japan. That would not be good for baseball. I don't know if it would be good for MLB.

ROBERT WHITING: The Japanese are responsible for their league, and if they had created a league where the players wanted to stay and not been so closed-minded, then maybe the stars wouldn't be so eager to leave. They've been mismanaged from the beginning. The teams are run by people who don't know anything about baseball. The purpose of the Tokyo Giants is to promote the newspaper the *Asahi Shimbun*. The Hanshin Tigers are owned by a railway. The purpose of the ball club is to promote the railway.

BOBBY VALENTINE: As far as taking a country in the industrialized world with over 130 million people that actually has baseball as its national sport—unequivocally the sport played by most, known by most, cheered for by most—to take away one of the life support systems of the professional leagues would be devastating for baseball.

ROBERT WHITING: Japan has its own problems. The teams are run like advertising vehicles for corporations. They're not run like businesses, like American teams, so they don't have the money to invest in deep farm systems. Each team only has one minor-league club, so they only have a total of 70 players under contract. So they don't have that much talent to lose.

And what about the possibility of a true World Series? One that pits the Japanese champions against the MLB champions?

BOBBY VALENTINE: A true World Series would be difficult. Not because of the talent or the need or the demand that the world's fans will make for it, but because of the money that has to be split up and the pride that has to be lost by one of these powers. I heard Bud Selig say that he believes there will be a true World Series someday. To get that conversation out in the open is a major step. The winner from Japan—because Japan is the league with the best infrastructure—should go to Hawaii and play the winner from North America. I'd like to see it done in a seven-game format and I'd like to see it done for charity. I'd like to see all the ticket and television money go into a pot that baseball worldwide could use to help develop the game around the world and inspire kids to be the next Ichiro or the next Derek Jeter. I think after that charity series was played and the attention that it gets is discovered I think that the size of the pot would be easier for everyone to visualize and they'd get to the table and see how to split it up.

KEN SINGLETON: I don't think we'll ever see a U.S.-Japan World Series, maybe an exhibition series. I know Bobby Valentine wants that. But how many play-off games can one team play? You want 19 in the States then seven more against a Japanese team? That seems like an awful lot. Maybe someday, but I don't know if we will see it.

BOBBY VALENTINE: There should be divisions of major-league baseball in Japan. There are stadiums and infrastructure. MLB should have a Japanese division in the National League and one in the American that takes players from the same pool. Free agents of the world get to sign with any one of the teams. You'd have these two winners go to the play-offs. Where those were played would have to be alternated in some way between Japan and the United States. You would have a system of worldwide international baseball then and it wouldn't be us against them, it would be all of us playing for the world championship to see who the best team is. This is nothing that can't be fixed. It's almost too simple to say it's not going to be done. What we all need is more women and more children caring about the game. If these games are now being played in the morning, then mothers and children would see the games and get more involved in the game. You see that in Japan to some extent, with games that are played in the United States.

HIDEKI MATSUI: That would be very interesting. I don't think it will happen soon because there are obstacles with the timing. But I know many fans in Japan would want that.

INDEX

Frank Robinson, 182, 184, 190,
191, 193, 195
Larry Doby, 183
player-managers, 195
Garcia, Dave
as Cleveland coach, 185, 190, 195
comments on Frank Robinson,
180, 191–92, 195, 201
Gehrig, Lou, 206–7, 223, 227, 230,
238, 243–44, 296
Giants (Tokyo), 275–76, 277
Gibson, Bob, 47, 48, 143, 150
Giles, Bill
Bud Selig's comments on, 168
comments on
designated hitter, 166–67, 168
grievance procedure, 122
Marvin Miller, 98
Player's Association, 91
Giles, Warren, 97, 104, 105
Gillick, Pat, comments on
Ichiro Suzuki, 263–67, 269
scouts, 263–64
Gladding, Fred
comments on
Ball Four, 82, 84
Jim Bouton, 57, 78
Larry Dierker's comments on, 76
Gonzalez, Mike, 33
Goodwin, Doris Kearns, 115
Goossen, Greg
comments on
Ball Four, 81–82, 83, 87
Joe Schultz, 66
John Kennedy, 60
nearly missing flight, 59–60
Jim Bouton's comments on, 77
Gorman, Lou, comments on
Cal Ripken Sr., 208
Grich, Bobby
comments on
free agency, 133–34, 135–36
reserve clause, 115–16
as Oriole, 133, 222
Grievance procedure, 118, 122–25
Griffith, Calvin, 97, 147
Griffith, Clark, 34
Groat, Dick, 47

H

Hall of Fame, designated hitters and,
169–71

Hargrove, Mike, 262
Hart, Jim Ray, 155, 163
Heid, Ted, 263–64, 271
Hernandez, Orlando, 52
Herzog, Whitey
comments on
designated hitter, 144, 146, 164,
165, 169
Frank Robinson, 181
success as coach, 201
Heydler, John, 142
Hickman, Jim
comments on
adversity, 29
Casey Stengel, 10
expansion draft, 4
losing, 19
playing Dodgers and Giants, 22
Ken MacKenzie and, 14
Hoak, Don, 47
Hodges, Gil, 7, 20, 21–22
Holtzman, Ken, 123
Hook, Jay
comments on
Casey Stengel, 12, 14–15
curveballs, 17–18
losing, 20
mumps contraction, 3–4
playing Dodgers and Giants, 22
Sandy Koufax, 23
spring training, 7
expansion draft selection, 3
record for 1962 season, 28
Hoscheit, Vern, 209
Houk, Ralph
comments on
designated hitter, 146, 147,
152–53, 163, 164–65
Ron Blomberg, 154, 155,
163
Rusty Staub, 162
Doc Medich's recollections on,
156
Ron Blomberg's recollections on,
153
Hovley, Steve, 60
Howard, Ellie, 154, 178
Howard, Frank, 70
Howard, Ryan, 261
Howsam, Bob, 101
Hoynes, Lou, 131
Hunter, Catfish, 123–24, 125
Hunter, Willard, 3